HOME BY CHRISTMAS?

The Story of US Airmen at War

F.W.190
ME.210
ME.110
ME.109

HOME BY CHRISTMAS?

The Story of US Airmen at War

Martin W. Bowman

PSL

Patrick Stephens
Wellingborough, Northamptonshire

Kriegie Lament

We won't be home for Christmas,
Don't depend on us.
We'll have snow
But no mistletoe
Or presents on the tree.
Christmas Eve will find us
Standing at apell,
We won't be home for Christmas,
We know that very well.

Frontispiece *Colonel Francis 'Gabby' Gabreski, a top US ace and a famous 'guest of the Third Reich'* (Harry Holmes).

First published 1987

British Library Cataloguing in Publication Data

Bowman, Martin W.
Home by Christmas?
The Story of US Airmen at War
1. United States. *Army Air Force. Air Force, 8th*—History 2. World War, 1939-1945 3. Escapes—Europe—History —20th century
I. Title
940.54'21 D805.E85

ISBN 0-85059-834-6

Patrick Stephens Limited is part of the Thorsons Publishing Group

Printed in Great Britain by
Butler & Tanner Ltd, Frome and London

Contents

'The loss of every Allied plane shot down over Europe was a tragedy—every member of a crew that was found and saved and sent back to us brought joy to all his comrades. To everyone who joined in this great work and to each member of his family and to all who shared, in those days, his risks and dangers I send assurances of my deep and lasting gratitude.'

Dwight D. Eisenhower

Author's Acknowledgements

The idea for this book was born eleven years ago during the Second Air Division Reunion in Norwich, England. At the time I was in the process of compiling my first book, *Fields of Little America.* It was Jim O'Brien, a pilot in the 44th Bomb Group and who features in 'Fields', who first suggested that while 'Fields' dealt with the actual missions, I should also write a book about what happened to some of these American airmen after they had been shot down. On his return to the USA Jim sent me his incredible collection of PoW memorabilia, some of which is featured in this book.

My researches for a book provisionally entitled, *'Home By Christmas?'* continued after the publication of *Fields of Little America* in 1977 and *Castles in the Air* in 1984; both books dealing with the American heavy bombing offensive in Europe in World War 2. *Home By Christmas?* takes some of those storylines further, into PoW camp, or via the escape and evasion lines out of Occupied Europe.

I am most grateful for the co-operation and friendship extended by the following: Bob Bishop; Bill Cameron; George Cooksey; Frank Cotner; Roy Davidson; Ralph Ernst; Rueben Fier; Robert Ferrell; Leslie Fischer; Vic Fleishman; Lee C. Gordon; Larry Grauerholz; Marshall Hamer; John A. Holden; John L. Hurd; the late Ben Isgrig; Lawrence Jenkins; the late Ron Kramer; General Curtis E. LeMay, USAF, Retd; B. L. 'Rusty' Lewis; Richard H. Lewis; Will Lundy; Frank McGlinchey; Bill Morris; Orlo Natvig; Jim O'Brien; Robert E. O'Hearn, author of *In my book you are all heroes*; Mike Olynik; Richard Olsen; Ralph K. Patton; General Delmar T. Spivey, USAF, Retd; Robert J. Starzynski; William B. Sterrett; Robert Sweatt; Joe Warth; Karl Wendel and 'Dusty' Worthen.

I am equally grateful to Roger Anthoine; Jacques De Vos; Lt Colonel A. P. De Jong; Armand Hardy; Cliff Hall; Harry Holmes; Ab Jansen; Guy Jacquemin; Henk Kwik; Edo van der Laan; Ian McLachlan; Tiny Mulder; Hans Onderwater; John Page; Bart Rijnhout; Hans-Heiri Stapfer Connie and Gordon Richards; Geoff Ward and Phil Walpole for their wholehearted contributions.

May 1986

Martin W. Bowman.

PRISON CAMPS

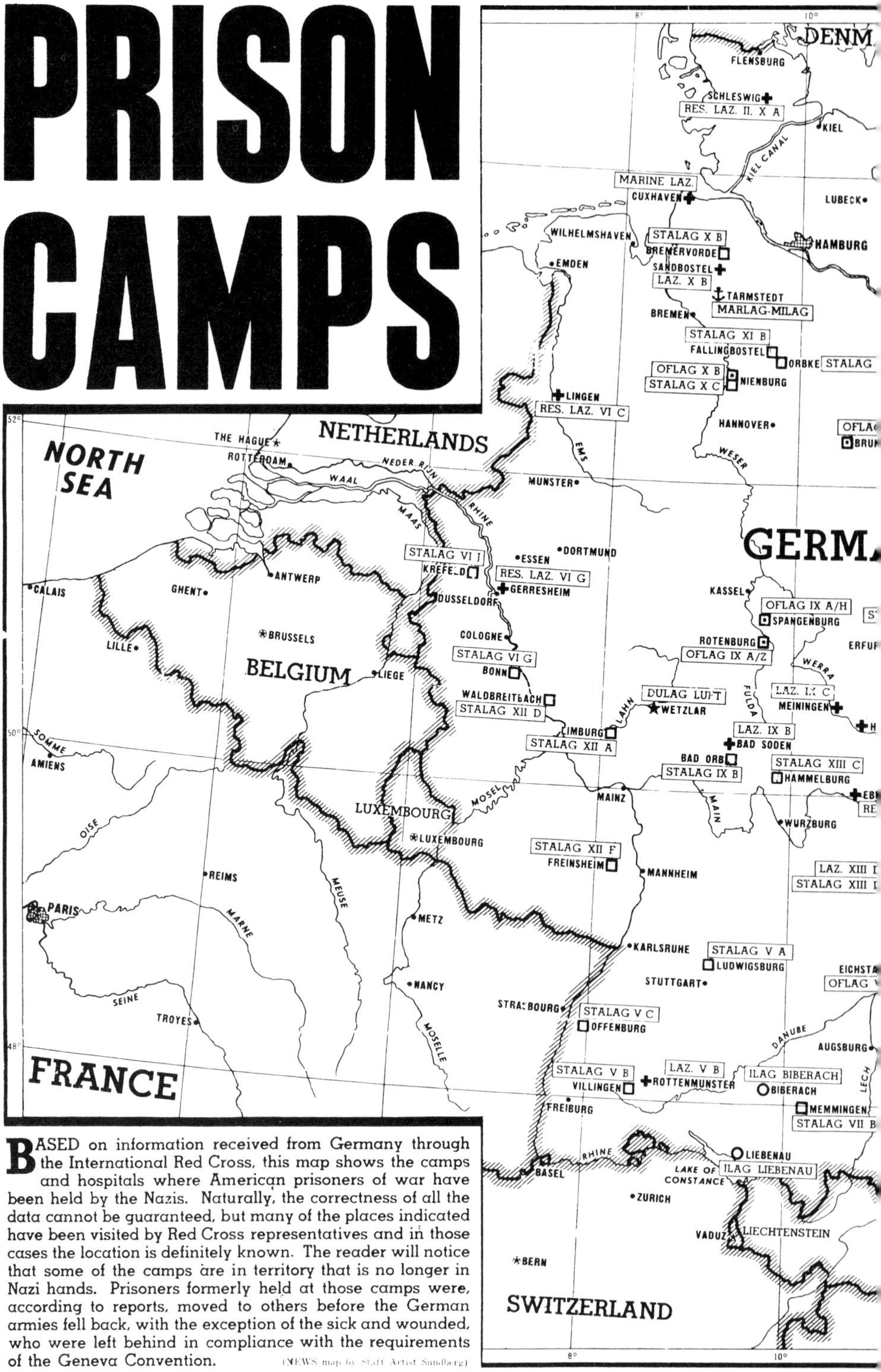

BASED on information received from Germany through the International Red Cross, this map shows the camps and hospitals where American prisoners of war have been held by the Nazis. Naturally, the correctness of all the data cannot be guaranteed, but many of the places indicated have been visited by Red Cross representatives and in those cases the location is definitely known. The reader will notice that some of the camps are in territory that is no longer in Nazi hands. Prisoners formerly held at those camps were, according to reports, moved to others before the German armies fell back, with the exception of the sick and wounded, who were left behind in compliance with the requirements of the Geneva Convention.

(NEWS map by Staff Artist Sundberg)

BALTIC SEA
EAST PRUSSIA
(GERMANY)
SASSNITZ
BARTH
STALAG LUFT I
GDYNIA
DANZIG
DANZIG
MARIENBURG
STALAG XX B
ALLENSTEIN
STALAG LUFT IV
GROSSTYCHOW
HAMMERSTEIN
STALAG II B
GRUDZIADZ
STETTIN
ODER
STARGARD
RES. LAZ. II
BYDGOSZCZ
SCHUBIN
OFLAG 64
TORUN
STALAG XX A
VISTULA
NETZE
NOTEC
WARTA
STALAG III C
ALT DREWITZ
WARTHE
BERLIN
STEGLITZ
POZNAN
WARSAW
STALAG III B
FURSTENBURG
WOLLSTEIN
RES. LAZ.
GRABOW
LUCKENWALDE
STALAG III A
LODZ
POLAND
STALAG IV D/Z
ANNABURG
RES. LAZ.
SCHMORKAU
STALAG LUFT III
SAGAN
STALAG VIII C
KALISZ
RADOM
PIOTRKOW
STALAG IV B
MUHLBERG
RES. LAZ.
KONIGSWARTHA
BODER
OSCHATZ
STALAG IV G
BRESLAU
ODER
BANKAU
STALAG LUFT VII
KIELCE
LAZ. IV A
HOHNSTEIN
STALAG IV A
CZESTOCHOWA
CHEMNITZ
STALAG 344
LAMSDORF
VISTULA
RES. LAZ.
BILIN
WISTRITZ
STALAG IV C
BLECHHAMMER
WK 8-BAB 21
KATOWICE
KRAKOW
TARNOW
ELBE
PRAGUE
MORAVSKA OSTRAVA
STALAG VIII B
TESCHEN
PLZEN (Pilsen)
MOLDAU
OLOMOUC (Olmutz)
CZECHOSLOVAKIA
BRNO (Brunn)
STALAG XVII B
KREMS
RES. LAZ. II
VIENNA
DANUBE
LINZ
PUPPING
STALAG 398
BRATISLAVA
KAISERSTEINBRUCH
STALAG XVII A
SALZBURG
AUSTRIA
MARKT-PONGAU
STALAG XVIII C (317)
RES. LAZ.
GRAZ
HUNGARY
LAZ. XVIII A/Z
SPITTAL
STALAG XVIII A
WOLFSBERG
LAKE BALATON
KLAGENFURT
MARIBOR
YUGOSLAVIA
SZEGED
GERMAN CAMPS WHERE U. S. PRISONERS HAVE BEEN HELD
FOR ENLISTED MEN
FOR NAVY AND MERCHANT MARINE
FOR AIRMEN
FOR OFFICERS
FOR CIVILIAN INTERNEES
HOSPITALS
THE FOLLOWING ARE THE MEANINGS OF THE ABBREVIATIONS USED ON THIS MAP:
STALAG: main camp (usually for enlisted men)
WK BAB: construction battalion camp
MARLAG: camp for sailors
MILAG: military camp
STALAG LUFT: camp for airmen
DULAG LUFT: transit camp for airmen
OFLAG: camp for officers
LAZ: hospital
RES. LAZ.: reserve hospital
ILAG: civilian internment camp
CAPITALS OF COUNTRIES
SCALE OF MILES
0 25 50 75 100
14° 16° 18° 20° 22°
54° 52° 50° 48°
Longitude East of Greenwich

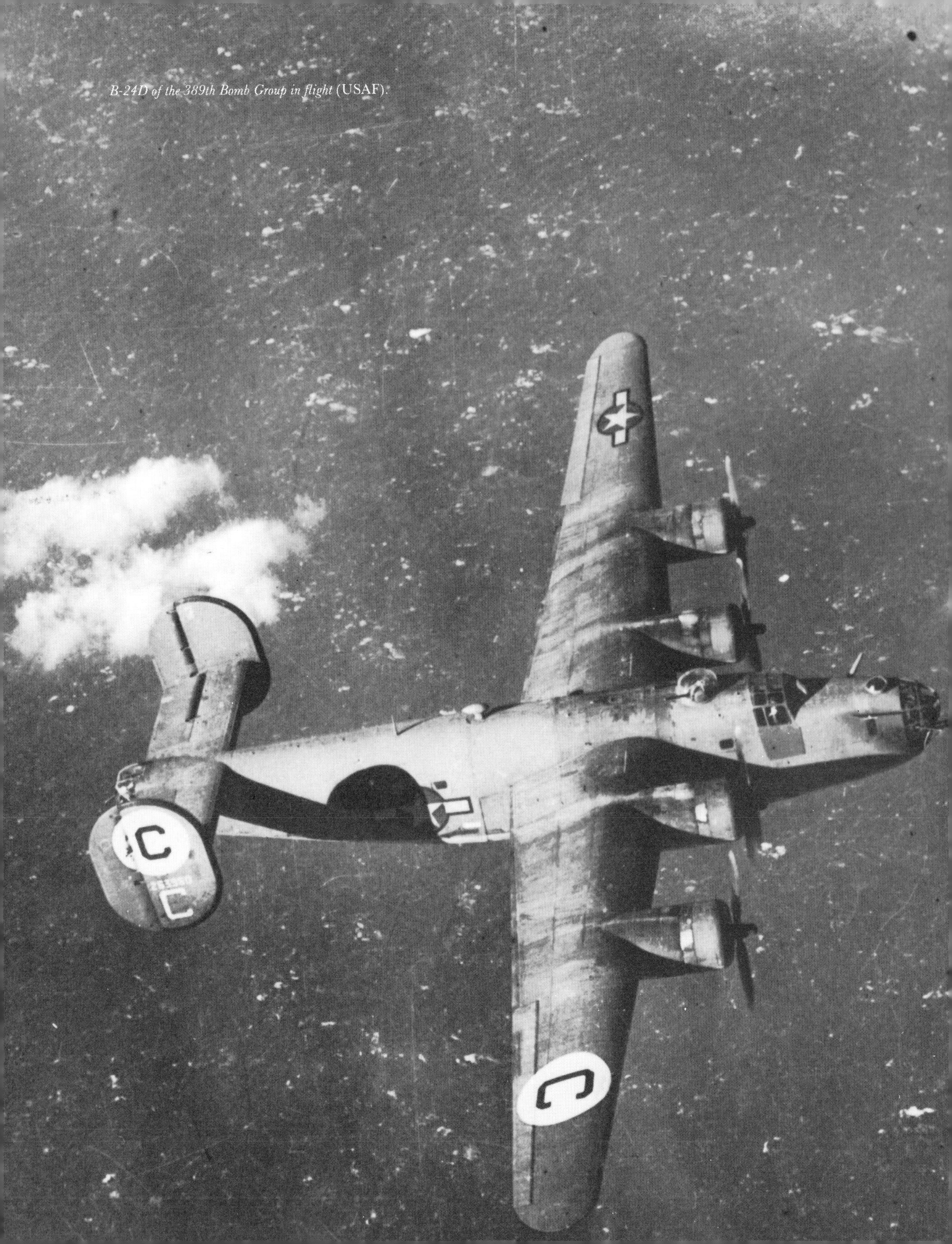

B-24D of the 389th Bomb Group in flight (USAF).

Part 1
LIFE BEHIND THE WIRE

1 The 'Bolero' mission

Throughout the winter of 1942-43 the B-17 Flying Fortresses of the United States 8th Air Force, numbering on average, 50 to 75 per mission and the same force's B-24 Liberator's, numbering only nine to eighteen per mission, attempted to prove that American daylight precision bombing of enemy targets in Europe could succeed. Opposing them was one of the most formidable fighter defences ever assembled in the history of aerial warfare. The American crews' only defence against the swarms of Messerschmitt Bf 109 and Focke Wulf Fw 190 fighters of the German Luftwaffe were their .5 inch calibre guns and tight formation flying for maximum concentrated firepower.

The Air Marshals at RAF Bomber Command, having had over two years' hard-won experience to call upon, counselled their American comrades in arms and prevailed upon them to join the RAF in area bombing by night. Even American instructors doubted that their fledgling force of 'greenhorn' crews could fight their way to the target, drop their bombs and then fight their way home again—all in broad daylight without fighter escort. However, both the four-engined B-17 Flying Fortress and the B-24 Liberator bombers, which formed the mainstay of 8th Bomber Command in England throughout the war, had been fitted with the much vaunted Norden bombsight for high-level precision bombing. Such was its accuracy during practice bombing in the clear blue skies over Texas that a new word in Army Air Corps nomenclature was coined. Unfortunately, 'pickle barrel accuracy', as it came to be known, was practically impossible in the often cloud-covered, fog-shrouded and highly congested airspace of enemy-occupied Europe.

Despite all the odds stacked against him, General Ira C. Eaker, Commanding General of the 8th Air Force in England, was determined that with the aid of RAF Bomber Command's night offensive, his 'round the clock' bombing strategy would work. Casualties would be heavy but acceptable. Losses of men and machines would be high whether they flew by day or by night—the only difference was that each B-17 or B-24 carried almost double the crew of an RAF Lancaster, Halifax or Stirling night bomber.

In one thing they were all equal. Shot down and captured airmen became, in Allied parlance, 'guests of the Third Reich'; or officially, in German, *Kriegsgafanganen.* As the Allied bombing offensive gained momentum throughout late 1943 and intensified in 1944, losses rose steadily. Captured Allied airmen were protected under the Geneva Convention but German citizens, who sometimes reached downed airmen before the military, could turn nasty and lynching was not uncommon. To the battered and severely ravaged populaces of Berlin, Hamburg, Dresden and a thousand other German towns and cities, the American aircrews had become *'terrorfliegers'* or *'Luftgangsters'*.

In the spring of 1943 all this was in the future. it was not yet practical or possible for the 8th Air Force in East Anglia to despatch its bombers further than Bremen or Kiel, approximately an 800-mile round-trip. In April 1943 the 'force' consisted of only six bomb groups; four equipped with the B-17 Flying Fortress and two equipped with the B-24 Liberator. One of these six, the 44th Bombardment Group (Heavy), equipped with the B-24D Liberator and based at Shipdham, Norfolk, was engaged, in addition to regular bombing sorties, in assisting RAF Coastal Command with raids on German shipping and naval forces.

One of those who flew on the shipping strikes was 24-year-old Lieutenant James E. O'Brien from Monongahela, Pennsylvania. By early May 1943 O'Brien, had already been in England eight months. He returned from a sortie 300 miles out to sea shadowing the German battleship, *Tirpitz*, to discover that he had been promoted to Major and given command of the 68th Bomb Squadron. The promotion came as quite a shock as O'Brien recalls: 'My only squadron experience other than flying, had been some additional duty as engineering officer at Barkesdale Field during our training days in the States.

'I had no sooner found out what a squadron commander was supposed to do, when word came on the calm night of 13 May 1943 recalling all the group crews for a maximum effort on the French port of Bordeaux. This would entail a long over-sea flight, a short quick climb to drop bombs on the U-boat pens and then out again. Other than the hurry to install bomb-bay tanks, this didn't seem too much of an order. However, at 02.00 hours the Field Order was changed to remove the bomb-bay tanks and load up with 4,000 lb of the new type incendiary clusters for a raid on Kiel, Germany. The obvious question was, "What good would indendiaries do at Kiel?"

'The explanation given at the briefing on the following morning at 05.00 hours, was that the B-17s were going to bomb the hell out of the U-boat pens, aircraft factories and seaport facilities and the B-24s were to kindle the fires. It was all very logical but it was a long trip without fighter escort.'

Following the change in orders Major O'Brien cancelled the recall of fellow crew members Lieutenants Tom Cramer and Bud Phillips, that had been put out earlier. It was decided that the 68th Squadron could put up six B-24s without calling on either of them provided that Jim O'Brien flew with his usual co-pilot, 'Mac' Howell, to check him out as first pilot for combat flying. 'Mac' had been 'cheated' out of many missions in his struggle to reach the magic 25 because senior officers had often ranked him out of the co-pilot's seat aboard O'Brien's ship, *The Rugged Buggy*. 'Mac' never really wanted to be first pilot.

Like countless others he just wanted to get back to the States to see his wife. Jim O'Brien was single and not concerned about his own welfare in the same way that 'Mac' was.

The crew of *The Rugged Buggy* was short one radio operator, so Lieutenant Ralph Ernst filled in. Ernst had flown to England with the 68th Bomb Squadron in September 1942. On 3 January 1943 the 'Flying Eightballs', as the 44th Bomb Group was nicknamed, had bombed Saint Nazaire and on the homeward journey the group was forced to land in Wales after running low on fuel. Ralph Ernst's Liberator crash-landed at Haverfordwest and was completely destroyed. The crew was taken to a Catholic hospital where the pilot, Lieutenant Camfield, died of his injuries. After a few weeks in hospital the survivors were returned to Shipdham where Ernst and the others were used as replacements for crew members lost on missions.

'The morning of Monday 14 May arrived (like most others),' recalls Jim O'Brien, 'with the night orderly banging on my door and shouting, "Mission briefing at 05.00!" I had only got to sleep at 04.00! After the ground crews under Captain Landrum and the armament crews under Lieutenant Thompson had worked all night taking out the bomb-bay tanks from the racks and reloading them with 100 pounders, we were briefed and ready for take off at about 09.00 hours. The 44th was putting up 24 ships for the mission. I showed up no so much as the squadron commander but as co-pilot of *The Rugged Buggy* in a "tail-end Charlie" slot–what a glorious way to go!'

A few of the crew members on 48-hour passes managed to get back to Shipdham before take off but were too late to be considered for the raid. One of them was Major Howard 'Pappy' Moore, pilot of the *Suzy Q*, one of the most famous Liberators in the group. *Suzy Q* was undergoing maintenance in Northern Ireland so 'Pappy' Moore's regular crew were re-assigned for the Kiel mission. Lieutenant Robert Brown, *Suzy Q*'s usual co-pilot, would take the pilot's seat aboard *Miss Delores*, a new Liberator which had sat at dispersal for some time. Lieutenant Hartley 'Hap' Westbrook would fly co-pilot.

Captain Bob Bishop, the navigator, plus seven others, all from the *Suzy Q*, completed the scratch crew of *Miss Delores* or *Q for Queenie* as it was known because of her call letter. Gilbert 'Gibby' Wandtke, the engineer, was not happy about the change in aircraft. He had been jilted by a Delores in the States and claimed *Miss Delores* would probably take them over the target but would not bring them back!

On previous missions the Liberators had bombed through the lower Flying Fortress formations. To prevent this, higher headquarters decreed that on the mission to Keil the Liberators would have to reduce their speed and fly behind the Fortresses. It was mooted that if the B-24s tried to slow down to the speed of the B-17s they (the B-24s) 'would drop out of the sky'. The B-24D's cruising speed was 180-185 mph indicated airspeed while the B-17s cruised at 160 mph indicated airspeed.

Above left *Major James E. O'Brien, CO of the 68th Bomb Squadron, 44th Bomb Group, Shipdham, April-May 1943* (O'Brien).

Left The Rugged Buggy *41-23819 in flight over the North Sea in February 1943* (O'Brien).

Right *During a visit to Shipdham airfield on 21 April 1943, Major General George E. Stratemeyer, Arnold's Chief of Staff, talks to Colonel Leon Johnson (CO, 44th Bomb Group), Howard 'Pappy' Moore (pilot of* Suzy Q*) and Lieutenant Robert Brown. In the background can be seen* Miss Delores *which Brown flew on the ill-fated mission to Kiel on 14 May 1943* (USAF).

Not surprisingly, the news that the B-24s would fly to the target behind the Fortresses, and the general rush in planning the mission, caused a feeling of anxiety among the crew as they walked to their pre-flight huts. Jim O'Brien turned over his personal belongings to the clerk and received his usual claim check. He kept the sixpenny bit and good luck charm which had brought him safely through his previous twenty missions and put it with his small escape compass.

Bob Bishop and the others walked out to *Miss Delores* and climbed inside. Once inside they began checking the equipment and settled in for the long flight. O'Brien's crew clambered inside *The Rugged Buggy* and also began carrying out their pre-flight checks. Their ship was already a veteran of a score of missions over the continent but this trip was something not previously attempted. As they taxied out behind Lieutenant George R. Jansen's ship, *Margaret Ann*, 'Mac' Howell was saying, 'If I get back from this trip, I'm going to get stinking drunk.' ('A new experience for him', recalls O'Brien). Dick Castillo, the rear-gunner, commented, 'Come on let's quit kidding, this will be just as tough as any we've ever flown'. Jim O'Brien thought too about Howard Moore's remark at briefing, 'I wouldn't go on this mission if I were you'.

Major O'Brien compares the mission to Kiel to Maurice Ravel's 'Bolero'. This is not to say it was like the *Charge of the Light Brigade*, a movie he had seen in 1939 with the 'Bolero' theme as background music, although there were certain similarities. Its comparison went back to the times the record had been played over and over again in the barracks at Shipdham.

Tom Cramer (killed two months later, in June 1943), Jim Dubard (killed in December 1943), Bud Phillips, Tom Landrum and O'Brien, had a stack of records ranging from Brahm's concertos to *Who threw the Whiskey in the Well?* When the 44th flew its B-24Ds to England from Grenier Field, New Hampshire in September 1942, the load had to be divided between aircraft because the breakable wax records were strictly non-regulation material and secondly, each B-24D was already seriously overloaded at take-off. O'Brien's crew, therefore, decided to carry the records over in *The Rugged Buggy* while Tom Cramer's ship transported the phonograph.

At Shipdham, the young American airmen discovered to their dismay that the 210 voltage in the Nissen huts only gave them about ten rpm! But they had not brought the valued collection of records to England in vain—they played them with a finger assist in the middle of the turntable to obtain a wavering, variable quality between 10-17 rpm.

At 09.00 hours 21 Liberators began taxiing out at Shipdham for the mission to Kiel. The early morning fog and rain which had cloaked the Norfolk countryside did not hinder take off. For twenty minutes the heavily laden bombers circled the field and gained altitude before falling into formation. Assembly completed they headed out towards the small fishing port of Cromer, perched high on the Norfolk cliffs. Land fell quickly away until some fifty miles out, the twin-tailed B-24s, flying as the low formation in the three-group 14th Wing, rendevouzed with over 100 B-17s stacked like pieces in a gigantic game of three dimensional chess. Pilots in the B-24Ds tried to settle down to a constant cruising speed of 180 mph while maintaining a height of only 500 ft to avoid detection by enemy radar. The task was made that much more difficult because they had to continually zig-zag twenty miles in one direction and forty miles in the other in order to remain behind the slower Fort's.

Despite this O'Brien noted that the flight over the North Sea was made in 'beautiful formation' and he thought about the 'Bolero' melody as the sea swept by beneath his speeding bomber: 'This was the quiet beginning where the drums beat a soft rythym and the flutes and piccolos spin their simple melody. About two hundred miles out we started our climb to 21,000 ft knowing that the Germans would have us tracked with radar from this point on. This was side two and three of the orchestrated rythym; less subtle and more colourful and romantic.'

'The 'Eightballs' should have avoided the Friesian Islands but the constant zig-zag course they had been forced to adopt caused them to stay off course and they overflew the islands at 19,000 ft. They were greeted with sporadic bursts of flak. 'We responded,' states O'Brien, 'with the usual appreciation of poor marksmanship from ground batteries.'

'My attention was diverted momentarily to Tom

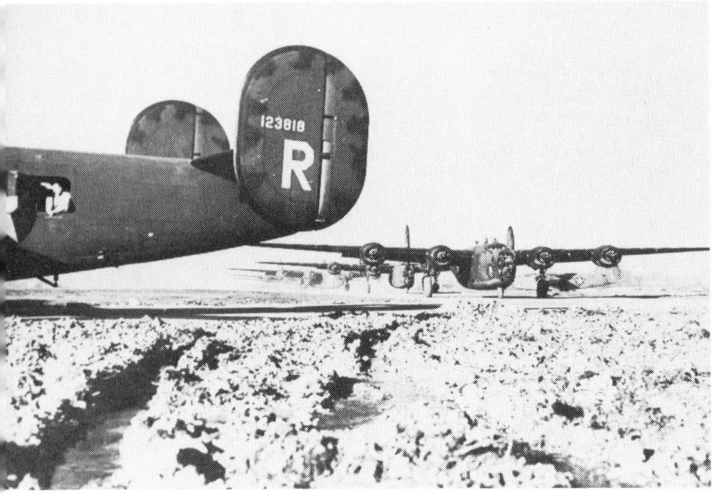

Holmes' ship, which took a burst of flak and appeared to have flames coming out of the bomb bay. (He managed to maintain height and re-cross the sea to England.) I was overly concerned with Tom's welfare but suddenly, our ship was rocked by two explosions. Side three of 'Bolero' increased in volume out of nowhere. A real indication of trouble was the manifold pressure on the two left engines which dropped to 15 psi and there was a sudden drag to the left which Howell and I struggled to correct. I had thoughts of feathering the two left engines but that would have been a sure give-away to German fighters waiting to come in for the kill.'

The intephone on board *The Rugged Buggy* was put out of action in the blast and all communication with the five men in the rear of the ship was lost. Unbeknown to O'Brien, flak had also blown a hole in the tail, knocking Sergeant Castillo out of his rear turret and almost amputating his foot in the process. Three crew members in the tail came to his aid and quickly realizing the extent of his injuries, pushed him out of the aircraft, pulling the ripcord on his parachute pack for him and then they too baled out. One of the three men, Sergeant Van Owen, the assistant radio-operator/waist gunner, baled out over the sea but he was drowned in Kiel Bay despite wearing a Mae West. Ironically, he had always had a fear of drowning even when wearing a life preserver. A German ship picked up his body and brought him ashore.

Despite the crew losses *The Rugged Buggy* and the surviving Liberators in the 44th Bomb Group continued to the target. Crews had been briefed to bomb from 21,000 ft but the constant zig-zagging now brought them over Heligoland Bay at 18,000 ft. As they turned into the strong wind for bombing they were down to 160 mph—almost stalling speed.

'The bomb bay doors opened', continues O'Brien, 'and the 44th let go its clusters of matchstick incendiaries. These only created more confusion. The clusters did not hold together for more than 200 ft before breaking up. As soon as they hit the slipstream they were all over the sky in a negative trajectory, flying back through the formation and bouncing off wings and propellers. Nothing worked better for the Germans at this point as the formation scattered to avoid these missiles.

'Meanwhile, we had dropped our own clusters of bombs and had plenty of trouble. The cockpit smelled of gasoline and our unspoken thoughts as Howell and I looked at each other were fire and explosion. We had now separated from the rest of the group after leaving the target and I noticed at least two other stragglers off to the right. One was Captain 'Swede' Swanson of the 506th Squadron.

'There was plenty of company joining us. Focke Wulf 190s were in formation on the left and Bf 109s off the right wing. 'Mac' McCabe in the top turret kept yelling through his oxygen mask to dip the wing so he could hit them with his .50s. Not knowing what else to do, Howell and I were just trying to keep the ship flying. We had been through this before and somehow fate had brought as through. In the past, we had outlasted German fighters until they turned back over the North Sea but now we were practically standing still in a 100 mph headwind on a 285 degree heading with lots of German soil still underneath.

'We had already turned to side four of 'Bolero' and the noise and the increasing crescendo had mounted to a deafening roar. There must have been two Jerries sitting off our tail end pumping a steady flow of cannon and .30 calibre bullets into us. I heard several .30s zing into the cockpit and bounce off the armour-plated seats. Mixed in with these .30s were some incendiary bullets which made a good mixture with

Left *The 'Flying Eightballs' taxi from their muddy dispersals at Shipdham early in 1943. B-24D,* 41-23818, *is* Texan II *which was lost on the raid to St Nazaire on 16 February 1943* (USAF).

Right *Crew of* The Rugged Buggy *Front row (L-R) LeRoy Richwine (tail-gunner); K. L. McCabe (assistant engineer); Norris Crisan (bombaimer) R. H. Wright (radio operator); Eddie White (waist-gunner). Back row (L-R): Grover Edmiston; Robert Billman (engineer); Jim O'Brien (pilot); Malcolm Howell (co-pilot); John Bledsoe (navigator); Van Owen (assistant radio operator)* (O'Brien).

the intense gasoline fumes and pretty soon we had a roaring furnace in the bomb bay.

'My first knowledge of fire was the intense heat all over the cockpit. I leaped out of my seat, breaking my oxygen hose in the process. I pulled open the top hatch directly in front of the top turret to get out, saw the whirling propellers and antenna wires and thought better of it. I stuck my head out of the hatch and my steel GI helmet, which we wore before the introduction of flak helmets, blew right off in the slipstream. If there was any time to take a second guess, it was then that I decided on some other exit.'

Meanwhile, Ralph Ernst, the radio operator, was trying very hard to extinguish the fire, using all the extinguishers he could lay his hands on. 'I managed to put out the fire temporarily between extinguishers but I figured we would have to bale out as the 'plane would explode at any moment. I tried to open the bomb bay door to make an easy exit but there was no hydraulic pressure and it wouldn't open. The fire was really heavy now and I sat down on the catwalk and used my heel to open the bomb bay door. The fire must have weakened the corrugated metal but it was still difficult to free. However, I did manage to get it open far enough for us to jump out.'

Ernst wasted no time and baled out of the doomed aircraft. On the way down he could see thick smoke coming from the Kiel shipyards. He landed on dry land, in a farmyard not far from a Danish village near the German border where he was captured immediately by German soldiers.

Jim O'Brien also availed himself of the open bomb bay doors but in his frenzied rush to escape the blazing bomber he snapped on a life raft dinghy instead of his parachute. 'I threw the dinghy back to the floor,' he recalls, 'found my chest pack in time and got into the nice quiet atmosphere outside the 'plane. This final emotional crescendo ended the 'Bolero' with the crash of symbols, horns, tubas, gongs and trombones. One momentary musical note at the end was the pulling of the ripcord and the patient wait for a jerk. There was no jerk and I was sure the thing had failed, especially with the handle in my hands having a little 12 in wire dangling from it. I was sure something had broken. This experience for every novice parachutist can take a few years from his life expectancy.

'Now all was peaceful and quiet as I looked up to see the secure strings of a parachute canopy lowering me to Mother Earth. The parachute training for 8th Air Force crews was nothing more than usual instruction on bale out procedure: intercom verbal signals, one steady ring of the emergency bell or "use your own judgement". I'm sure that 99 per cent of the 30,000 airmen PoWs never had time for bells or verbal signals. It was generally a spur of the moment decision reached when everything else had gone kaput.

'On the way down I decided that I should have my back to the wind. I experimented with the shroud lines, trying to turn the canopy so I was facing downwing of my drift. All this did was make a violent swing that almost spilled the canopy. That experiment ended quickly.'

All kinds of debris was falling around him and a small piece of engine cowling narrowly missed O'Brien. He felt a sharp pain in his side and thought it might have been caused by a piece of shrapnel but it turned out to be nothing more than a stomach muscle strain caused by the exertions of the parachute descent.

'Shortly after I realized I had an open 'chute,' continues O'Brien, 'I looked up and saw another 'chute coming down beside me with one nylon panel torn open from top to bottom. I couldn't determine who it was. I landed in a Danish farmyard about thirty miles north-west of Kiel and was captured at about 12.30 hours.'

The 44th's cargo of incendiaries had required a shorter trajectory and a two mile longer bomb run than the B-17s. Flying a scattered formation the B-24s were exposed to fighter attack. Altogether, five 'Eightball' Liberators were lost, including three B-24Ds belonging to the 67th Squadron, which brought up the rear of the formation. The first to go down was Lieutenant William Roach and his replacement crew flying in *Annie Oakley*. There were only two survivors.

Miss Delores was hit by flak over the target. One burst hit 'Gibby' Wandtke and he fell from the top turret with shrapnel wounds. John L. Susan, the radio operator, took over manning the turret. Unfortunately, Susan's guns would not fire between the two vertical stabilizers and Roy L. Klingler, the tail-gunner was dead. Six German fighters continued to fire at the ailing bomber from the rear. Two other gunners, George R. Millhausen and Richard Cate, were killed.

Just after Haldon R. Hayward, the bombardier, dropped his bombs, Bob Bishop spotted a fighter boring in and shouted at Hayward to duck. A shell exploded on the Plexiglas nose and Hayward was struck in the face by fragments. Bishop had the paint stripped from his steel helmet by the blast. As *Miss Delores* fell behind, the left wing started to burn. Brown gave the bale out order but unknown to the crew, the flak burst had also knocked out the intercom.

Wandtke, although wounded, made his way aft via the open bomb bay at the height of the battle to warn the gunners to abandon ship. The survivors proceeded to evacuate the aircraft. The time was just one

Right *Lieutenant William Roach and the first replacement crew to join the 44th Bomb Group. Back row (L-R): Roach, Tenney (co-pilot); Kissinger (navigator); Kennon. Kissinger was the only survivor from this crew who were lost on their first mission, to Kiel, on 14 May 1943* (Will Lundy).

Below right *The ill-fated* Annie Oakley *pictured here with her ground crew on 24 April 1943* (Will Lundy).

Bottom right *Crew of the* Suzy Q. *Back row (L-R): George Millhausen (KIA 14 May); August Ullrich (PoW 14 May); Gibby Wandtke (PoW 14 May); Bob Bishop (PoW 14 May); John Susan (PoW 14 May); David Collie. Front row (L-R): Unknown; 'Gentleman' Jim DeVinney (PoW 16 August 1943, Foggia); 'Pappy' Moore; Roy Klingler (KIA 14 May)* (Bishop).

o' clock. Bishop made his way to the nose wheel bay where he looked out and saw a 'red carpet of tracer'. He paused for a moment until the German fighter ceased firing and then jumped. (Bishop knew the German pilot could not fire for long without his guns seizing up.) Feet up and head down in case the German should open fire on him, Bishop folded his arms into 'wings' thinking it would aid his descent, but the reverse happened and he tumbled.

Bishop quickly reverted to his former position and groped for the ripcord. He was horrified to discover it was not there! In his haste to leave the stricken Liberator Bishop had put his RAF type chest parachute on upside down! However, he located and pulled the ripcord after free falling to about 5,000 ft to avoid being fired upon by German fighters.

'It was like standing on a motorbike doing 120 mph, when suddenly, a little handkerchief came out. I thought it was rather small for a parachute—then the big parachute opened out and reduced my speed to practically nil in a split second.' His flying boots went spinning off. Bishop decided to inflate his Mae West before he hit the water—a dangerous manoeuvre as the sudden force could have broken his ribs. Nevertheless, he hit the water safely and was hauled aboard a Danish trawler where he collapsed on top of a bundle on the deck. The Danes shouted and gesticulated and he found he was sitting on a wounded German fighter pilot who had been shot down in the same raid!

John L. Susan was pulled by his shroud lines from the sea by a fisherman after going underwater. Brown, Westbrook, Hayward, Wandtke and August Ullrich, the assistant radio operator gunner, were also rescued.

The third 67th Squadron Liberator lost was *Little Beaver*, piloted by Captain Chester 'George' Phillips, which was shot down after leaving the target. Only four men from the eleven-man crew survived after three explosions rocked the ship. One of them was caused by a 20-mm cannon shell which exploded in the nose and ignited the hydraulic fluid accumu-

Left *Chester 'George' Phillips in the pilot's seat aboard* Little Beaver. *He was among those killed in three explosions that rocked the ship after leaving Kiel.* (Bill Cameron).

Below right *Technical Sergeant Mike Denny (standing, left) who became a PoW following the Kiel mission. George Price (standing, right), Ed Phillips (kneeling, left) and First Lieutenant Tom Bartmess (navigator) who drowned in Kiel Bay, were all victims of the 44th BG's mission to Kiel on 14 May 1943* (Bill Cameron).

Below *Crew of the* Little Beaver *22 March 1943. Back row (L-R) Unknown; First Lieutenant Ed Mitchell (co-pilot, interned in Turkey after Ploesti raid 1 August 1943, KIA 13 November 1943); Unknown; Staff Sergeant Barney Grabowski (tail-gunner, KIA 14 May 1943); Leonard Broussard; Technical Sergeant LeRoy Winter (assistant engineer, shot down 16 August 1943, Foggia, Italy, escaped and returned to England). Front Row: Staff Sergeant Chuck Forehand (PoW 14 May); First Lieutenant William Hill (Bombardier, PoW 14 May); Captain George Phillips (pilot, KIA 14 May); Staff Sergeant Ed Phillips (KIA 14 May); Technical Sergeant George Price (KIA 14 May)* (Bill Cameron).

lators. The flight deck became a mass of flames and Philips and Everett W. Wilborn Jr, the co-pilot, were killed. The aircraft went into a flat spin. Mike Denny, the engineer, put on his parachute and then tried to extinguish the flames but his efforts were in vain. He then had to save himself. Denny could not get the bomb bay doors open and was forced to crawl right through the bomb bay and bale out through one of the waist windows.

William 'Chubby' Hill, the bombardier, was only saved by his steel helmet. Tom Bartmess, the navigator, baled out of the aircraft and about three minutes later, Hill followed. The short delay was crucial. Bartmess landed in the water but got caught in the shrouds of his parachute and drowned. Hill landed on dry land suffering from blows on the forehead caused by the opening of his parachute and the landing, a bruised back and shock. He joined Dale Glaubitz, the assistant engineer, and Charles Forehand, one of the waist gunners, as the only other survivors.

The fifth 'Eightball' Liberator lost overall and the only 506th Squadron aircraft lost on the mission was *Wicked Witch*, flown by Captain John W. 'Swede' Swanson. Flak had damaged the number two engine before the target but Swanson maintained formation and was able to salvo his bombs. As the group turned off the target *Wicked Witch* was finished off by enemy fighters making head on attacks. Swanson and three others were the only survivors from the nine-man crew. Two of the gunners were thought to have drowned.

Scrappy, piloted by Lieutenant John Y. Reed, from the 66th Squadron, became the sixth and final loss to the 44th Bomb Group. Badly damaged over the target, Reed nursed the B-24 back to Shipdham where ten of the crew baled out. *Scrappy* had to be shot down by RAF Spitfires. Adam Wygonik, the engineer-top turret gunner, had been hit by 20-mm cannon fire on the bomb run and badly wounded in the head, eyes and arms. Sergeant Alan Perry, the radio operator, put a parachute on Wygonik's harness and shoved him out of the aircraft while they were still over the Kiel shipyards. Bleeding profusely and without his

oxygen supply, it is doubtful he would have survived the long flight back to England.

Wygonik landed in the target area and was soon picked up by German soldiers. (Later, his right eye was removed at hospital in Vienna before he was eventually repatriated). The Germans methodically rounded up all the other survivors and drove them away in police wagons. Jim O'Brien recalls; 'We were held in prison for three hours. I found Norris Crisan, Bledsoe and McCabe but 'Mac' Howell didn't show up. A German medic brought in his dog tags and asked me, "Do you know a little man in a yellow suit? He is *toten* (dead)." I kept hoping that the story was a bluff to get us to talk so we all acted as if we did not know "Mac" and stuck to the "name, rank and serial number routine" throughout all interrogations that followed.'

'After extensive questioning by the English-speaking medic and some waiting around the town, eight of us were placed in a canvas-covered Renault diesel truck and proceeded to another town along dusty roads. We continued for about an hour to a point where we picked up some more prisoners including Ernst, Husselton, McCammand and Castillo.'

Ernst had been held in a farmhouse where a housewife washed his hair and face blackened by the fire in the aircraft. The Gestapo and two Luftwaffe officers arrived and took him away in a patrol car. Castillo was lying on a stretcher with his foot and leg bandaged and bleeding.

O'Brien continues; 'We carried on and after a few miles the truck stopped again. Sergeant Crisan was ordered to get out. He came back after viewing the wreckage of *The Rugged Buggy* and whispered that the radio set was intact after the crash and they simply wanted him to identify it. He didn't help them too much because he was the bombardier and loyal to the "name, rank and serial number" bit. Castillo was taken to hospital where his foot was later amputated. I never heard from him again except the rumour that he was repatriated in a prisoner exchange in 1944. That night we arrived in an improvized military camp south-west of Kiel where we stayed overnight with the lights on and the guards over us.'

The following day the survivors from the Kiel raid were put on a train for Dulag Luft I, the German interrogation camp at Oberusel near Frankfurt in south-west Germany. The journey provided an opportunity for the men to admire the beautiful countryside and witness the results of Allied bombing at close quarters as the train steamed through the hard-hit cities of Hamburg, Hannover and Kassel.

At Hamburg station O'Brien and his fellow 'Eightballers' were transferred to another train while an American heavy bombing raid was in progress. Their train got away safely and there were many opportunities to escape but everyone felt uncertain and lost. The train finally pulled into Frankfurt railway station at the end of their tiring journey. The prisoners were forced to spend the night sleeping on the overcrowded and very cold station platforms.

At around eleven o' clock on the morning of 16 May, just two days after being shot down, Jim O'Brien and his fellow prisoners arrived at the little railway station near Dulag Luft. They disembarked and were made to walk to the camp itself. They enjoyed the walk because it was the first opportunity they had had to stretch their legs after the cramped confines of the train and sleeping rough in railway stations. They were admitted into the camp compound and immediately put into the 'cooler' where they were searched. They were issued with wooden clogs and old Polish uniforms. Jim O'Brien reflected ruefully that this was to be his permanent fate as a 'Kriegie'.

However, that evening he was given back his combat clothes and some food was issued. It consisted of two slices of black bread for lunch and five cooked potatoes in jackets for supper plus a kind of soup made from grains of barley, oats and potatoes. O'Brien was later moved to the regular 'cooler', really a tight shut cell with bars. Despite the hard bunk he slept well that night.

He spent all next day in the cooler under constant questioning by his captors. O'Brien saw a 'V' marked on one of the walls and he began re-marking it. This did not please the guard, who immediately turned on the electric heater until the prisoner was almost roasted. Despite this and the constant intrusions for questioning O'Brien now had time to collect his thoughts, reflect on his shooting down from start to finish and review his life up to then. He wondered if his predicament would be permanent and his thoughts turned to escape.

On 18 May O'Brien awoke from a good night's sleep to more questioning. Reaction was beginning to set in and the American Major complained about his treatment. However, he received no sympathy from his German captors, who moved him and some other prisoners to the camp lager that evening. Everyone was suspicious of everyone else, especially towards the British officers who were administering the lager. However the move meant better food and the internees tasted the best of Red Cross cuisine including mashed potatoes, carrots, spam, cheese and tea. They slept well that night with the improved food inside them.

On 19 May the officers were separated from the enlisted men. Next day O'Brien, Bishop, Brown, Westbrook and their fellow officers were ordered into railway boxcars for the journey to their permanent

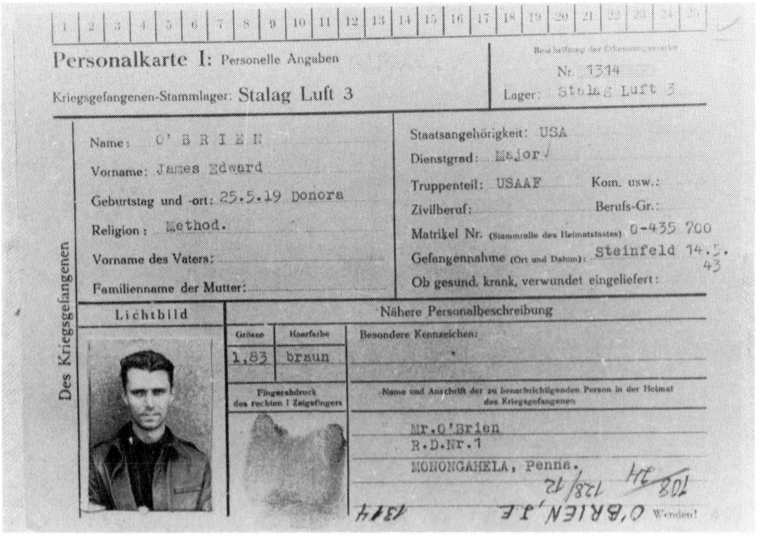
Personalkarte I: Personelle Angaben
Kriegsgefangenen-Stammlager: Stalag Luft 3
Nr. 1314
Lager: Stalag Luft 3
Des Kriegsgefangenen
Name: O' B R I E N
Vorname: James Edward
Geburtstag und -ort: 25.5.19 Donora
Religion: Method.
Vorname des Vaters:
Familienname der Mutter:
Staatsangehörigkeit: USA
Dienstgrad: Major
Truppenteil: USAAF Kom. usw.:
Zivilberuf: Berufs-Gr.:
Matrikel Nr. (Stammrolle des Heimatstaates): 0-435 700
Gefangennahme (Ort und Datum): Steinfeld 14.5.43
Ob gesund, krank, verwundet eingeliefert:
Lichtbild
Nähere Personalbeschreibung
Grösse: 1,83 Haarfarbe: braun
Besondere Kennzeichen:
Fingerabdruck des rechten ! Zeigefingers
Name und Anschrift der zu benachrichtigenden Person in der Heimat des Kriegsgefangenen
Mr. O'Brien
R.D.Nr.1
MONONGAHELA, Penna.
1314 O'BRIEN, J.E. Wenden!

Jim O'Brien's identity card at Stalag Luft III (O'Brien).

camp at *'Stammenlager' (Stalag) 'der Luftwaffe'* (Luft) III at Sagan near Breslau in occupied Poland. The prisoners' shoes were confiscated to help prevent escape and the officers were closely guarded. Despite their privations, the prisoners sang and joked to pass the time during the day and even managed a little sleep standing up.

It was a monotonous trip as O'Brien recalls, 'We rode all day on the 20th at about 5 mph. We passed through many important towns and beautiful countryside. We slept on the train, feeling very dirty and miserable. Next day we rode unil 13.00 hours, when we reached Sagan. After a body search we were put in the American compound where I saw many old friends from the 44th Bomb Group and some of my old flight school classmates. It was a very exciting day in some ways. 'Swede' Swanson and I, were put in a two-man room at the end of Major Sage's block.

'On 22 May I was able to settle down more and gave the latest to the news-hungry prisoners. I felt very strange and out of place having the rank of Major among men of lower rank who had been in the service a lot longer than me. There was plenty of time for reading and many lectures were held outside under the trees (before the Germans cut them down). There were church services, discussions and debates and the opening of a reference library with books provided by the YMCA.

'Classes were held in many subjects from German to Meteorology. Gramophone concerts were held with swing and classical numbers being played and there were community sing-songs by the fire pool. A play, *Turn back the clock*, was presented with the opening of the new theatre. It was very good and the theatre itself helped put the war to the back of men's minds. The girl parts were excellently played by the men.

'For the first few months it was a very leisurely life with plenty to eat, what with German issues of potatoes, occasional soup, bread and Red Cross parcels. I got plenty of sleep, going to bed at 12.00 most nights and getting up at 09.00 hours.'

The first few weeks of imprisonment were also taken up with a great deal of correspondence home to waiting wives and relations, especially anxious to learn the fate of their husbands, brothers and sons. One such letter, written by Gibby Wandtke, five days after he was shot down on the same Keil raid as O'Brien, informed his mother, Mrs Lena Wandtke, in his home town of Manawa, Wisconsin, that he was a PoW:

'Dear Mother,
By now you've probably been informed that I'm a PoW. Our 'plane was pretty well shot up and we "hit the silk" over the sea. Landed in the water and what a swim it was. Got picked up by a boat. Got hit in the leg but it's coming along nicely and I'm on my feet and okay . . .'

As the weeks passed Gibby found time to write to old friends like Bill Voss and often in a humorous sort of code!

'Dear Bill,
You ask me to write something about life as a PoW . . . The part of the country our camp is in, is real nice. It is quite like the area a few hundred yards past the old Bigford Farm [swamp] . . . We live in large barracks, about the same as the big barracks

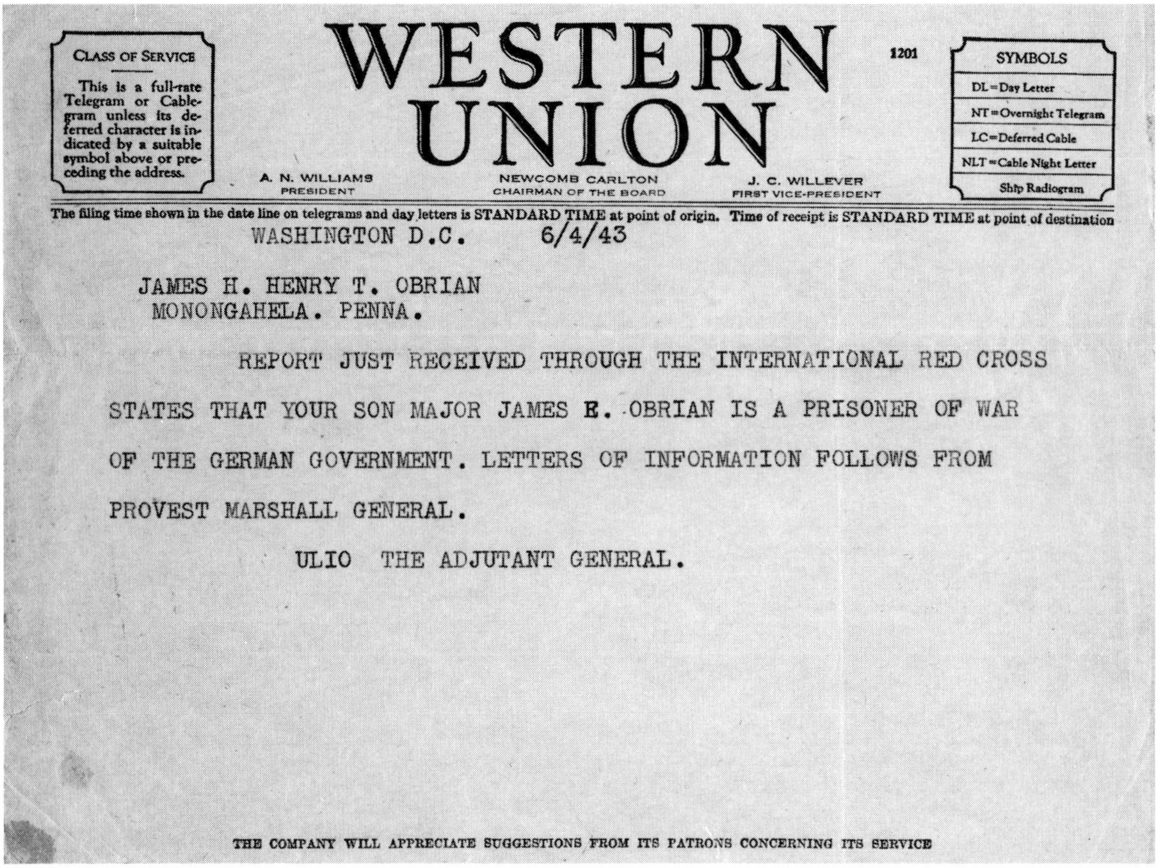

CLASS OF SERVICE
This is a full-rate Telegram or Cablegram unless its deferred character is indicated by a suitable symbol above or preceding the address.

WESTERN UNION

1201

SYMBOLS
DL = Day Letter
NT = Overnight Telegram
LC = Deferred Cable
NLT = Cable Night Letter
Ship Radiogram

A. N. WILLIAMS, PRESIDENT — NEWCOMB CARLTON, CHAIRMAN OF THE BOARD — J. C. WILLEVER, FIRST VICE-PRESIDENT

The filing time shown in the date line on telegrams and day letters is STANDARD TIME at point of origin. Time of receipt is STANDARD TIME at point of destination

WASHINGTON D.C. 6/4/43

JAMES H. HENRY T. OBRIAN
MONONGAHELA. PENNA.

REPORT JUST RECEIVED THROUGH THE INTERNATIONAL RED CROSS STATES THAT YOUR SON MAJOR JAMES E. OBRIAN IS A PRISONER OF WAR OF THE GERMAN GOVERNMENT. LETTERS OF INFORMATION FOLLOWS FROM PROVEST MARSHALL GENERAL.

ULIO THE ADJUTANT GENERAL.

THE COMPANY WILL APPRECIATE SUGGESTIONS FROM ITS PATRONS CONCERNING ITS SERVICE

Western Union telegram informing Jim O'Brien's parents on 4 June 1943 that he had been made a PoW (O'Brien).

which burned down next to the old hotel Manawa [livery stable] so you can see we are well housed... German rations are about the same as the ones at the new plant built in 1941 near the old Borden Plant [Sewage Disposal Plant]... The discipline is about the same as Waupun Prep School [Wisconsin State Prison].

The guards are pretty good fellows. Both they and the civilians I have seen remind me of that settlement near Weyauwega [Insane asylum]... Hope Bill that your line of work will be plentiful over here... Regards, Gibby.' [Bill was an undertaker!]

Meanwhile, Jim O'Brien was also thinking of home but waiting for news of a differing kind. 'My sleep was filled with dreams about the folks back home, my shooting down and about Howell. I was constantly hoping and praying that he was alive.'

2 Life behind the wire

By the end of August 1943 PoW camps throughout the Reich were beginning to burst at the seams. At Sagan, downed American crews were arriving in the camp with alarming regularity. The Germans could not believe their luck when on 12 August a 92nd Bomb Group B-17 piloted by Lieutenant Gene Wiley, was shot down with Colonel Delmar T. Spivey on board. The 92nd had started out for the marshalling yards at Gelsenkirchen but bad weather forced them to bomb a target of opportunity at Bochum. Wiley's B-17 was hit by flak just after bombs away and they crash landed in Holland.

Spivey, who was on only the second of his five scheduled missions as part of an inspection trip, recalls: 'All the crew survived although several of us, including me, were wounded. Interrogation was normal—all senior officers (and those with special knowledge) were given especially tough interrogations. It was startling how much detailed information the Germans had on us. In my case I was on secret orders. Not even the crew I was flying with had ever heard of me. Yet after sweating it out in the "snake pit" at the Dulag Luft interrogation centre I was taken out of solitary and treated like the senior Colonel I was.

'I was cleaned up and given a good room, books, food and clothes. Then the questions. After two days the interrogator became angry with nothing but "name, rank and serial number". He told me I was a fool to be in the ETO on an inspection trip instead of having my feet on my desk at Training Command headquarters. Then he told me my life history, correctly and in detail, winding up by giving me my young son's birthday and the fact that my wife should be told I was safe—which he would do if I co-operated. Many PoWs were so impressed with such information that they confirmed the interrogator's information and gave him more. Thus they added to the great store the Germans had already acquired from previous interrogations, papers, magazines and official registers of service etc, which they could get in neutral countries and from spies and friends in Allied countries.

'I was put in the North Compound at Stalag Luft III with the SBO (Senior British Officer), Group Captain Massey. All American flyers were with the British until the autumn of 1943 . There were so many of us the Germans had to build a new compound. On 1 September 1943 about 700-800 of us were moved to the Centre Compound and I was SAO (Senior American Officer). My duties were to act as representative of the all-American compound in dealing with the Germans, the Protecting Power (Swiss government), Red Cross and the YMCA. The Red Cross got all the praise and glory, whereas the YMCA did equally good work. In effect, I was the Commanding Officer of all the PoWs in the Centre Compound until our evacuation in January 1945.

'The compounds were very similar. The senior officers organized the men along military lines—forming squadrons, and arranging staff for welfare, morale, escape (the most important of all the activities), education, athletics, entertainment,

Two German sentries stand guard beside Lieutenant Wiley's B-17 (42-30081), 407th Bomb Squadron, 92nd Bomb Group, which was brought down near the Dutch border with Colonel Delmar T. Spivey on board on 12 August 1943 (via Bart Rynhout).

Stalag Luft III (Sagan).

religion etc. I worked very closely with Group Captain Massey. He was an excellent SBO in every respect. The German Kommandant respected him and so did we all. I liked all the SOs but Massey was the ''old man'' for all of us until his repatriation. He did not involve himself in escape and was thus always ''clear'' with the Germans.

Although the SOs collaborated at Stalag Luft III they had different philosophies about their duties. I knew one SAO at Barth [Stalag Luft I] who stated to all concerned that it was the duty of all PoWs to taunt, aggravate, inconvenience and impede everything the Germans did regardless of the consequences to PoWs. Massey believed, and I agreed with him, that working in harmony with the Germans frequently paid off in better treatment for the PoWs. We believed it was our duty to do that which in the long term, would ensure the welfare and safe return of our PoWs while at the same time not compromising in any way our duty to our countries and their efforts to defeat the enemy.

'Collaboration with the enemy was never practiced or condoned when such action would aid or comfort him. We tried to live by the Geneva Convention and insisted, frequently without success, that the Germans do the same. In general, the Luftwaffe lived up to the Convention whenever they could.'

Late in September 1943 Major Jim O'Brien, received the news he had been dreading. A letter informed him of the tragic news that 'Mac' Howell had been killed on the Kiel raid. More bad news was to follow. On 15 October newly shot-down crews, including some from the 44th Bomb Group, arrived in the camp. They told O'Brien that in four months beginning January that year O'Brien's squadron, the 68th, had lost nine Liberators with only four survivors from the ninety men in them. O'Brien wrote, 'No friends left it seems'.

In October the first of two famous escapes from Stalag Luft III occured. On 29 October three men escaped from the British Compound through a tunnel which started close to the wire. This had been ingeniously achieved by placing a wooden vaulting horse in position with two tunnellers inside. During exercise periods the men had dug a tunnel and at the end of the sessions, sealed it up and covered the trap door with sand. This operation continued until the tunnel was outside the wire. Three men were then transported to the exercise area concealed in the horse and after crawling the full length of the tunnel they got clean away and made it safely to Sweden. The full story has been excellently chronicled in *The Wooden Horse*, by Eric Williams, one of the three escapers.

The morning after the escape the RAF prisoners were called to parade in the usual fashion. It did not take the Germans long to discover that three men had escaped. Group Captain Massey told his men that the Germans were going to make an identity check against the identity photos to discover who were missing. Massey instructed his men to make this check as difficult as possible for the Germans. Chaos reigned with tables being knocked over and ball games in progress. The prisoners would not come to order and the guards fired shots into the air. In desperation the German Kommandant called in about 100 fully armed soldiers to restore order. In no time at all the guards dispersed through the eight huts in the compound with orders to shoot. With this the 'Kriegies' tumbled out and stepped into their parade positions.

The Kommandant started to read the riot act. Then two British prisoners stepped from the squad, sat down on the sand in front of the Kommandant and began to play chess! One of the guards brandished his rifle and rushed across, obviously with the intention of shooting both players. OberFeldwebel Glemnitz took his life in his hands and kicked the chess game 'from here to Christmas', as one observer put it, and told his men to take the two prisoners to the cooler. Without the officer's intervention they would have been shot dead.

The Germans later made attempts to photograph the PoW's for their records. When their backs were turned for a second the camera was stolen, complete with film and the PoWs used it to good advantage for their escape passports. The Germans were furious and demanded its return. Group Captain Massey said they could have the camera back minus the film if no further action was taken. Rather than risk reporting the incident to higher command, the offer was accepted. It was 'goon baiting' at its morale-boosting best.

Meanwhile, the Allies continued pounding German cities. On 18 November mass formations of 8th Air Force Liberators and Fortresses were seen. Thousands of PoWs watched the four-engined bombers overfly the camp and felt the weight of their bombs when concussions and vibrations were experienced at Sagan. Four days later the 8th Air Force returned and followed this with raids throughout November and early December. A '*Luftangriff*' on 14 December was audible in the camp and spirits soared. That night singing could be heard in the blackout mingled with renderings of Lieutenant Runner's trumpet to fuel the fires of German discontent. 'Kriegies' derived great satisfaction when the Germans were under the hammer.

On Christmas Eve heavy bombing could again be heard in the distance. It proved a better Christmas present than the PoWs could have hoped for. Although the war would not be over by Christmas they believed that the end could not be long in coming. It led to even greater enjoyment among the prisoners who attended carol services, saw a Christmas play and enjoyed meals of banquet proportions.

On Christmas Day there was even bacon, sausage and toasted bread for breakfast and the Germans entered into the festive spirit by waiting until 11.00 to hold *appell* [roll call]. At night celebrations got into full swing. Many different nationalities used the occasion to climb the wire fences into adjoining compounds and it became so bad that gunfire was heard. Next morning counts and recounts tried to establish the imbalance between British and Polish personnel in the American compound. Many prisoners were marched away to the cooler while others rapidly consumed the last of the home-made alcohol before it was confiscated.

By the afternoon of New Year's Day, snow began to fall and added to the post-holiday gloom. *Appell* was held indoors and the lighting and hot water supplies were cut off. Hopes of a quick end to the war were rapidly diminishing. The Germans remained in good spirits and some guards joined in with British, American, Russian and other nationalities in a huge snowball battle. Meanwhile, the real battles continued. On the fighting fronts Germany still felt secure behind the Atlantic wall while in the PoW camps throughout the Reich, the other battle, for survival, went on.

At Sagan no escape attempts were made during the long winter months but plans were laid for a full-scale breakout from the North Compound in the spring. The mastermind behind this operation was Squadron-Leader Roger Bushell, a South African born ex-barrister who had outwitted the Gestapo on several occasions but whose experience had left him a marked man. 'Big X', as he was known in the camp for security reasons, intended to cause the Germans as much trouble as he possibly could. Bushell reasoned that a large-scale breakout would pin down thousands of troops and reserve forces throughout the Reich and cause maximum disruption.

Bushell elected to build three tunnels, called 'Tom, Dick and Harry.' By the spring of 1944 all three were well under way. The tunnels were remarkable engineering feats created by men working with only meagre tools. The biggest job was disposing of the sand. Because of its colour it was easily recognizable but was camouflaged or hidden upon excavation. Usually, it was carried from the tunnel entrance in small bags hidden under the prisoners' clothes. They could only carry limited amounts but there was a great amount of manpower available.

Jim O'Brien recalls: 'A favourite trick was to fold the sand into a blanket for sunbathing, slowly mixing the sand with the dirty surface soil under the blanket as you sat in the sun. I remember doing this on cold, cloudy days when nobody with any sense would be sunbathing. But the Germans never seemed to understand the actions of the Americans and British. Once we loaded sand in an attic in a building used as a cookhouse until the ceiling collapsed. We mixed sand and ashes from fires used for cooking. At one time so much sand was mixed with the ashes (much lighter than sand) that a horse-drawn truck attempting to move the ashes could not budge it!'

All this work could not go on unnoticed for ever. On 11 March 'Tom' was discovered by German ferrets. Work stopped on 'Dick' and the prisoners concentrated their efforts on 'Harry'. On 25 March Bushell and 75 other Allied PoWs crawled through the tunnel and out of the camp limits before a premature discovery ended the hopes of hundreds more in the queue. Hitler was so incensed by the mass escape he ordered that all the escapees must be executed. This was later rescinded to fifty and among the victims was Bushell. Only three prisoners made 'home runs' but the operation achieved all of Bushell's aims.

FOOD PARCELS

ONE PER WEEK PER MAN

RED CROSS

BRITISH		AMERICAN		CANADIAN	
Condensed Milk	1 can	Powdered Milk-16oz.	1 can	Powdered Milk	1 can
Meat Roll	1 can	Spam	1 can	Spam	1 can
Meat & Vegetable	1 can	Corned Beef	1 can	Corned Beef	1 can
Vegetable or Bacon	1 can	Liver Paste	1 can	Salmon	1 can
Sardines	1 can	Salmon	1 can	Cheese-8 Oz.	1 can
Cheese-4 oz.	1 can	Cheese	1 can	Butter-16 oz.	1 can
Margarine or Butter	1 8oz.	Margarine-16 oz.	1 can	Biscuits-soda	1 box
Biscuits	1 pkg.	Biscuits--K-Ration		Coffee-ground-8 oz.	1 bag
Eggs-Dry	1 can	Nescafe Coffee-4 oz.	1 can	Jam	1 can
Oatmeal	1 can	Jam or Orange Pres.	1 can	Prunes-8 oz.	1 box
Cocoa	1 can	Prunes or Raisins	1 can	Raisins-8 oz.	1 box
Tea-2 oz.	1 box	Sugar-8oz.	1 box	Sugar-8 oz.	1 bag
Dried Fruit or Pudding	1 can	Chocolate-4oz.	2 bars	Chocolate-5 oz.	1 bar
Sugar-4 oz.	1 box	Soap	2 bars	Soap	1 bar
Chocolate	1 bar	Cigarettes	5 pks.		
Soap	1 bar				

REICH ISSUE

WEEKLY RATION

Army Bread-1 loaf	2100 grams	Soup-Oatmeal, Barley or Pea	3 times
Vegetables-Potatoes	400 grams	Cheese	46 grams
Other Seasonal	?	Sugar	175 grams
Jam	175 grams	Mare	215 grams
Meat		Salt	
Flour---on occasion			

Right *An extract from the Pittsburgh Press of 23 December 1943 reports Nazi threats to execute US airmen held as PoWs.*

THE PITTSBURGH PRESS, THURSDAY, DECEMBER 23, 1943

NAZI REPRISALS AGAINST SEIZED YANKS FEARED

Breakdown in Agreement On Treatment of Prisoners Is Threatened

By JOHN A. REICHMANN
United Press Staff Writer

WASHINGTON, Dec. 23—Official circles today expressed concern over Nazi threats to take reprisals against captured American and British fliers as an answer to Russia's execution at Kharkov of three German prisoners for atrocities against Soviet citizens.

The threat was regarded primarily as a German move to split the United Nations by holding Anglo-Americans to answer for Nazi grievances against the Soviet Union. It was seen also as a gesture to bolster morale of the German people, who might find some form of satisfaction in seeing executions of the airmen who helped give the Reich the same type of aerial punishment that the Germans inflicted on London earlier in the war.

'War Without Quarter'

But despite the Nazi motives, it was said, the threat can precipitate a breakdown in the Geneva Convention for treatment of war prisoners and substitute war without quarter for the more humane practices that have evolved over the years.

Japan already has violated principles of the Geneva Convention by executing some American pilots captured after the raid on Tokyo. Germany has threatened to follow suit—and now has renewed the threats in connection with the Kharkov executions.

Complicated Problem

The settlement of prisoner cases, however, is complicated because negotiations must be handled through neutral powers. Germany and Great Britain became involved in such a dispute after the shackling of each other's soldiers following Dieppe. It is still unsettled and some German and British prisoners still are in chains.

Germany, it was said, may base the threat of executing Allied prisoners on the idea that she now holds more war prisoners than the Allies and therefore could inflict the greater harm. But new and larger Allied operations are impending and the German prisoner list may soon be dwarfed.

'Day' Is Coming

Thus, it was said, the day will come when Berlin finds itself faced with an interpretation of the laws of war which it proposed but which no longer worked to the German advantage—just as it is now faced with all-out bombing of cities on the same "legal" basis that the Nazis proclaimed when they bombed London.

All reports indicated the Russians gave the German prisoners every legal consideration at the Kharkov trials—far more, in fact, than Nazi courts give foreigners. Officials here, however, were not as much concerned with fine legal points as with forestalling a wave of indiscriminate executions of prisoners.

REPULSING GERMAN COUNTER-ATTACKS, the Russians today reported they had captured more towns in the vicinity of Vitebsk (1) and Korosten (3), while standing their ground and repulsing an enemy drive on Zhlobin (2). Other Nazi forces wedged Soviet positions southeast of Kirovograd (4), but were later reported "liquidated."

Allies Will Send Notes to Berlin

LONDON, Dec. 23 (UP) — The United States, Britain and Russia will send representations to Berlin on Germany's implied threat to punish, perhaps execute, American and British fliers in retaliation for the hanging of three German war criminals at Kharkov, the London Daily Express said today.

The Allied attitude will be transmitted to Germany through Switzerland, the protective power in the Reich, the diplomatic correspondent of the Daily Express said.

The Daily Express did not speculate whether the representations would take the form of threats of counter-retaliation or some other type warning.

The Stockholm newspaper Aftontidningen suggested that Germany was attempting to force the United States and Britain to intervene with Russia to prevent further war guilt trials of German prisoners.

Finland and Hungary Warned by Russians

MOSCOW, Dec. 23 (UP)—The political review "War and the Working Class" in its first issue since the Teheran Conference, today warned the Axis satellites Finland and Hungary that they must decide immediately either to break with Hitler or to go down with him.

"These vassals must understand before it is too late that the double-dealing policy they have pursued in recent times cannot save them," the publication said.

Left *Red Cross rations were not always received and the German food issue could also be restricted. Nevertheless this table gives some indication of the food allocations officially available to the PoWs of Britain and her North American allies.*

The 'Great Escape' marked the end of Colonel von Lindeiner's career as camp Kommandant. He was removed for court martial and replaced by Lieutenant-Colonel Cordes. He served as acting Kommandant for a few weeks until Oberst Braune assumed full-time command of Stalag Luft III. Braune was a tall man, about fifty years old, with a lined, sad and patient face and thinning fair hair. He wore the Iron Cross First Class on his left breast pocket. Although strict he behaved reasonably well at all times towards the prisoners.

Other far-reaching effects of the Great Escape included the introduction of three *appells* a day and lock up was brought forward to 21.00 hours. The arrival of 120 new prisoners from Dulag Luft placed an even greater burden upon the camp and soon all ten-man rooms were full and six-man rooms overloaded. It was not until the end of March that fresh rations and some bulk issues of Red Cross parcels were received. The arrival of 1,400 letters from home was also a big boost to morale.

On 6 April a Memorial Service was held for the fifty PoWs murdered by the Gestapo. Afterwards, prison life returned to its normal uneventful existence. Prisoners continued their slow walks around the perimeter wire, looking across the countryside and glancing now and again towards the sky as the drone of aircraft could be heard in the skies. On 11 April the entire camp watched the 8th Air Force fly over on one of their mass daylight raids.

Soon overcrowding in the West Compound prompted the Germans to introduce three-decker bunks. Each bunk started life with nine slats but these were soon reduced as they were burned for fuel or used in the construction of tunnels. The mattresses were made of burlap and filled with uncomfortable wood shavings. Two lightweight German blankets were provided, together with an American issue but the prisoners still had to sleep with their clothes on to keep warm.

The *Vorlager*, or Front Camp, consisted of several administrative buildings and storehouses. The Red Cross parcel building was situated among them and a group of prisoners were permanently assigned to prepare and distribute the parcels. Red Cross food parcels saved the life of many a prisoner. The Germans made certain that all cans were pierced to prevent them being stored for escape purposes. Two holes were punched in the tops of all cans except fish, which received a single hole. The prisoners sealed all the holes with margarine to stop the contents going bad.

All the food was brought into the camp on horse-drawn wagons or ingenious wood-burning trucks. 'Food Acco', the camp trading post, had its headquarters in the cookhouses, although the camp library, also located there, was eventually moved to the theatre building.

The cookhouses was situated near the centre of the camp, adjacent to the fire pool. German rations were issued from this building. Black bread was the usual issue. Reputedly made of sawdust and other *ersatz* ingredients, it tasted sour but when toasted it was bearable. Potatoes, *kohlrube* (similar to turnip), margarine, jam, sugar, occasional blood sausage (really congealed blood with a few slices of onion added) and a few green vegetables in season, were also given out by the Germans. Issues of pea and barley soup, usually wormy, were made every other day at noon. Occasionally there was cooked millet. Each prisoner was given an eating bowl and cup engraved with swastikas.

The Germans also made available a small quantity of seeds and these were planted more in hope than anything else by the prisoners. The pine needle saturated soil tended to produce poor vegetables and disappointed gardeners produced ears of corn only four inches long at the most!

The cookhouse issued cooked potatoes nearly every day, although on occasions they were distributed uncooked. The cookhouse boilers made hot water for use in individual rooms where the stoves were inadequate. The cooks experimented with new dishes but generally the 'Kriegie' diet was monotonous. Improvization took many forms. Toothpowders were used in cake baking, although it sometimes affected the flavour, and indigestion tablets were used successfully as a leavening agent. Crackers ground to a fine powder were used as flour. Even ice-cream was made with fresh snow and powdered milk and sugar. It was whipped up with jam. Pancakes were made from Canadian biscuits soaked in water for three hours inside 'Klim' (milk spelt backwards) tins and then dipped in milk and fried.

Despite the poor diet and shortage of kit and equipment (shorts were made from overcoat linings), various sports like volleyball and softball were played in the compound and inter-barrack competitions were held, with the winners receiving accumulated cigarettes and candy bars as prizes. Swimming was held in the camp fire pool until it became stagnant and infested with vermin. Boxing and gymnastics were held on special occasions like 4 July and Labour Day. Kite flying gained in popularity but it was soon stopped by the Germans to prevent messages being passed between compounds.

BBC news broadcasts were relayed between each barracks by a newsman whose arrival in a prearranged room was greeted with 'Soup's On!' This signal was changed from time to time to allay suspicion. Each group would send its own representative to listen to the news and he then repeated it to his

Right *Hut inspection at Stalag Luft III* (Sagan).

Below right *The* Play Boy *crew, 466th Bomb Group. Back row (L-R): Fiskow; Mount; Doring; Heafner; Pipes. Kneeling (L-R): Cotner; Duran; Everding; Roth* (Cotner).

room mates. Not surprisingly, the 'Kriegies' went to great lengths to hide their radios. A crystal set was even concealed inside a cigarette packet. The *Vorlager* also passed on its own version of the war news. Each day a radio broadcast was delivered over the loud-speaker system to the cookhouse. The news was written down and read to assembled groups at roll call in the afternoon.

Another source of excitement were the unpredictable but constant searches made in the compound. The Germans would gut a whole block looking for concealed radios, escape items and other illegal items. Even ceilings were pulled down but the searches often proved fruitless. 'Ferrets', German guards clad in blue overalls, clambered underneath the prisoners' huts probing with steel rods for possible tunnels.

This was a further opportunity for 'goon baiting', as Frank Cotner, a B-24 Liberator pilot in the 466th Bomb Group at Attlebridge, England, recalls: 'After the "Great Escape" the Germans dug tunnels under our barracks for the "ferrets" to lie in and overhear our conversations to glean valuable information. However, we had already established a system whereby when one of the "ferrets" entered the compound the whole camp knew about it in advance. The minute he went under one of the barracks the men in the hut would get an overwhelming desire to scrub the floor! The floors of course had many cracks in them and when we heard a "goon" underneath we would throw hot water onto the floor and start scrubbing and singing. Many times the angry "ferrets" would jump up and hit their heads on the beams!'

★ ★ ★

Frank Cotner and the *Play Boy* crew had been shot down on 29 April 1944 on only their eleventh mission, to Berlin. At the IP *Play Boy* received a direct hit from an 88 which knocked out the number three engine. Despite this Cotner continued his bomb run before heading for England. But *Play Boy* could not maintain speed and had to drop back out of formation. Cotner tried to tag onto the end of a Fortress formation but he could not get sufficient speed from his ailing bomber.

Out on a limb and alone, *Play Boy* came under attack from about twenty Fw 190s. A handful made their attack from 6 o'clock, pumping 20-mm shells into the stricken B-24. Robert F. Pipes, the engineer, and Sergeant Mount, the tail-gunner, hit back with .5 calibre ball, tracer and armour-piercing rounds. Two, perhaps three, fighters fell away on fire but the German pilots had found their mark. The tail turret received several direct hits and caught fire. Mount was hit, suffering burns while Sergeant Falk, flying his first mission with the crew as waist gunner, was killed instantly by a shot through the head.

Other German fighters knocked out the number two engine before they were forced to retire by escorting P-47 Thunderbolts. The damage to *Play Boy* was considerable. Cotner asked Pipes to check out the fuel supply. Pipes told him there was only enough for another thirty-forty minutes' flying time—not enough to reach England. The bomber lost height rapidly but Cotner decided to fly on the two good engines for as long as his fuel supply held out. He would not risk ditching in the Channel.

When the fuel supply finally ran out *Play Boy* was down to only 9,000 ft. Cotner gave the bale-out order and gripped the stick while the co-pilot, navigator, bombardier and radio-operator jumped. Pipes was sent to the rear of the ship to make sure everyone had left. Two of the crew were standing on the catwalk at the rear of the bomb bay and one could not bring himself to bale out. He was helped out by Pipes and H.L. Heafner. Heafner followed him out while Pipes went forward to check on Cotner. He was already on his way from the flight deck after trimming the aircraft. Pipes baled out, linked up with H.L. Heafner and the two of them evaded capture for the rest of the war.

Frank Cotner followed Pipes out of the bomb bay. 'When I baled out I could see that there was a hole approximately three feet in diameter between our number three and four engines. There was a similar hole through the bomb bay doors which might have had some effect on my ability to control the bomber in level flight. I could see that the fuselage had sustained thousands of holes and the right stabilizer was almost destroyed. The left was severed near the middle. This damage was a result of the attacks by the Luftwaffe.' [*Play Boy* made a soft belly landing at Daarle in Holland with the body of Falk still aboard].

'I landed in a little farming community in Holland and was almost instantly surrounded by very friendly Dutch civilians. I had injured my left side in the landing and this made walking very difficult. Some farmers brought a door and laid me on it and carried me into a large house. I was there only a few minutes when one of them spoke to me in English. He said, "We could help you to escape except that you are so badly hurt". Another fellow arrived and came to the centre of the group. He looked down at me and said, "Hi buddy, where are you from?" I told him I was from the United States, to which he replied, "Well I'm from Chicago myself!" Apparently, like a lot of Americans, he had got caught in Holland when war was declared.

'The villagers took me to a small hospital at Almelo. I was put into a hospital bed and I had a typical Dutch grandmother with white hair and rosy cheeks take care of me. During my short stay she told me that if my leg had been broken the Germans would probably have allowed me to stay in hospital until it mended. However, since it was only severely strained she thought they would take me away almost immediately. She then made me a strange proposition. With my permission she would take a sledgehammer and break my leg so that they would have some excuse to keep me in hospital!

'Before anything like that could be done the Germans arrived and took me into custody in Amsterdam. The prison looked like it was about two blocks square. I was placed in solitary confinement and served warm tea and some sort of soup twice a day. I was only there for a short while before being transferred to Frankfurt and placed in solitary confinement once more.

'Prior to my interrogation a German Major brought out a book showing photographs of the commanding officers and many of the pilots in the 466th Bomb Group. The Major said, "Lieutenant, we know just about everything we want to know about your mission, except how many bombs you carried". I told him I had no idea because I wasn't the bombardier. I was sent back to solitary confinement. Again and again I was called in, asked the same question and I always gave the same answer.

'This went on for over a week and a half until one day I looked out of my window and saw the Germans working on what I believed to be an RAF blockbuster bomb. It had a delayed action fuse and was only about 30 ft from my cell. Next time I was called in I said we had been carrying fifty 100 lb bombs (we had in fact been carrying 75 anti-personnel bombs). The Major said that was all he needed to know and I could join my comrades.'

Another arrival at Stalag Luft III during May 1944 was 21-year-old Rueben 'Ruby' Fier, a B-17 navigator in the 94th Bomb Group at Bury St Edmunds, Suffolk. Fier was shot down on his tenth mission, on 31 December 1943 over Cognac in *Pacific Steam*. His pilot, Edward J. Sullivan, co-pilot Cliff Robinson and Elmer Shue, the flight engineer, were captured on landing by parachute. The remainder of the crew evaded capture and escaped over the Pyrenees into Spain and were subsequently returned to England. Fier evaded capture for two months by living in various parts of France with Maquis groups and others who risked their lives to hide him.

Like Frank Cotner, Fier's account is another in a series of 'horror stories' told to fellow prisoners at Sagan. 'Many times I was moved elsewhere as the Germans approached to conduct a search for downed fliers reported hiding in the area. When travelling with the Maquis, I carried a sten-gun because I was informed it was every man for himself if we engaged in a fire-fight with the enemy. Fortunately, it did not happen in my case, though I recall the night a French gendarme "eye-balled" several of us sitting in a car on a dark street. We all had guns pointing at him if he decided to challenge us. Apparently, he thought better of it and continued on his way.

'Many times while commuting from one location to another by bus or train, I would be rubbing shoulders with German military personnel—if they only knew! Once, I had just disembarked from a train in Carcassone and left the station as a convoy of Vichy police pulled up to the station and threw a cordon along the street, checking everyone as they entered or left. I was across the street from the station and took it all in. A week before my capture, I managed to send a disguised Red Cross telegram to an uncle in the States letting him know I was still alive.

'Unfortunately, after an unsuccessful attempt to cross the Pyrenees, in which I developed frost-bitten toes, three of us were apprehended by French gendarmes on a road between Axat and La Pradelle. Levi Collins, a B-17 gunner, Flying Officer Clifford Tucker, an Australian Hawker Hurricane pilot, and I, were transported by taxi to the local jail in Axat and given a warm meal in the office of the Chief of Police. For a while we hoped they would assist us in making our way to Spain but one of the three gendarmes who apprehended us was apparently a Nazi collaborator who intimidated the others.

'We were locked up for the night and early the following morning the other two arresting officers visited us in our cell and with what appeared to be genuine tears running down their cheeks, begged our forgiveness and put the blame for our present predicament on the Adjutant, who insisted we be turned over to the Germans. They also informed us that several members of the Gestapo would arrive soon to take us away. (The Adjutant of the Police Department in Axat who was allegedly responsible for turning me, Collins and Tucker, over to the Gestapo, was executed by the Maquis in the evening of 16 March 1944 as he left the Police station.)

'Four Gestapo men arrived and put the three of us in handcuffs. They transported us to Gestapo headquarters in Carcassonne in a canvas-covered truck with the rear flap drawn down to obscure our view of the outside and anyone else's view of us. After questioning, being threatened and being smacked a couple of times because of my responses, I was taken to Paris by train and then by bus to Fresnes Prison on the outskirts of the city.

'During my stay at Fresnes Prison, Levi Collins, a Dutch Sergeant and I, were caught trying to cut our way out of our fifth floor cell. The Dutch Sergeant was taken from our cell and I never saw him again. Levi Collins and I were removed to individual cells on the first floor of our section of the prison. I was put in a darkened cell with all bedding removed and my hands were handcuffed behind my back.

'After four days' confinement Collins and I were taken to the Kommandant's office and after a "royal chewing" through an interpreter, were told that we would be confined to solitary on half rations for a week as punishment for our attempted escape. Though we were told our punishment would be in solitary, Collins and I were put in a corner cell in the condemned row, without bedding and with a damp, cobblestone floor. After many attempts to obtain bedding by banging on the door and yelling in general, the door opened and the guard threw four blankets into our cell. Two were spread on the damp floor and the other two were used to cover us when we lay down, which is what we did most of the time.

'What really concerned me was that the food was better in the condemned prisoner's cell, in comparison to the rations we received in our fifth floor prison. Our meals consisted of "coffee" for breakfast and supper, while we were given soup or a piece of bread on alternate days for lunch. Our commode in the corner of our cell also served as a sink with a water-spicket about 18 in above the commode. Writings and scratchings on the walls of the cell indicated others condemned to death by German tribunals had been occupants of the cell prior to our incarceration there.

'After one week, Collins and I were taken out of our punishment cell and placed in different cells but still on the fifth floor of the prison. During my stay in Fresnes Prison I was interrogated two or three more times as the Gestapo attempted to learn where I had been for the two and a half months I was on the loose and who had aided me. Needless to say, they obtained no information from me and I got a few clouts across the face. After spending five weeks in Fresnes Prison I and eighteen other Allied fliers who were captured after a period of evading, were removed to Frankfurt-am-Main by train.

'En-route, while waiting to change trains at Darmstadt station, a group of civilians on the platform looked us over. We were in civilian clothes, surrounded by armed guards and handcuffed. When they found out we were downed fliers their invectives came our way. If the guards hadn't kept the growing crowd back, I believe we would have been lynched. Bombing results were evident everywhere.

'At the Frankfurt-am-Main jail we were placed in individual top-floor cells for 21 days. During air raids we were left in our cells while other prisoners were removed to shelters. Viewing the raids was exciting but knowing you were in the middle of a raid by your own people was very frightening. Fortunately, the jail was not hit while we were there. I underwent my last two interrogations by the Gestapo and was removed to Dulag Luft.

'After one week at Dulag Luft, without being interrogated, I was sent to Stalag Luft III, arriving there on 14 May 1944; four months and fourteen days after being shot down. The feeling of security which came over me on entering Luft III and joining thousands of other Allied fliers, was tantamount to being home free after the interrogations, getting cuffed about and threatened with execution as a spy and saboteur.'

Among the new intake of prisoners at Luft III on 29 May 1944 was Captain Ronald V. Kramer from the 448th Bomb Group. On 9 May, during a mission to

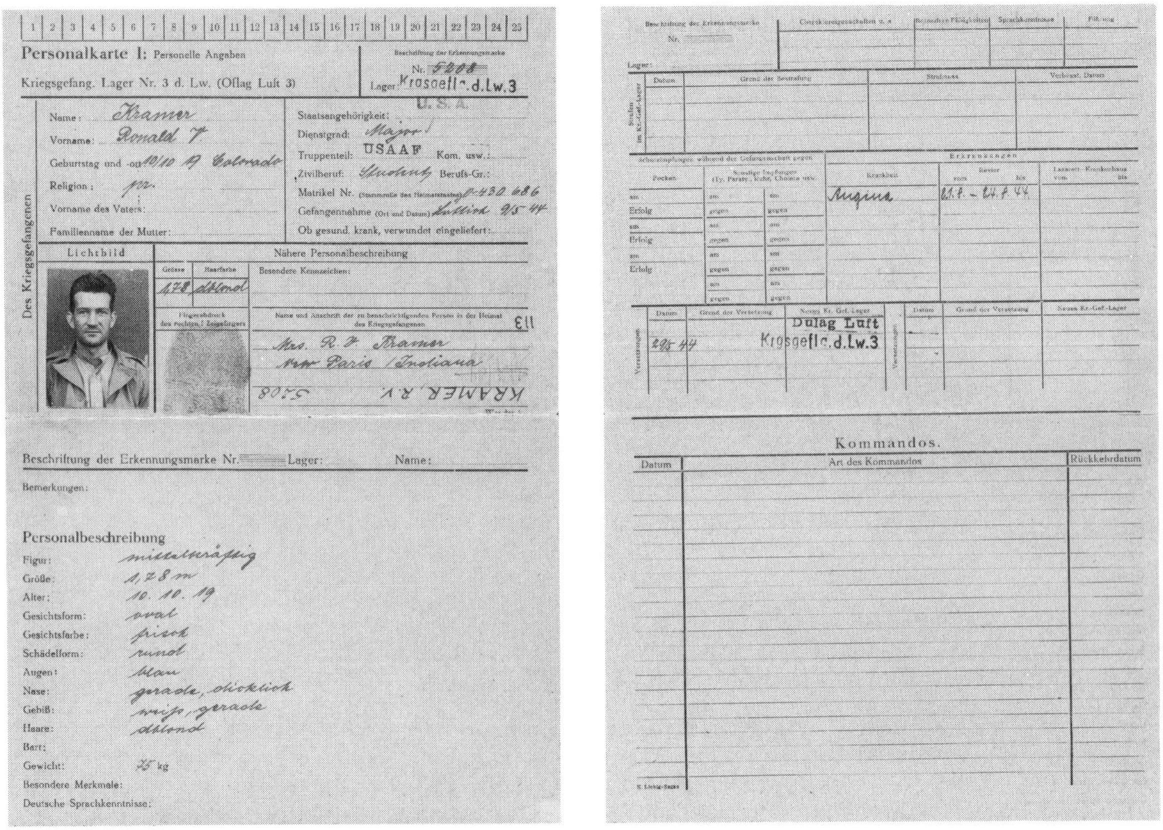
1 2 3 4 5 6 7 8 9 10 11 12 13 14 15 16 17 18 19 20 21 22 23 24 25

Personalkarte I: Personelle Angaben

Kriegsgefang. Lager Nr. 3 d. Lw. (Oflag Luft 3)

Nr. 5208

Lager: Krgsgefl.d.Lw.3

U. S. A.

Des Kriegsgefangenen

Name: Kramer

Vorname: Ronald F.

Geburtstag und -ort: 10/10 19 Colorado

Religion: pr.

Vorname des Vaters:

Familienname der Mutter:

Staatsangehörigkeit:

Dienstgrad: Major

Truppenteil: USAAF Kom. usw.:

Zivilberuf: Student Berufs-Gr.:

Matrikel Nr.: 0-430 686

Gefangennahme (Ort und Datum): Lüttich 9/5 44

Ob gesund, krank, verwundet eingeliefert:

Lichtbild

Nähere Personalbeschreibung

Größe: 1,78 Haarfarbe: d.blond

Besondere Kennzeichen:

Fingerabdruck des rechten ! Zeigefingers

Name und Anschrift der zu benachrichtigenden Person in der Heimat des Kriegsgefangenen

Mrs. R. F. Kramer

New Paris / Indiana

KRAMER. R.V. 5208

Beschriftung der Erkennungsmarke Nr. Lager: Name:

Bemerkungen:

Personalbeschreibung

Figur: mittelkräftig

Größe: 1,78 m

Alter: 10. 10. 19

Gesichtsform: oval

Gesichtsfarbe: frisch

Schädelform: rund

Augen: blau

Nase: gerade, dicklich

Gebiß: weiß, gerade

Haare: d.blond

Bart:

Gewicht: 75 kg

Besondere Merkmale:

Deutsche Sprachkenntnisse:

Krankheiten: Angina 21.7. – 24.7.44

Versetzungen: 29.5.44 Dulag Luft Krgsgefl.d.Lw.3

Kommandos.

Datum	Art des Kommandos	Rückkehrdatum

the railway marshalling yards at Liege, Belgium, his Liberator had been hit by flak and burst into flames just as they released their bombs. All attempts to control the fire proved futile and the crew were ordered to bale out. Kramer wrote, 'We were at 18,000 ft. It looked a long way to the ground but I did not hesitate. I jumped and dropped several thousand feet on my back. There was a terrific jerk after pulling the rip cord. Everything seemed very quiet after the terrific noise a few minutes before. I saw the burning pieces of our aircraft falling and tremendous palls of fire and smoke coming from the target. It was a lonely feeling to see our bombers disappearing in the west when in another hour I knew they would be back at Seething.

'I guided the 'chute to an open field. Several Belgian farmers came running and helped me to my feet. I told them I was an American and they shook my hand and kissed me. They took me into a nearby wood immediately because German soldiers were

Above *Captain Ron Kramer's ID card at Stalag Luft III* (Kramer).

Left *Colonel Joe A. Miller CO of the 453rd Bomb Group who was shot down on 18 March 1944 and made PoW* (USAF).

scouring the countryside. A civilian suit was brought for me and we started walking through the fields in the direction of France. The Belgian who accompanied me was presumably an underground agent to be returned to England. At about 12.30 we were intercepted by two German soldiers. They examined the Belgian's papers but they did not hold up and he was later shot.'

Kramer was arrested, searched and taken to Luftwaffe headquarters in Brussels. He was questioned repeatedly and threatened with execution if he did not give them information. Kramer was incarcerated in an old stone jail. When he was taken through the Belgian capital for further interrogation he was winked at by the Belgian people, who seemed very anti-Nazi. The air raid sirens sounded repeatedly during his stay as American bomber formations headed for the railway yards. The German soldiers were either very young or very old and Kramer's opinion of the 'master race' took a big drop.

On 13 May Kramer was moved by train to Frankfurt interrogation camp with a number of other American airmen from Brussels. The journey through Holland and along the River Rhine was pleasant with old castles and vineyards nestling along the river. Thoughts of war were far from their minds until they reached the war torn cities of Cologne and Frankfurt. At Frankfurt Kramer started ten days' solitary confinement in a dirty cell with only a daily diet of four slices of bread and a bowl of watery soup to eat. He was often questioned but still he refused to give his captors any information. As a reprisal he was refused washing and shaving facilities. The many lonely hours were silently passed with prayers and thoughts of home.

On 24 May he was finally released and taken to Wetzlar distribution camp with 100 other American flying officers where they were able to make contact with the American Red Cross and receive food and clothing. After Frankfurt it seemed 'better than Christmas' but on 29 May when Ron Kramer arrived at Stalag Luft III, it seemed like 'a life sentence'. The only consolation seemed to be meeting several old friends from the 448th Bomb Group and catching up on their news.

Kramer discovered many fellow Liberator crewmen at Stalag Luft III. Most had been shot down, captured and then processed prior to being sent to Luft III where they came under Luftwaffe supervision. However, airmen who were caught in civilian clothes were passed to the Gestapo to prove their military identity or be shot as spies. The Gestapo was not subject to the Geneva Convention.

One airman at Sagan in June 1944 who endured this treatment was Colonel Joseph A. Miller, CO of the 453rd Bomb Group at Old Buckenham. On 18 March 1944 he was leading Liberators of the Second Combat Wing to Fredrickshaven on only his fourth mission. After bombing, Colonel Miller's B-24 Liberator got into difficulties and dropped out of formation. The crew baled out and Colonel Miller landed in a French field. He was soon in the hands of the French Resistance and disguised as a priest, made his way across France to Perpignan. He was captured by a German border patrol as he waited to cross into Spain. Because he was in civilian clothing, Miller was handed over to the Gestapo.

He was sent to Fresnes Prison where the Gestapo treated him harshly, certain that a man of his rank would have information invaluable to them. Colonel Miller stuck to 'name, rank and serial number' and his captors' patience began to run out. While in his cell Miller thought back to 1938 when three German officers were attempting to set a new record flying from Berlin to Tokyo. Everything had gone well until over the South China Sea their Heinkel developed engine trouble and they were forced to land in the Philippines. Their distress calls had already been picked up by the American Army Air Corps in Manila and a rescue mission was launched. It was Colonel Miller who found them and who arranged for their eventual return home. Miller told his Gestapo interrogators of the incident.

Because of the Luftwaffe's insistence that the Gestapo release downed airmen to Dulag Luft with the minimum of delay, the Gestapo chief of the Paris region, T.T. Schmidt, drove to Oberusel to discuss the matter. The deputy commander at Oberusel was Major Junge who, before the war, had been a Focke Wulf test pilot. In 1938 he had been the pilot of the record-attempt from Berlin to Tokyo. After the meeting Schmidt asked Junge to tell him about it. Junge recounted the rescue and Schmidt casually remarked that he was holding an American Colonel in Paris by the name of Joe Miller. Junge was convinced it was the same man who had rescued him in 1938. Schmidt arranged for Miller to be taken to Dulag Luft and Junge made a positive identification. Miller was put under house arrest at a nearby hotel before being sent to Sagan. (After the war Junge was sentenced to prison for war crimes. However, before the war ended he had managed to get his family to Switzerland and on to Ecuador. Shortly after the war ended, Miller, who was head of the American Military Mission to Ecuador, learned that Junge's family were in need of money and he assisted them to return the favour!)

June 1944 at Luft III began with sunny days and thunderstorms in the evening but by far the biggest noise seemed to be on the morning of 6 June. Prisoners seemed to be running in all directions and gradually word spread that the Allies had established

Views of Stalag Luft III, Sagan, Germany (via Bart Rynhout).

Above *Senior American officers in the South Camp, Stalag Luft III, June 1944. Jim O'Brien is fourth from the left, back row.* (via O'Brien).

Opposite and overleaf *Collection of items relating to PoW life: money, cigarette and tobacco packets, Red Cross parcels and cartoons from the* Gefangenen Gazette; *the prisoners' own Luft III magazine.*

a bridgehead in Normandy. Every prisoner in the Reich had waited for this day. Celebrations followed and soon almost everyone was laying bets that the war would be over by Christmas. Morale received another boost when, on 21 June, almost 300 8th Air Force bombers flew overhead, their silver wings glinting in the sunlight. It only increased everyone's hopes that the war would soon be over.

A news room situated in the West Compound theatre, which was completed by Russian prisoners in June 1944, displayed maps of the war fronts taken from German propaganda hand outs. The camp also enjoyed hand-printed weekly newspapers called the *'Kriegie Klarion'* and the *'Stalag Stump'*. Both contributed greatly to morale. The Germans also provided two Berlin newspapers, the *Deutsche Allgemeine* and the *Volkischer Berbachter*. The only publication printed in English allowed on the camp was the *OK*. ('Overseas Kid'), which was a German propaganda newspaper with selected news from America. All the German publications succeeded in doing was to keep out rain when wedged in various parts of the huts! Prisoners were also allowed to watch some American-made films such as *Orchestra Wives*. They were such a welcome change, no-one seemed to mind the continual malfunctions of the camp projector. The 'Sagan Players' also presented three one-act plays and drew attentive audiences for a Shakesperian production and a minstrel show.

News of the capitulation of the German garrison at Cherbourg and the capture of 73,000 German troops three miles south of Caen reached the camp. In the east Russian forces were rolling ever westward on a 400 km front. It all sounded very encouraging to success-starved ears. Further bulletins announced that American fighters and bombers based in Russia had bombed an oil refinery in Poland and in Italy there was an uprising.

It all called for a celebration and it was fortunate that most prisoners had saved their food and cigarette rations so that on 4 July they could celebrate American Independence Day. Jim O'Brien recalls, 'We made liquor from potato peelings and sugar from our Red Cross parcels to mark our celebrations. We distilled it through a trombone supplied by the Red Cross but the first batch was undrinkable. It was so strong it took the plating off the instrument! A German guard was not so smart and wanted to drink our first, strong batch. It nearly killed him. We took his gun and credentials, knowing full well he would not tell his superiors.

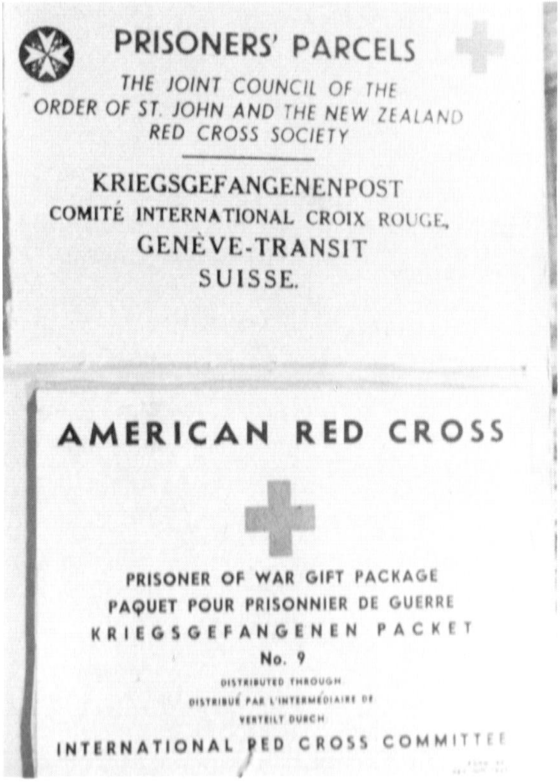

Gefangenen Gazette

SPECIAL SUPPLEMENT TO
PRISONERS OF WAR BULLETIN

Published by the American National Red Cross for the Relatives of American Prisoners of War and Civilian Internees

Washington, D. C. — September 1944

Col. Delmar T. Spivey, senior American officer at Stalag Luft III, sent to the editor of Prisoners of War Bulletin a complete file of the *Gefangenen Gazette* from October 15, 1943, to April 9, 1944.

Gefangenen (Prisoners') *Gazette* is produced, by hand and typewriter, three times weekly, with a Sunday supplement of colored cartoons, by American airmen-prisoners at the Center Compound. When sending the file, Colonel Spivey wrote:

Credit for this paper is given to 2nd Lt. Ronald T. Delaney, who, under most adverse circumstances as to material and subject matter, has shown persistence and initiative to a commendable degree.

There are some 4,500 young American airmen at Luft III, and the articles and cartoons in the Gazette throw a vivid light on camp conditions and on how the men there are temporarily adapting their lives to an atmosphere that must be completely alien to them.

It is unfortunately a physical impossibility to make the complete file available to all families of the men at Luft III, and to the many other families of American prisoners of war who would surely find it intensely interesting. Prisoners of War Bulletin, however, has prepared this special supplement made up entirely of extracts, drawings, and cartoons taken more or less at random, from the *Gefangenen Gazette*. No editing has been done here, but, of course, every issue has to be approved by the German commandant before it goes on the camp bulletin board.

Stalag Luft III, which, like all other camps for airmen, is under the control of the Luftwaffe, is probably the best-established camp for Americans in Germany. Enlisted men in the Stalags and especially on work detachments have much less opportunity for study and play than officer prisoners have.

Gilbert Redfern, *Editor*
Prisoners of War Bulletin

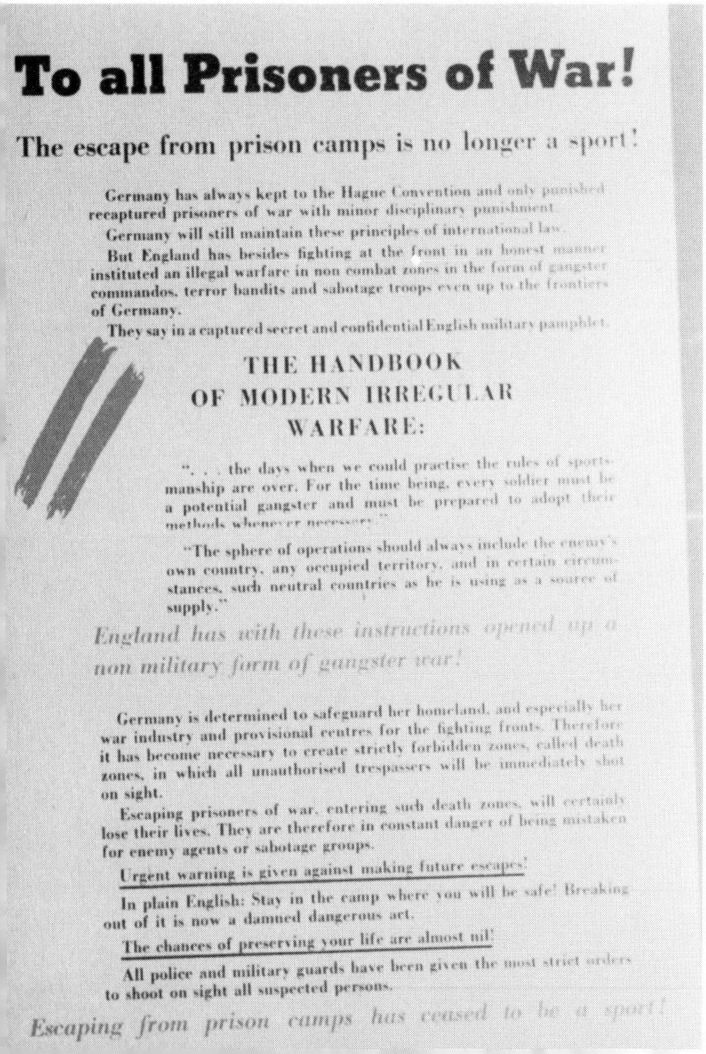

To all Prisoners of War!

The escape from prison camps is no longer a sport!

Germany has always kept to the Hague Convention and only punished recaptured prisoners of war with minor disciplinary punishment.

Germany will still maintain these principles of international law.

But England has besides fighting at the front in an honest manner instituted an illegal warfare in non combat zones in the form of gangster commandos, terror bandits and sabotage troops even up to the frontiers of Germany.

They say in a captured secret and confidential English military pamphlet,

THE HANDBOOK OF MODERN IRREGULAR WARFARE:

". . . the days when we could practise the rules of sportsmanship are over. For the time being, every soldier must be a potential gangster and must be prepared to adopt their methods whenever necessary."

"The sphere of operations should always include the enemy's own country, any occupied territory, and in certain circumstances, such neutral countries as he is using as a source of supply."

England has with these instructions opened up a non military form of gangster war!

Germany is determined to safeguard her homeland, and especially her war industry and provisional centres for the fighting fronts. Therefore it has become necessary to create strictly forbidden zones, called death zones, in which all unauthorised trespassers will be immediately shot on sight.

Escaping prisoners of war, entering such death zones, will certainly lose their lives. They are therefore in constant danger of being mistaken for enemy agents or sabotage groups.

Urgent warning is given against making future escapes!

In plain English: Stay in the camp where you will be safe! Breaking out of it is now a damned dangerous act.

The chances of preserving your life are almost nil!

All police and military guards have been given the most strict orders to shoot on sight all suspected persons.

Escaping from prison camps has ceased to be a sport!

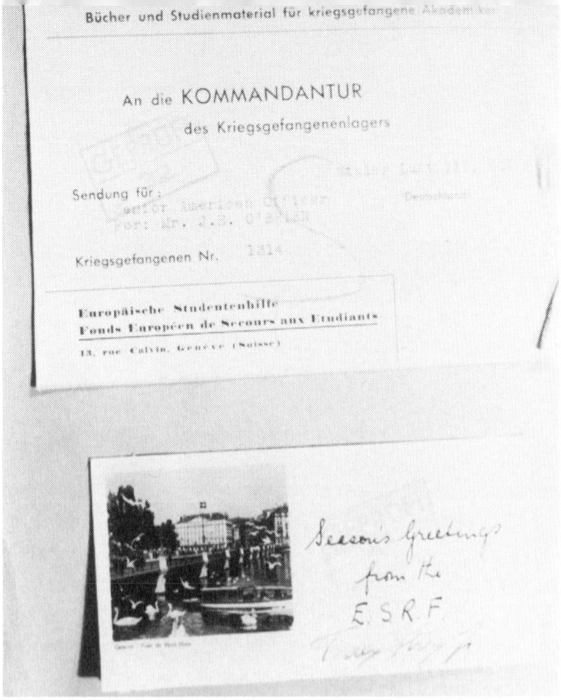

Above left *A mailing to Jim O'Brien and* **above** *a postcard received from Switzerland by successful escaping PoWs from Stalag Luft III* (O'Brien).

'One hears of blind drunks and our home brew tasted so good, after a few drinks on empty stomachs the liquor caused temporary blindness! Drunks lying around the camp were thrown into the fire pool and the habit soon spread. Everyone, including all the senior officers, was thrown in. The Yankee Doodle "Spirit of '76" band played "Dixie jazz" as they marched through the barracks. At first other nationalities thought we were crazy but soon they were in it more than we were.

'The most evocative moment of all came when we were allowed to sing the *Star Spangled Banner* at the end of the programme. A lump came to many a throat.'

3 Italian interlude

While Jim O'Brien and his fellow prisoners continued to languish in the South Compound at Stalag Luft III his contemporaries in the 44th Bomb Group carried the war into all parts of the Third Reich. Since his shooting down over Kiel in May 1943 the 'Flying Eightballs' had led an eventful and sustained bombing offensive from England, together with other B-24 and B-17 groups of the rapidly growing 8th Air Force. However, in June 1944 the veteran 44th and 93rd Bomb Groups, whose crews were familiar with high altitude precision bombing techniques, were surprised to learn that they were to begin low-level practice missions over East Anglia. Together with the newly-arrived 389th Bomb Group, the Liberators were soon skimming the Norfolk and Suffolk landscape at less than 150 ft en route to their target range over the Wash.

Rumour and speculation gained momentum as the ground crews began removing the Norden bomb sights and replacing them with low level sights. Heavier nose armament and additional fuel tanks in the bomb bays gave the men clues as to their new role. In fact the 44th, 93rd and 389th were being prepared for 'Operation Statesman', the low-level attack on the oilfields at Ploesti in Rumania. By increasing the Liberators' fuel capacity to 3,100 gallons they could just make it to the target from North Africa.

Training over, on 30 June 124 B-24 Liberators departed Portreath in Cornwall for the long flight to North Africa. Aborts reduced the Liberators' ranks and among those which had to seek sanctuary in Portugal was a B-24D belonging to the 44th Bomb Group with William Morris on board and a 389th Liberator piloted by Captain Wilhite whose crew included Robert H. Sweatt. (Both Morris and Sweatt's subsequent adventures are featured in this book). The Iberian Peninsula fell behind and crews flew on to the Libyan desert where they came under the control of the United States 9th Air Force. Relationships between the two commands were never good but the 8th steadfastly entered into the African campaign, which began with missions in support of the Allied invasion of Sicily. Most of these missions were flown without fighter escort and soon losses began to assume the proportions sustained at the height of the raids on the U-boat pens.

On 19 July the Liberators made the first air attack on Rome with a visit to the capital's Littorio marshalling yards. Because of Rome's cultural and religious significance, the briefing for the raid was the most detailed and concise the combat crews had ever received. The raid was an unprecedented success and only one bomb had 'got away' and slightly damaged a basilica.

The Liberator groups were later withdrawn from the campaign in Sicily and training for the Ploesti raid began in earnest. Finally, on the morning of Sunday 1 August, 175 Liberators belonging to the 44th, 93rd and 389th Bomb Groups of the 8th Air Force and 98th and 376th Bomb Groups of the 9th Air Force, took off from landing strips in the Benghazi area on the ten-hour round-trip to Ploesti.

This famous raid has passed into American Air Force folklore (the part played by the three 8th Air Force groups is also chronicled in *Fields of Little America*, Patrick Stephens Ltd). Colonel Leon John-

Above *Life for the 44th Bomb Group at Benghazi, Libya in July-August 1943 was in sharp contrast to the life they had left behind in Norfolk* (Warth).

Opposite left *B-24D of the 389th Bomb Group in flight* (USAF).

Below left *Maintenance is carried out to* Southern Comfort *at Benghazi beneath the shade of the wing. Joe Warth facing the camera* (Warth).

Below right *Crew of the* Southern Comfort *having a pre-mission talk* (Warth).

son, who led the 44th Bomb Group in *Suzy Q*, was awarded the Medal of Honor for his leadership on the raid, as was Colonel 'Killer' Kane of the 98th Bomb Group. Posthumous Medals of Honor were awarded to Colonel Addison T. Baker, Commanding Officer of the 93rd Bomb Group and his co-pilot, Major John Jerstad. In the 389th Bomb Group, which scored a great success at its target at Campina, Lieutenant Lloyd D. Hughes was also awarded the Medal of Honor posthumously. All groups received the Distinguished Unit Citation.

The casualties, which were high because of ground fire, fighter attacks and other losses caused by B-24s being engulfed in explosions from delayed action bombs dropped by preceding groups, were soon made good. Replacement officers as well as gunners who were left behind in East Anglia to allow more fuel to be carried aboard the Liberators, were posted to the hard hit campaigners. After a well-earned leave in Cairo the B-24 crews flew further missions against Axis targets in Italy and Austria, including a raid on the Messerschmitt factory at Wiener Neustadt on 13 August.

On 16 August the B-24 groups were given Foggia in southern Italy as their target despite reports that the Axis had been moving defences and concentrating them in Foggia. On previous sorties into this territory the missions had taken on the nature of a 'milk run' and only the day before another bomb group had gone in without opposition. However, 16 August proved far different, as Charles Joe Warth, a gunner in *Southern Comfort* piloted by Lieutenant H.W. Austin in the 506th Bomb Squadron of the 44th Bomb Group, recalls: 'We were told that the raid would be a ''milk run''. We were ''fat, dumb and happy'' to go there. But conditions change rapidly in

Above left *Final mission preparations are carried out by the fuselage of* Southern Comfort. *Standing, H. Austin: Kneeling, facing (L-R): A. Fabiny; D. Lee; J. Jett. Kneeling (back) Joe Warth (L) and possibly Singer (R)* (Warth).

Above *The 'Eightballs' lived in tented accommodation while in the Libyan desert* (Warth).

a combat zone and the German High Command, getting word we were returning, laid a little trap for us.'

Joe Warth had missed the Ploesti raid because all 44th Bomb Group aircraft carried nine-man crews to permit more fuel to be carried. He was the only member of the crew to stand down that day. Foggia would be Austin's crew's twelfth mission of the war.

At around 06.30 on 16 August 25 'Eightball' aircraft began taking off from their desert airfield at Benina Main, one of Mussolini's former airfields fifteen miles from Benghazi. The roar of the Liberators' Twin Wasp engines produced great sand clouds as they taxied from their dispersal points. Hundreds of wrecked Axis aircraft still littered the area for miles around and on the walls of the hangars were inscribed the words, 'Believe, Obey, Fight'.

Shortly after take-off two Liberators were forced to jettison their bombs in the Mediterranean after developing mechanical troubles and returned to Benina: 23 aircraft, including Warth's ship, *Southern Comfort*, headed for their target, the satellite airfield at Foggia North. The target was reached at 10.33 and the Liberators released their 45-second tail-delay and fragmentation bombs from 20,000 ft. The enemy flak guns were well aimed and accurate and several B-24Ds suffered minor damage.

Light, scattered clouds over the target area afforded no protection at all and upwards of fifty Bf 109s, Ju 88s and Me 110s, using the unlimited visibility to good advantage, tore into the 'Flying Eightballs'. Joe Warth recalls, 'Our Liberator took an uncountable number of direct hits from the German fighters, which came at us from every direction. I know we shot down at least three of them when we heard the bale-out klaxon sound; three of our engines were shut off and on fire and the bomb bay was a blazing inferno. In the rear of the aircraft we were completely cut off from the rest of the crew. I made it to the camera hatch, turning round to see the door to the bomb bay vaporize in the flames. The four of us in the rear wasted no time in getting out, Staff Sergeants Lee and Purcell going out of their waist windows.

'I was sure the parachute would not open so I tried to knock myself out so that when I hit the ground I would be unconscious. But after what seemed minutes my 'chute filled. First the drone then the main 'chute. When I was on my way down I looked about and saw that the sky for many miles around was a mass of burning and still fighting aircraft and a patch of white parachutes. Some aircraft were on fire while others were pressing home their attacks. Others tried to fight them off. [Altogether, the 44th Bomb Group lost seven B-24s, including the seemingly indestructable *Suzy Q* in the hands of a new crew.]

'*Southern Comfort* was a mass of flame as she spun down, crashing into an Italian hillside. There was a final blast of flame and noise as if she had but one desire left; to return to the earth as the ore from which she came.' [*Southern Comfort* lived on in the 44th Bomb Group throughout the rest of the war as *Southern Comfort* I, II, III and IV.]

'I hit the ground and rolled over. There was only a nick on my leg. I rolled up my parachute and tried to walk away. I got down a hillside and was met by two German motorcyclists who had seen me land. They were on the scene within about two minutes. They searched me and although I couldn't understand German I knew what a machine-gun pointing at me meant. I held up my hands while my money and other articles were taken from me. They took me down the hillside. I was more scared now than when I had bailed out of my airplane. I was put on a motorbike behind one of the Germans in front who did the driving. The other sat at the back with his machine-gun in my ribs. We drove down the hill and met up with some more Germans and their American prisoners from the raid. All ten men aboard *Southern Comfort* baled out but Lieutenant P.S. Singer, the navigator and Lieutenant S. Finder, the bombardier, never reached the ground alive. Both their bodies were later found by the Germans who reported that their parachutes were bullet ridden and had failed to work properly.

'About half a dozen of us were taken to a small holding area surrounded by a mix of German and Italian soldiers. We sat there a long time before being loaded onto a heavily-guarded truck and taken to a small compound about twenty miles away. We were given a brief interrogation from a German who had lived in St Louis for a time. He spoke English fluently.

'That night we met our radio operator, Staff Sergeant Ray Whitby in jail. He had only arrived at Benghazi the day before, on Sunday 15 August. Our regular radio operator, Edgar L. Shaw, had been taken sick on the way to the plane and Whitby had replaced him. Next day we were moved to Bari, a coastal town on the "heel" of Italy, for a more thorough interrogation at Gestapo headquarters. Despite our unwillingness to talk they produced details of our group and knew everything about us.

'Austin and our co-pilot, Lieutenant A.T. Fabiny, were sent away to an officers' camp. Hickerson, the tail gunner, J.W.B. Jett, the top turret gunner, Lee, Purcell and I, were sent north to Sulmona, an old prison camp at Aquilla ("Valley of the Eagle") which had been used during the First World War to hold German prisoners. It was next to a concentration camp used by Mussolini for housing political prisoners. We were the only Americans at Sulmona but there were 3,000 British troops, some of whom had been captured in the North African desert. We were given complete British uniforms and food rations and met the Senior British Officer of the camp. An Australian named "Blackjack" ran the camp and had a private army to do it. Our guards issued orders through him.

'It was a well organized camp. We lived in long huts, sleeping on the floor in palliases. We were fed one bowl of macaroni and 100 grammes of bread each day. Fortunately, we had as much fresh water as we could drink. We also received Red Cross parcels from England, Australia and New Zealand. I celebrated my 21st birthday in Aquilla on 3 September 1943 with rice wine. It was potent and a little bit went to the

Charles 'Joe' Warth pictured in December 1942 (Warth).

head!

'We knew we would be moved to Germany when the Allies invaded southern Italy so everyone was thinking of one thing: escape. It was debated for days and in the mass of confusion a lucky chance came up. One morning our Italian guards, hearing that the British Army was coming, left the gates open and scurried around. 'Planes had flown over the camp the day before. There was no way to identify the camp from the air and no flags were put up in the camp. In the confusion a few of us managed to escape. I took off with Barry Shillito, a British commando, and covered quite a few miles in the first day. (All six of my crew got out of Aquilla but curiously, only about ten British got out.)

'We knew it was unsafe to travel in groups so we split into twos. I could think of no-one better equipped than the commando so I stayed with Shillito. None of us "Yanks" had been trained in escape and evasion procedures.

'By chance we ran into some Italian partisans who surprisingly, were pleased to see us. They took us in and took good care of us. The leader had been one of Al Capone's mobsters and had lived in Chicago until he was deported. He was willing to do anything to help an American get away to further his cause to return to America after the war. He took us down the mountains to Castillini sul Berferno ['Castle by the River Perferno'].

'By this time I was pretty sick with malaria, yellow jaundice and dysentry. My commando friend knew it was time to get some rest because I was down to under 100 pounds. I could not walk a hundred yards without having to stop. Arrangements were made by the leader for me to be taken to an Italian home. I stayed for more than a week and the rest restored my health. The Germans came to the house every morning at 8 o'clock and issued their demands for food rations. The Germans did not bring their own food in from Germany—they got it from the land they lived on. Every afternoon at about 5 o'clock a German truck would call to pick up the food.

'Several people in the village knew I was staying at the house. My British friend had left several days earlier. One of the Italians who was evidently a Fascist, decided it was time to report me to the authorities. The Germans returned late one night and started a house-to-house search. Word spread and within moments of the Germans' arrival at one end of the town I was out the other, down the mountains. I was pointed in the right direction and proceeded alone for about four days, finally reaching a little valley. On one side the Germans were shelling the British on the other, and *vice versa*. I stayed in the bottom of the valley and waited for the shelling to stop. At the end of the battle I went up what I hoped was the British side and met an advance patrol from the 8th Army. They were a very welcome sight to a 21-year-old kid from Kentucky.

'From then on I was OK. I went home via Sicily and North Africa, where I was admitted to hospital for eight days. Early in November, when I was fit to travel again I was despatched to the west coast of Africa where I boarded an aircraft for London. I was met by MI6 and underwent heavy interrogtion for two days. They checked my story repeatedly because at this stage in the war very few PoWs had got back to England. I was turned over to the 44th Bomb Group at Shipdham who verified that I was a *bona fide* airman. Colonel Leon Johnson sent a driver to London to pick me up. I stayed at Shipdham for one day and then returned to London for transportation back to the USA. I was home by Christmas, arriving in Miami on the night of 25 December 1943.'

4 Journey to Krems

Ralph Ernst, Jim O'Brien's replacement radio-operator who was shot down on the Kiel raid on 14 May 1943, had little reason to celebrate. Ernst and the other enlisted men from the *Rugged Buggy* had been parted from O'Brien and his fellow officers at Dulag Luft. After interrogation, the enlisted men had been put on a train for Stalag Luft I on the Baltic. Ernst had remained there for six months before being transferred to Stalag VIIA, Moosburg, a few miles north of Munich in southern Bavaria.

The barracks at Moosburg were overcrowded and the beds were made of crude, rough, wood. Fleas and bed bugs were everywhere. The mattresses were filled with straw and dunlap while wooden slats served as springs. The prisoners never undressed on cold days or during the winter months because there was little heat. What warmth there was came from small stoves made out of tin cans which burned wood from the attic.

While at Moosburg, Ernst made an abortive escape attempt. His reward, in June 1944, was a transfer to Stalag XVIIB, Krems, 85 kilometres south-west of Vienna. From 1938 until 1940 it was used as a concentration camp. Ernst and his fellow prisoners walked from the railway station, up into the foothills to the camp near the village of Gneixendorf. The new intake of prisoners were run through the delouser and marched into the camp proper.

Krems was bursting at the seams with 4,500 prisoners of all nationalities herded into twelve compounds—five of them holding Americans, the others Italians, Russians, French, Serbs and Poles. The barracks, built to accommodate 240 men, were just like cattle sheds and at least 400 men were crowded into them. Only boards and battens hid the cracks and the floors were made of wood. Just as at Moosburg the prisoners' straw-filled palliases were a wonderful haven for fleas.

However, the Americans were quick to organize themselves, as Ralph Ernst recalls, 'Our American compound had a camp leader and helpers. An army was designed in case of emergency and set up like a military organization. Master Sergeant Norris Crisan, the bombardier on O'Brien's crew, was our barracks chief.'

Orlo Natvig, a radio operator in the 91st Bombardment Group, was team leader to twenty men at Krems and was responsible for dividing the food rations: 'It was fairly easy to ration the soup because not too many prisoners wanted it but bread was different. They took a great interest in seeing that every slice was divided evenly. Whenever we received any meat it was the same. Food was the essence of the day —there was little else that broke the monotony.

'When I first arrived at Stalag XVIIB it was in a deplorable state. The floors were covered in mud and

Orlo Natvig pictured in May 1943. (Natvig).

we were given brooms made out of twigs to sweep out the barracks. The camp was built on a hill and it was just as well there was something worthwhile to look at because leisure facilities were virtually non-existent in the early days. One of the few things we could do was walk around the compound. Later, we dug a few trenches for air raid shelters and even talked the Germans into letting us build a chapel. Father Stephen Kane, a real fine Catholic chaplain, had been captured in North Africa.'

Natvig had been one of the first Americans at Stalag XVIIB, having been captured on 27 September 1943 when his B-17, *Local Girl*, was shot down over Holland after a raid on Emden. The night before, Natvig had a premonition this mission would be his last and so he had caught up on his correspondence and had sent home to his mother all the loose money he had in his bill fold. His premonition was well-founded. After dropping their bombs on the target *Local Girl* was attacked by Bf 109s. They made their attacks from below because the ball turret was out of action: the gunner having passed out through lack of oxygen. The number two engine was set on fire and a shell exploded in the ratio compartment. Splinters missed Natvig by inches. The intercom was knocked out and most of the crew began evacuating the aircraft.

Lieutenant Peagram, the pilot, remained true to his word that in the event of an emergency, he would remain at the controls to allow the rest of the crew to bale out. (The brave pilot was later found dead among the wreckage of the bomber.) Eight men baled out of the doomed bomber over the coast of Eems. For some it was a close shave, as Natvig recalls, 'The

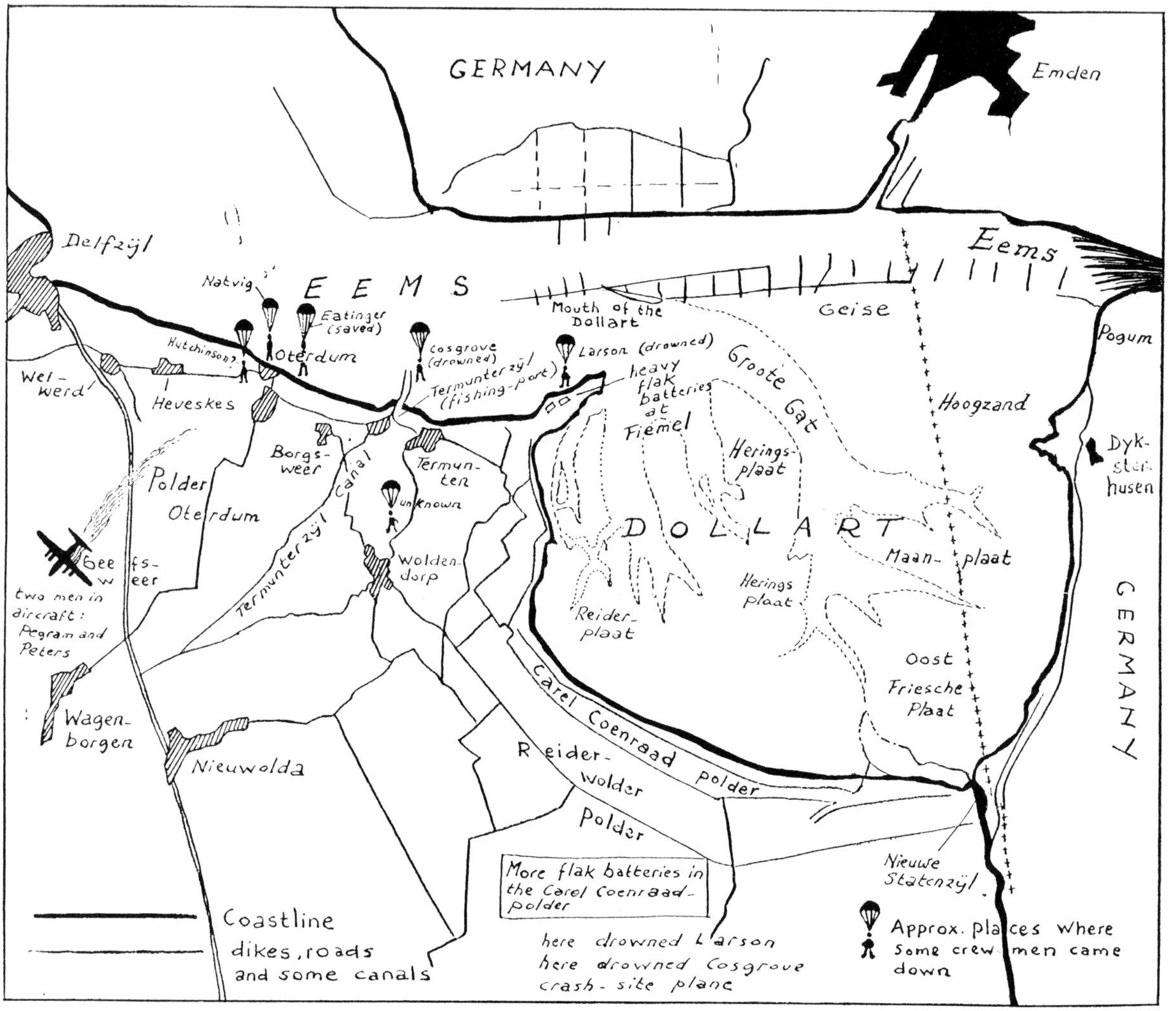

Right *Aerial photo showing the exact location where Orlo Natvig landed on Dutch soil. A few hundred yards more and he might have suffered the same fate as Cosgrove and Larson who drowned in the River Eems. Arrows show the route the captured Natvig was teken into captivity* (via Natvig).

Below left *Map showing* Local Girl *crew landing sites in Holland.* (via Natvig).

Below right *A German sentry stands guard beside the wreckage of* Local Girl (via Natvig).

waist gunner, Staff Sergeant Hutchinson, and I, put a parachute on the ball turret gunner and pushed him through the waist door hatch, pulling his ripcord as he went. I pulled at the coveralls of Melvin Peters, the other waist gunner, to get him to go with us but he made no effort to follow us and we did not have time to force him, as he was still hanging on to his waist gun.' (Peters went down with *Local Girl*, firing his gun to the end.)

Larson, the engineer, and Cosgrove, the navigator, drowned when the cords of their parachutes became entangled in the *'botschuttings'* or 'flounder fences'; a device of twigs and branches to catch fish, and in their heavy clothing they were powerless. Norman Eatinger, the bombardier, was more fortunate. He was rescued by a Dutch fisherman who at that moment was fishing on the Dollart and rushed to the scene.

Natvig recalls, 'It's a remarkable thing what goes through your mind when you bale out. I recalled the time I had signed on at seventeen. My mother had been very upset and had said, "You'll probably end up getting shot down". I also thought about my friend Curtis, who belonged to a fighter group near London. We were going to meet in London that coming weekend for a birthday party for an English friend at High Wycombe.

'As I drifted down I thought that if I undid one of my boots and threw it down, it would tell me in which direction I would land. I watched it for as long as I could and it headed for land. I was heading for a little town. I had seen some German parachutists who had baled out over London and they had slammed into the side of buildings. I thought how ironic it would be if I did the same, in this, a small town of only about thirty buildings. There was little I could do but I was glad I wasn't heading into the water.

'As it turned out, I came right over the top of the buildings and landed on a "*kwelder*" behind a dyke about 200 yards outside the village of Ouderdom. I had missed landing in the water by only a hundred feet. It was raining at the time but my appearance did not bother five contented cows who looked up once and then continued grazing! I noticed a group of people coming towards me. I got out of my parachute, gathered it together, and walked over to meet them. One of the group was a policeman so I raised my arms to show I had no weapons. I handed over my parachute to the civilians and gave away my escape and emergency ration kits. One of the Dutch people later made a wedding dress from my parachute and another used part of it for a christening set.

'I asked a young Dutch lad about half my age if there was any chance of escape. He said the area was

Above *Local Dutch citizens pose in front of* Local Girl *and a very young German sentry* (via Natvig).

Left *German officers examine ammunition collected from the wreckage of* Local Girl. *Two Dutch policemen, van Klaveren (standing) and Max van Diederhoven (sitting on wing), look on* (via Natvig).

Below and above right *Two elderly guards pose in front of the wreckage of* Local Girl. *Two propellers missing on these photos were later recovered by the Dutch and used as a memorial to the crew. Long after the war Orlo Natvig was given the blades and he had them shipped to the USA where they now stand in his front garden!* (via Natvig).

heavily defended and the Germans would arrive shortly. I was taken to the cafe of Jan van der Laan and taken prisoner by the Germans who lost no time in getting to the scene. It was quite a shock to have a fully fledged German officer walk up to me brandishing a .38 pistol and cocking it before he reached me. He stuck it in my stomach and my blood turned to water.'

Natvig and five others were transported to Dulag Luft at Frankfurt, stopping off at a German fighter base at Jevers. 'We were placed in an old guard house on the base for three days and then taken to the local train station. While we were on the platform some civilians wanted our skins. We backed up by a concrete wall and our guards stood out in front pointing their rifles with bayonets fixed. I did not blame the civilians because I had been told by the truck driver on the way from the airstrip that some of our bombs had fallen in a schoolyard. He also said an aircrew member who had baled out in the vicinity had been strung up on telegraph poles. He may have been trying to scare us but judging by the attitude of the civilians, I am sure they would have had our hides but for the guards.

'At Dulag Luft we were placed in solitary confinement. I was put in a room about 5 ft wide by about 13 ft long and spent six days there. It was quite surprising to me, talking with my interrogators, to discover they actually knew more about the 91st Bomb Group than I did. It came as a real shock that they could list the history of my 324th Squadron commander who was of Jewish descent. I am sure there was little they could gain from me and pretty soon I was taken to a holding camp. There I met an English-speaking Luftwaffe officer who had been a salesman for an optical firm in Iowa. He had even travelled through New Hampton, my home town. It was quite amusing for him to show me a photo he had of his car parked in the main street. He maintained he had been caught up in the war after he had gone back to Germany to visit his parents.

'During my sojourn in Frankfurt, the 8th Air Force paid us a visit and bombed a propeller works. That night the RAF dropped flares preparatory to their raid on the factory and one of them became entangled in the wire fence surrounding the compound. I asked some RAF personnel, "Why the flares?" They told me everything inside the ring of flares was the bombing zone! This did not make me feel too good because bombs would be hurtling down within a block of our camp. When the bombs began to fall it seemed as if the barracks were bouncing up and down from the vibrations. A German flak post firing nearby added to the noise and debris falling on the compound. I sat right down on the floor with the rest who were trying to stop their knees knocking.

'Apart from quite a bit of fire in the downtown area we came to no harm. Later that night we were put on a train and told that we were on our way to a permanent camp. The train was so overcrowded that we had to take it in turns to occupy the seats. On the outskirts of Nuremberg we ran into more bombing. I swear the Germans backed our train right into the main part of the city in the hope that we would get caught up in it.'

Natvig and the other prisoners survived the raid and were transported to Krems to sit out the rest of the war. To guard against escape attempts, the American prisoners were not allowed out of the camp to join work details. As a consequence they had no opportunity to procure food. Instead, they had to depend on other nationalities who were allowed out and paid them in cigarettes for any goods brought back.

New arrivals joined Natvig and Ernst in the American compound at all-too-frequent intervals. On 13 October 1943, 1,350 American non-commissioned officers arrived from Stalag VIIA. The next day the second Schweinfurt raid (see Chapter 9) claimed many more airmen and some would find their way to Krems in the next few weeks. One of them was Marshall Hamer, a gunner in the 96th Bomb Group, who was captured immediately on landing; 'Fortunately, I landed in a ploughed field. Unfortunately, in that same field German soldiers were on manoeuvres. All careful plans for escape were blasted by shouts of "*Luftgangster, Luftgangster*".

'Prison camp was a learning experience. We were fed once a day with something called soup, for lack of a proper description. It was brought to us in a half barrel and set in the middle of the barracks for 200 men to make a dive for their share. It was a sort of vegetable soup. We will never know what was put into it, although we could recognize some items. After everyone had eaten we would pull things from our pockets that we found in the soup; bits of an animal that had gotten too close to the cooks.

'Nature was kind to us in that if some meat or vegetables were spoiled, the maggots would float to the top and we could scoop them off and go ahead with the meal. If the soup was so bad no one would eat it, one could always wash his socks in it, or shave with it since it was hot. We were also given a bread ration once a day. This black bread was very functional as well as nutritious. You could use it for a pillow (hard) or as a hammer. It never got stale unless it was cut for the crust was like concrete. The Germans baked it in huge pans and stored it for future use. Dates stamped on the bottom indicated its age. Finally, the Germans ran out of stored bread and baked fresh bread, which was worse due to the sawdust added to the flour. We ate it just like fuel.

'For nineteen months I never had a hot bath or a change of clothing. I still managed to keep myself clean. For one hour each morning, noon and evening we were allowed to have water, though it was cold. Those who wanted could wash clothing in cold water without soap. We showered under a cold spigot. In the winter we had to clear out the snow first since we had torn the windows out of the bath house. Showers were brief and infrequent.

'Our worst enemy was boredom. We got used to the guards and the machine-guns. In fact we used to harass them for excitement. We lost most of our men who could not cope with emptiness and nothingness. I learned soon after my arrival at camp that I would have to take care of myself. I walked in circles around the compound winter and summer. I figured there was no way out of camp except to walk out. When the time came I wanted to do just that. Keeping mentally in shape was more difficult. We never talked about the past, as that would bring feelings of self-pity. The future offered little to talk about. We lived a moment at a time.

'Washing clothes was the biggest event of my prison life. I planned days ahead which day of the week would be best for washing socks, shirts, etc. Simple as it was, it kept me thinking and gave me something to do.

'Many men took imprisonment as an opportunity to do that which they always wanted—nothing. In between roll calls, which could be as often as six times a day or night, these fellows stayed in their bunks. I need not tell you what nineteen months of rest will do for the body. When the time came to go they were unable to move and were left behind in their bunks.'

Another new arrival at Stalag XVIIB was Bill Morris, who had been returned to combat status in England following his crew's internment in Portugal in July 1943 while en-route to North Africa. His luck had held until 1 December 1943 when he was shot down on the mission to Solingen in the Ruhr Valley flying as a replacement tail gunner for another crew. Bill Morris recalls, 'There was heavy flak over Solingen and our Liberator took a hit. We lost formation and were jumped by fighters. We manged to get back as far as Belgium but we were forced to bail out over Antwerp. I baled out over the English Channel, hoping that the wind would blow me towards England. It didn't! Instead, I was blown inland over Belgium. I came in over the main street of a small town and some locals came out to help me. I buried my parachute and personal items as per the routine we had been taught.

'I checked my bearings by the sun and decided I had to head south. I hoped that I might be able to get to France and join the Underground. I went as far as I could, swimming several ditches and dykes. I got soaked through but I figured that someone would eventually recognize my uniform and hide me until I got my clothes dry. I saw one of my crew members about half a mile away and ran over to him. He was in a barnyard when I reached him. Before I could ask him if he was hurt and how many had got out etc, fifteen to twenty Germans with sub-machines-guns appeared over the hill. I had been free for only half an hour. I was surprised how composed I was but at eighteen one doesn't bother so much about things.

'We were taken to the local jail and were there for about three days before being taken to Antwerp. From there we went by troop train to Frankfurt and Dulag Luft. I was put in solitary confinement for a few days and underwent the usual interrogation. There was very little food and no bathroom facilities.

'The journey by troop train to Krems was a harrowing experience. The weather was bitterly cold and we had little food. There were only small pot-bellied stoves in the boxcars and there must have been seventy men in each boxcar. It was a nightmare trip that seemed endless. One day it would be freezing and the next it would get so hot that we would have to open up the doors to get a little air. The guys had diarrohea and nausea and there were no toilet facilities.'

Morris arrived at Krems to begin what would be one and a half year's imprisonment. It was also his first Christmas behind barbed wire. During Christmas 1943 the Germans entered the festive spirit by playing some music over the camp tannoy system. One tune which had a significant meaning for the prisoners was Bing Crosby singing, *I'll Be Home For Christmas, If Only In A Dream.*

It was a dream, and soon the prisoners were trying to settle down to a long, cruel winter. It was during the winter of 1944 that some would-be escapers were caught, shot and hung on the wire as a deterrent against future escapes. Orlo Natvig recalls, 'Three or four guys were going to crawl along the fence and cut through the wire. It was snowing at the time and I watched them through one of the barrack room windows. I saw the shadowy figures sliding down the fence, heading for the boundary. With that I went to my bunk and lay down. About fifteen minutes later shooting started, followed by wild screaming. The Germans had caught them in the open and had shot two or three of them. They fired a lot of rounds into the barracks and at least one man, who was in bed, was hit. I rolled on to the floor as soon as the shooting started and although I was the first one down, there were plenty more on top of me!'

Despite this, discipline was usually maintained. Kaptain Poleger of the Luftwaffe was in charge of the camp and Natvig recalls, 'He was straight in his dealings with prisoners and about as fair as we could expect in the prevailing climate. His home was on the southern German-Austrian border. One day when his family were to make a visit to Stalag XVIIB by train it was strafed by P-38 Lightnings and they were killed. After this he became quite ruthless with us. He could no longer treat us impartially and he asked to be transferred. Another German commander at Krems was Oberst Kuhn who we called "Captain Bluewood" because he had a wooden leg.'

The Germans also delighted in tormenting the prisoners as Natvig recalls: 'They would keep us outside in the snow all day and run dog tag checks or search the barracks. The guards would delight in running their bayonets through our food supplies which we had kept back from the Red Cross parcels. In effect they were forcing us to eat the contents of the cans to prevent us stockpiling them for escape purposes.

'Escape was always in our minds but the Germans were very clever and forestalled many attempts before they had begun. Either they had a spy in the camp or they had seismographs, because each time we got near the wire they probed around until they found the tunnel. They got the Russian prisoners to clean out the latrines and pour the contents down the tunnel to prevent us using it again.

'One day we discovered that the Germans were going to de-louse us and shear everybody's hair off. We therefore mixed some sand and margarine and pasted everyone's hair flat on their heads. When the German barbers started cutting, their scissors were well and truly blunted! The only thing that went wrong was that they carried on with blunt scissors, practically tearing out the men's hair and not cutting it! When they saw what was happening those that remained cut their own hair to spare their ordeal at the hands of the demon barbers.

'Several times the Germans collected our excess clothing and hauled it away on a wagon. We soon got wise to it and on the next occasion men threw lighted cigarettes in the back until the wagon was well alight.'

During the winter of 1944 the prisoners had little coal for heating water. In desperation they cut down the sub floors in their huts and even their bed slats for fuel. Insides of bathrooms were ripped out before the situation got so bad that the Germans had to put a stop to the practice.

Winter 1944 gave way to spring and prisoners poured into Stalag XVIIB. John L. Hurd, a B-17

Lieutenant Francis Shaw's crew, pictured at Wendover Field, Utah in December 1943 when it was part of the 750th Bomb Squadron, 457th Bomb Group. It was transferred to the 614th Bomb Squadron, 401st Bomb Group in February 1944. Standing (L-R): Hansen (navigator); Autry (bomb aimer); Cole (co-pilot); Francis Shaw (pilot). Kneeling (L-R): Kneese (tail-gunner); Gorden (waist-gunner); Macomber (radio operator); John L. Hurd (ball-turret gunner); Seagren (waist-gunner) (Hurd).

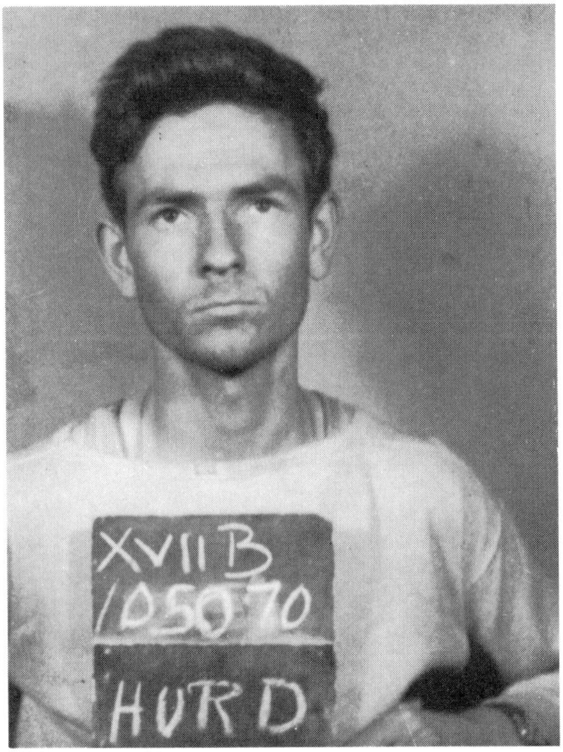

Sergeant John L. Hurd entering 'Kriegiedom' at Stalag Luft 17B, Krems 17 April 1944 (Hurd).

ball-turret gunner in the 401st Bomb Group at Deenthorpe, arrived at Krems on 17 April after he was shot down on his eleventh mission, to Politz, on 11 April. It was the start of a very degrading routine as Hurd recalls: 'After my picture was taken, my hair was cut off and my clothes were put in a gas chamber and deloused. My clothes had a strong odour of gas about them when I put them on again. I was then taken to a barracks where other PoWs were already living and stayed there several days until the Germans opened another compound with four empty barracks. I finally got my own bunk in Barracks 31B.

'I was given a bowl and spoon and cooked my meals in the washroom near my bunk. With others cooking, the room became quite smokey. We had no cooking stove at this time. We got hot water from the camp kitchen and the Germans gave us boiled potatoes or boiled rutabagas for our noon and evening meals. Sometimes we would get spinach or pea soup. The pea soup had bugs in it and we threw most of it out or gave it to the Russian PoWs. They were so hungry they ate it eagerly.

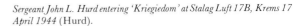

'Every day we got a ration of dark bread from the Germans. I would try a piece and put a slice of cheese and fried Spam on it. It was good. Sometimes we got blood sausage but I did not eat much of it. A few mornings we got barley for breakfast. For dessert I would cut up some chocolate "D-Bars" and mix with C-rations (crackers), powdered milk and water for a pudding. Several weeks after entering Stalag XVIIB another PoW and I pooled our food and we cooked and ate together from then on. Later, a third prisoner joined us and we formed a three-man combine.'

Despite the privations and poor food, during the early part of 1944 the prisoners at Krems were in reasonably good physical condition. They played softball and volleyball and other games. If anyone hit a ball into the stagnant fire pool it was no pleasant task to retrieve it. The '*Kriegies*' also called it the swimming pool but few men actually swam in it.

John Hurd kept reasonably fit by running around the compound several times a day: 'We played baseball and attended boxing matches. Another PoW and I teamed up to play in bridge tournaments. We had a well-stocked library in camp and I read about twenty books. We also had school classes. I took a thirteen-week course in Algebra and got my diploma and also a six-week course in civics. We had a theatre called the "Cardboard Playhouse". I attended several plays and German movies there. Some Sundays I went to chapel.

'One of our pastimes during cold weather was heating water for coffee. We had a small stove in the barracks for heating a large can of water. To be eligible for a ration of water a person would have to furnish something to burn in the stove. Sometimes I furnished soap, German bread, cardboard or wood from the barracks. I made my coffee cup from two different-sized butter cans. One fitted inside the other with cardboard set between the sides for insulation.'

In June 1944 rumours of an Allied invasion prompted John Hurd to start a diary. On Tuesday 6 June he wrote: 'Rumour going around that the invasion has started. After supper it was confirmed by news man. . .'

The 'news man' was the last link in a chain set up at Krems to pass on the day to day news to the prisoners to keep up morale. The source began with a crystal set made by Ralph Ernst. Crystal sets abounded in every prison camp but Stalag XVIIB boasted one which was powered. Only a select few knew of its existence and one of them was Ralph Ernst. 'I was an experienced radio man and I made the small crystal set from material obtained from French workers in exchange for goods. A bunk mate of mine could speak German well so we used my crystal set to tune into the German networks for news. This way we kept track of Allied movements on the continent. The news was relayed to all the barracks by runners at noon each day.'

Messages from the outside world were also used for

other reasons, as Ernst explains: 'At headquarters, which we called the "White House," I helped in the radio communications department. We had a two-tube radio which I modified to receive BBC transmissions on short wave. Secret messages were received in this way. A certain letter from the first word was formed into a message. Each PoW camp had a designated call letter. We located German airfields and factories near to us and we sent their location to London. A few weeks later we would discover that our messages had been passed on to the RAF because they bombed a German airfield to the east of us.'

The RAF and the American bomber forces continued their raids on Austrian targets including Vienna. Most were made in daylight by the 15th Air Force based in the Foggia region of Italy where Liberators and Fortresses took off on raids against the 'soft underbelly' of Europe. News was also received via the crystal set of other missions and the war news generally during July 1944 gladdened the heart of every PoW.

'Uncle Joe driving towards the Baltic'—'25 German Generals killed or captured'—'B-29s bombing Japan'—'7/8ths of Saipan is ours—it's only 1,200 miles from Tokyo' clamoured the headlines. As if sensing the news was predominantly bad for them, the German PoW authorities issued a tremendous amount of propaganda about the American 'terror gangsters', saying they had been recruited from the American underworld. Prisoners remarked that all this was happening while the biggest gangster of them all, Adolf Hitler, had narrowly escaped assassination at the 'Wolf's Lair'. News of more Russian advances filtered through the airwaves to be followed with the resounding declaration that Germany had enough oil to last them until the end of the year.

By 5 August the Russians had reached Warsaw but it would not be until the war's end that the prisoners held captive in German PoW camps would learn of the Poles' valiant but futile insurrection. However, news from the western front was good. The Americans had broken out of the beachead and had driven across the Brest Peninsular to St Nazaire. In Italy, Florence was given up by the Germans to preserve its cultural heritage. In the Pacific, news came through that the Americans had landed on Guam. On 16 August it was announced that 'Operation Anvil' had succeeded in landing at Toulon on the French Mediterranean coast. 'Apparently,' went the report, 'There is little resistance.' Nine days later Paris fell and the German armies were in full retreat.

On 2 September Rumania severed relations with Germany and came into the war on the Russian side. The Red Army marched on and captured Ploesti and Bucharest. One week later the Germans withdrew from southern and western France and the American and British armies in northern and southern France joined forces. The British and Canadian forces pursued the German armies across Belgium to Antwerp.

German reverses in Italy resulted in thousands of Allied PoWs being transferred to Austria and parts of Germany. By October some camps were housing prisoners in tents. Doubling up became the standard practice as door panels were removed and triple decker beds were installed. In all the excitement and confusion some took the opportunity of removing much needed items for escape and an inventory was made of tin cans for escape tools and bed boards for propping up tunnels.

The weather turned much colder and the coal ration was reduced to only a few lumps per hut per day. On 8 October ominous reports of 'little activity' on the fronts filtered through on camp radios. Prisoners hoped this meant that preparations were being made for the final push. Meanwhile, the Germans were making 'fantastic' claims about a new secret weapon 'to be unleashed soon' to end in 'ultimate victory for the Axis'.

On 9 October 1944 the prisoners' long dreamed of push began with violent battles being waged on the western front. The Russians were moving in the Balkans and the Baltic states but 'Kriegies' had now been on half rations for several weeks. Time was running out for the prisoners at Krems and throughout the Reich. Victory was still not in sight even though on land and in the air, the Allied armies and air forces were enjoying great success. Everyone played their part but the constant daylight bombing raids by 8th Air Force Liberators and Fortresses were having a devastating effect on Germany's manufacturing capability and its oil industry in particular. However, there was a price to pay. And it was the young men of the 8th Air Force who were paying it.

5 Into enemy hands

'7 October 1944. Position, Merseberg, Germany. Time 12.30 hours. Altitude, 28,000 ft. Magnetic heading, 170 degrees', twenty-year-old navigator Karl W. Wendel, recorded. This was a maximum effort to knock out German synthetic oil refineries. The flak, which had been stalking the B-17s of the 447th Bomb Group across the sky, closed in. Someone sang over the interphone that the flak was thick enough to land on. The group leader was shot down and Wendel, who had flown his first mission, to Berlin, only the day before, found himself momentarily in the position of lead navigator; the youngest in the 8th Air Force. However, his new role was taken away as quickly as it was thrust upon him.

Wendel recalls that his ship, *TNT Kate*, one of the oldest B-17s in the 8th Air Force, was going great until the first direct hit. Half the oxygen system went out and there was a scramble to connect the oxygen masks to another supply. The ball-turret gunner screamed for help. He could not breathe. The radio operator helped him. 'Engineer to pilot, gas leaking like Hell from the wing tanks!' There was a violent shudder and yaw and then the waist-gunner reported, 'There's a hole big enough to drive a Jeep through back here!'

The very heavy flak kept tracking them. Number three engine was out and number two's propeller was out of control and windmilling frantically. Oil flowed like venomous bleeding. From his position in the nose Wendel could see it congealing. *TNT Kate* dropped from formation and the crew started throwing all loose equipment overboard to lighten the ship. On two engines they could not even maintain their altitude. The bombardier salvoed the bomb load over the suburbs as the formation pulled away and proceeded to the alternate target because clouds obscured Merseberg.

'Navigator to pilot', Wendel announced, 'Course two-nine-zero; heading to nearest safety is 290 degrees, if we can make it.' 'Roger', returned the pilot above the noise of the engines and flak as the B-17 turned on the new course. The navigation plan was to head west to a 'dead reckoned' position near Eisenach, then to change course to 240 degrees to cut south of 'Flak Valley' (the Ruhr) and to fly into southern France. This plan was the best possible since the wind was from 040 degrees at 50 knots (a strong tail wind) according to the division report at the last control point.

The B-17 dropped like a stone. Number four engine was hit and caught fire. Out of all this the prosaic sound of a ringing bell added to the confusion and excitement. Wendel asked, 'Are we baling?' but the pilot and co-pilot did not reply. Wendel was not alone: 'I heard the lonesome kid in the tail-gun position. Fleming was scared and asked repeatedly if we were baling out.'

'Bale Out! Bale Out!' Wendel ordered him as he watched Art, the bombardier, beckon to him and then slip out the navigator's hatch. Slowly, Wendel unfastened the connections to his oxygen mask and electric suit so he could jump the diminishing 22,000 ft. The parachute pack was hooked properly. 'Must unstrap and take my watch from the "G" Box,' Wendel's mind clicked.

Dropping from the navigator's hatch as he usually did when they landed, he was surprised to find that his feet did not strike the ground as he left the aircraft. 'Take it easy and don't get panicky,' Wendel cautioned himself. In the quick rush of air he found his hands tightly on the parachute pack. The navigation watch which he had in his hand a moment before was gone. Wendel threw off his flying helmet because the goggles were banging around on his head. He was not afraid. He could think clearly. 'Better hold my breath until I'm down out of this rarefied atmosphere. I'd better delay pulling the ripcord until I'm down where breathing is easier. Strange, but this excitement doesn't fit in with the tranquil blue sky, the few far off clouds and the quietness here above the earth. A heck of a time for philosophy and observation,' he thought, 'but somehow I was enjoying this.'

'Where's the ground,' Wendel thought. He was falling backwards. 'I don't want to fall too far.' The problem was to turn around so he could see the ground. Easily, he rolled over and was falling face down. His altitude was only about 1,200 ft when crack went the 'chute as it arrested his descent. His flying boots did not jerk off as he had been told they would in such a case. Wendel was drifting fast towards a house with an orange tile roof. He attempted to drift away from it but did not get very far as he was afraid of 'spilling' the 'chute so close to the ground. In a moment he struck the roof of the house, knees buckled and he bounced off into the back yard. The yard was small and it was closed in with a high chicken wire fence. Getting up from the dusty ground where he had rested an instant or two, he was surprised to find himself unhurt.

Many tow-headed youngsters came from all over and watched him from outside the fence and from afar. Then came civilians with a varied assortment of weapons. They entered the yard and several of them wanted to beat him, especially a comical old man with a broomstick. Speaking in German, Wendel told them, 'I'm an officer; what do you want?' It stopped them short. They looked at each other quizically and talked among themselves . At that moment a policeman came up and assumed responsibility. Wendel was comparatively safe now, although he had been unaware of the danger before the mob. He had even been arrogant.

Wendel was searched a number of times before spending the remainder of the afternoon in a schoolhouse in Weissenborn (near Nordhausen). The civilian guards were disgusted to discover, to Wendel's amusement, that he was in fact American. A multitude of children passed through the schoolhouse to see the American *'Terrorflieger'*. Late in the afternoon, Fleming and the co-pilot, Kelley, entered the schoolroom. Wendel sensed by their faces and by the way they both snapped to attention for the police sergeant when he walked into the room that they were afraid. 'I believe I was a bit bold and conscious of my rank as an officer because I realized that the Germans went for this sort of thing,' Wendel admitted to himself.

When boarding a train for Frankfurt-am-Main later that afternoon Karl Wendel and his two companions found the rest of their crew except for Art, the bombardier, George, the ball-turret gunner, and Russ, the engineer. They hoped that these missing comrades were alive and well. Some Luftwaffe officers who boarded the train at one of the villages took over the prisoners. The *'Luft Gangsters'* as the prisoners were called, amazed the guards by their joviality and good spirits. They sang and joked all the time. They even sang derogatory songs about the Germans.

That night, when the train stopped at a small town, Wendel was informed, since he was the only member of the crew who understood German, that two or three of the missing men had been killed. They intimated that they had been beaten to death by civilians. One man was still missing. Wendel recalls, 'We hoped it was Art and whichever one it was, that he was OK.'

Wendel was analytical: 'Glad I did my damndest in navigating this time,' he reflected. 'St Francis, patron of birds and birdmen, however, had not been with us this day. The Luftwaffe guards and the place evidenced the fact that the whole thing had happened but somehow it was unreal. Two things had happened in my life. I had been born and I had been shot down. The mind must try to avoid strong consciousness of unpleasant things because the permanent position I was in still seemed imaginary. It was as if everything on this last mission had happened to somebody else. Somehow I was detached from it all.'

The navigator's pals were astounded to see Wendel eat the foul smelling cheese and coarse black bread and the blood baloney which was served to them. The rest of the crew could not bear to eat any of it. Wendel told them about the good old days when he used to eat all sorts of German foods at his grandmother's house.

After two days' travel they arrived at the interrogation centre at Oberussel where they were thrown into solitary confinement cells to soften them up for questioning. They were fed very little—only a cup of soup and four thin slices of black bread a day. There was a severe penalty for marking the walls of the cell. Upon close inspection one could find small bunches of straw stuck in the moulding around the wooden floor. Each straw represented a day and each bunch of straw represented some prisoner's stay in the cell. The average stay was two days. The longest, according to the straw records, was ten days. Wendel hungered there for two cold weeks. 'Solitary gets monotonous after a few days and the threats of being turned over to the Gestapo made me think but the Germans had not noted my lack of dog tags or identification.'

One night after Wendel heard the guard go past his cell, he shouted and the man in the next cell heard him. He replied that he was an RAF fighter pilot named Frank Barwise. He and Wendel formed the 'Odd Thirties Club' (the cells on their side of the corridor were the odd number thirties) the purpose of which was to inform new prisoners in solitary of the falsity of the Gestapo threats, to warn them against giving any military information to the false Red Cross representative, who was at the interrogation centre, and to generally encourage the new and unwary. The communicating with new prisoners was done by shouting through the walls when the guards had passed at night. Word was then shouted from cell to cell progressively until the whole intake knew what went on.

Karl Wendel and Frank Barwise saw each other once. They looked good despite a week without a shave and two weeks without a wash. They used to sing to each other all the time through the walls. The fleas kept them awake anyway and they had to pass the time. Finally, they ran out of songs. It was then that Karl Wendel started to sing some German songs which his grandmother had taught him long ago. Soon after, the guards heard him and they listened to him for quite a time before they opened his cell door and complimented him. Wendel insisted that the guards sing in return for their listening. They did. From that time on he frequently had visits from guards who came seeking information about their relatives in the States and conditions there. Wendel told them all he knew and more, about every place they wished to know about. They liked him and brought him extra food rations.

Wendel's interrogator was a German Major. He wanted to know all the details about Wendel's squadron, group, last bombing mission, where he baled out and when. The Major confirmed the death of two of the crew and said that Russ, the engineer, had been captured five days after the crew baled out. The Major realized that Wendel had the Military Intelligence he wanted but because he refused to talk, Wendel remained a guest of the Major's for fourteen days in solitary. A relief from the constant tension and discomfort was the 'symphony' he heard every morning when hundreds of American heavy bombers droned overhead on their way to their target. 'Damn, that is a reasurring and inspiring sound,' thought Wendel.

At last, on 23 October, Wendel and a bunch of American and RAF fliers were shipped out to the distribution centre at Wetzlar. On the train journey Wendel became the interpreter for the Senior Allied Officer, an RAF Wing Commander. At Wetzlar they ate food from Red Cross parcels for three days but many men were sick because their stomachs had shrunk after two weeks in solitary confinement. 'The RAF and RAAF men were good sports and I played chess with everyone for almost all the time I was at Wetzlar,' recalls Wendel. 'Then the Luftwaffe shipped us to the now famous Stalag Luft III at Sagan. Sleeping on the luggage rack of the train was a new experience for me and I fared better than most who could not lay down during the two-day journey.

'The quarters in the South Compound at Luft III were terrible. 200 men were living in barracks containing sixteen rooms with one night latrine each. The rooms were dim, smoky and poorly ventilated. Several of the men went crazy from the confinement: others developed complexes.'

Robert O'Hearn (see Chapter 10), a gunner in the 96th Bomb Group who had been shot down on the second Schweinfurt mission on 14 October 1943, recalls: 'The monotony of confinement was relieved by discussions on everything from farming to philosophy. We seemed to have experts in many fields. The PoW experience was an education.'

The prisoners were also very adept at organizing themselves for escape as Karl Wendel recalls: 'The military organization created by the prisoners was a gem. The chain of command was from the ranking American Colonel on down and the discipline remained intact. There was a committee and an officer for all the military departments. The most important were Food Supply, Administration, Clothing Supply, Security and "X" (or Escape).'

The 'X' committee tunnel project had been successful in the North (RAF) Compound and had led to the 'Great Escape'. The Americans in the South Compound organized their 'X' Committee in much the same way. Lieutenant Colonel 'Flamingo' Clark, a tall red-headed West Pointer, known as 'Big X', was in charge of all escape activity including approval of escape plans. His assistant was Major 'Tokio' Jones, who was known as 'Little X'. 'Another key man,' recalls Bob O'Hearn, 'was Major Jerry Sage, a bigger than life Army paratrooper. But although we had a dedicated organization our tunnels were discovered and destroyed before we could use them.'

So secret was the work of the 'X' committee that nine tenths of the men in the compound were never aware of the project although in almost every hut there were prisoners who were involved in the escape activities. Bob O'Hearn's hut was no exception. 'Two roomates were engaged in "X" work. I sometimes did lookout duty while they were in the tunnels, or I recited the "Gen" (BBC news reports received on a secret radio in another part of the camp). The guards probably didn't want to see too much but they were not ignorant. Once a guard warned a couple of indiscreet "Kriegies" to keep their mouths shut or they would lose that "damned canary".'

Another of the men who worked for the 'X' organization was Lieutenant Robert L. Ferrell, a twenty-year-old lead navigator in the 458th Bomb Group, who had been shot down one week after Karl Wendel, on 14 October 1944. Ferrell recalls, 'I worked on the "X" committee's tunnel-digging assignment. Specifically, I was in the dirt-hauling-away detail with pockets sewn in each trouser leg interior and a small hole in the bottom of each pocket with a draw string to keep the hole closed until you wished the dirt to start trickling out.

It was a far cry from a few weeks before, when on the night of 13 October Ferrell had returned to his

Second Lieutenant Robert L. Ferrel pictured in April 1944 (Ferrell).

base at Horsham St Faith after an evening in Norwich. 'Even though it was 11.30 pm when I returned to base, I had to view the crew status board on the wall. The board that would spell out the names of the crews which would mount the mission the next day. Damn it, there we were; Lieutenant Klusmeyer's crew. We hadn't flown in three days so I really couldn't complain. Oh well, up the stairs two steps at a time and down the hall to Room 23 and hope that I don't awaken Ernest Sands, the bombardier, who is sacked out.

'Sleep came hard for me for Patricia and I had broken up earlier in the evening. She had lost her pilot brother on an RAF raid the night before and she felt she could not stand the anguish of maybe losing two people from her life. We had leaned against the rock wall that surrounded the park where the 6- × -6 trucks picked us up and expressed our love for each other and I vainly tried to understand her feelings in the matter. I kissed her goodbye, leaving with her my flying scarf that I had made from an old white parachute—a parting token.

'All these thoughts kept running through my mind as I tried to fall asleep for two or three hours. God, don't tell me that squeaking Jeep brake is the one announcing the arrival of the ''wake-up'' sergeant. The door opens, the flashlight beam crosses the small room and the booming voice announced, ''Lieutenant Sands, Lieutenant Ferrell; 03.30 hours. Sign the wake-up sheet here. No over here. Up and at 'em men!'' The door slams behind him and I feel like I could sleep forever. Feet on the floor, lights on, grab the olive drab coloured towel and down the long corridor to the communal bathroom for the morning ablutions and back to the room to dress. The thoughts of what awaits me in the Officers' Mess is not heart warming. Those same damned powdered eggs, cooked three tons at a time, the greasy bacon that would slide off a gravel driveway and that steaming black coffee with the hard English rolls. Oh well, I bet the Roman gladiators were fed better than this ''but there's a war on Mac''.

'Push the meal down against an already nervous stomach and head out for the side door and over to the War Room. I never wanted us to be a lead crew anyway. It's just too much work on the navigator and bombardier and an easier task for the pilots. The MP's give you the once over and check your ID card as you troop into the Base War Room with its momentary secrecy. Here the Group CO [Colonel James H. Isbell] the Exec', the various squadron commanders, the lead crews and the deputy leads are present.

'We are soon hearing what the regular crews will hear some of in a couple of hours from now. It's the Group deputy lead for us today and that is a better tune. I look about and wonder if we can win this war with all of us 19, 20 and 21-year-old officers? Sure hope so. The CO is a full Colonel and ancient—every bit of 28 and a West Pointer of course. A regular amongst this sea of reservists but that doesn't mean five cents to me now for I'm too green to really understand.

'The target—Cologne. Be sure and do your best to miss the Ford Motor Co factory and the famous cathedral. The whole 8th Air Force will be airborne this day and over 600 enemy bombers will be hitting the immediate Cologne area. The briefing is soon over with its usual precise monotony. A short walk and I am in the crew briefing area and around the corner to the Personal Equipment Section. The parachute, the parachute bag, the oxygen mask, '45 and shoulder holster, three clips of ammo, the new two-piece electric flying suit, flak helmet, three flak vests (two to stand on) and all my navigational paraphenalia. Then off to the Briefing Room.

'The crews begin to gather and soon the Catholic chaplain is giving the prayer to all of us Protestants. Announcements over and with the gestures of a sculptor undraping a new statue, the Exec' pulls aside the pool-table-green-coloured cloth to expose the routing, the IP (Initial Point), the target, the RP (Rendezvous Point) and the course home. The Intelligence officer gives his estimate of the number of stationary flak units as well as his guesstimate of the number of mobile flak railway batteries that will be rushed into the target area. The near reverent silence is broken by the in-sucking of air by the astonished crewmen. What a way to earn a living but there is more mileage in an ounce of patriotism than in a ton of money. ''Pilots stay in here for your briefing. Navigators, bombardiers, radio operators and gunners to your respective sections for sectional briefing. Crews dismissed!''

'All the navigation work is done and now to drag that parachute bag out to the 6-×-6's waiting bumper to bumper to transport some 500 of us crewmen out to the bomber hardstands. I note the refuellers are still topping off the tanks on the three birds on our hardstand area. The armament men are still putting the standard 500 pounders in our bomb bays. The incendiaries are already loaded on the top shackle — one per stanchion. The red flag streamer is attached to each incendiary to denote to the aircraft behind us that we are a lead crew. Sergeant Sills, the tail turret gunner, will not be flying with us today as he received permission to visit his wounded paratrooper brother who had been brought back from the debacle earlier at Arnhem. But no need to worry for we will be well covered by the ships coming along behind us since we are flying up near the front as deputy lead. I look at the ball-turret gunner; a mere boy of 17. The oldest man on the crew is middle aged—he is the 24-year-old engineer top-turret gunner. He is also second generation German as is our first pilot.

'Everyone is in his position and the flares arch skyward from the walk around area just outside the control tower. The engines start on the 49 B-24s; a maximum effort this day of four squadrons and twelve airplanes per squadron plus the stripped down and gaily-painted assembly mother ship that will leave us and return to base in about an hour. We roll down the runway aboard *The Jolly Roger* just after the lead ship is airborne. It's 07.52 and wheels are up and in the wells.

'The laborious and time-consuming task of assembling the 48 bombers is accomplished by the time we are outbound from a point north of London heading for the Dutch coast. The placidity of the deputy lead ship is soon broken by the radio crackling, ''Lincoln Red Leader to Foxtrot Two: Take over the lead as we are going down with engine trouble. Acknowledge.'' I jam my flak-helmeted head into the deep plastic bubble on the port side of the navigator's compartment to see the lead drop its wing and turn down through the clouds to the left. It was swiftly soaking through to me, so I got up on my tip toes and peered out the astrodome. God, the sky is filled with bombers and they are following us. Us—who is guiding us? Me!

'The sobriety of the crew is awesome. Through the breaks in the undercast we can see the Zeider Zee below and with tradition, we clear our machine-guns by firing down into the Zee. The left gun on the Emerson nose turret, being occupied by Millard C. Miller, my second navigator, proves to be frozen. Miller has been put on the crew just for today's mission and he is too provide me with an extra set of eyes, keep the fighters off our nose and provide me with current pilotage data.

'We are now two minutes behind the master

As another formation of Liberators assembles overhead, B-24 Liberators of the 458th Bomb Group prepare for take off on 24 December 1944 (USAF).

schedule but when we approach the IP we can pick it up by shortening the corner. The cold in the compartment and the heavy anti-aircraft firings help to keep my mind off of my awesome responsibility. Graduating second in my class is not much comfort to me right now with a reported 587 of the original 600 bombers still left and following along behind us. With the plastic code flimsy in my hand, I call the radio operator sergeant and read the hourly code to him and we discuss the message that he is to transmit when we reach the IP. Well, here it comes—the IP—still alive and intact. Cut the corner short now. Straighten her out, level it up.

'Since our *Jolly Roger* is a B-24J, I am facing forward and the navigator's table folds down to provide work space and to allow the second navigator to crawl across it to get through the two narrow doors into the Emerson nose turret. William Klusmeyer turns the aircraft over to the bombardier and we start running straight and true, hoping the flak will allow us to pass through to the target. Keep an eye peeled for those Bf 109s and Fw 190s. The target is almost below us now and we could get out and walk around on the flak—it's so heavy. Looks like a box barrage.

'With his eye glued to the Norden sight, the bombardier shouts, "Bombs Aw. . ." The Plexiglas of the Emerson nose turret turns red with blood, the bombardier is blown from over the bombsight back into the nose wheel well, my left hand is showing blood through my gloves from three shrapnel piercings and the smell of cordite seeps through my oxygen mask. There is a wind blowing inside the aircraft, the communications are knocked out so I can't check with the rest of the crew. I crank the nose turret to the '0' position, push the bar handle holding the two tiny doors closed down to full open, slip my hands under the second navigator's arm pits and pull on him. His head falls back against my right shoulder. I look at Miller and vomit into my oxygen mask and nearly drown from it. I have never seen a human head hit by a shell. I pull him out and lay him on the strewn

Colonel William B. Luper, CO, 457th Bomb Group (right) (Douglas).

floor of the navigator's compartment. Taking a scrap of paper, I write a terse note to the pilot to send some help forward and then I pass the paper through the crack between our compartment and the pilots' feet.

'Sergeant Pohler, the engineer upper-turret gunner, crawls forward on his hands and knees through the tunnel that connects us with the rear of the flight deck area centre and behind the radio operator's position. He shakes his mask loose from his walk-around oxygen bottle and shouts in my ear that the second shot of flak has blown a large hole in the aircraft at the radio operator's station below the right wing root, the third shot hit below the ball turret and drove it almost out the top of the airplane and the fourth shot exploded rearward of the tail turret and blew its glass away. Fortunately, the gunner was not inside the ball turret at the time since the fighters steer clear of the heavy flak. The last I see of the second navigator is when Pohler is dragging him by his harness back up through the tunnel and toward the flight deck. (Miller was thrown out the bomb strike camera hatch opening after Pohler secured a 25 ft static line clip to his "D" ring).

'With a note of the macabre, I make an entry into my navigation log explaining the absence of the required number of fixes. I write it in the blood lying on my table. All this time the aircraft is making a slow, wide turn to the right because its controls are shot away and the number three engine is knocked out. We are slowly losing altitude. The noise of the wind blowing in through the holes in the front of the airplane creates an awesome, ghostly sound. The stun of the incident is blown away by the sound of the three rings on the bale-out bell.

'Sands and I crawl through the tunnel, enter the flight deck and see that all are gone except the first pilot. He motions us to go rearward for bale-out. We try to get through the bomb bays but the raging fire drives us back. We return to the front compartment and pull the emergency handle on the nose wheel doors but they fail to open in response. This is our only way out now. The bombardier stoops over and jumps up and down on the nose wheel doors. They begin to part and fly away. He drops through the opening until his outstretched arms hold him momentarily. He looks at me and shouts above the noise, "This sure as hell pisses me off!" then he drops out and away. I crawl over to the opening and turn to face the front of the ship and follow the same procedure. Then out I go.

'What did the training people back at Pueblo Army Air Force Base, Colorado say to us? "Do not open your parachute until you have fallen far enough to be able to readily recongnize the objects on the ground for if you open sooner you run the risk of the Germans shooting you while you are descending." What did the altimeter last read—25,000 ft, 23,000 ft? Hell, I can't remember now. I am falling and tumbling and falling. My past life rushes through my mind's eye. Why had I not done more with my life? Why hadn't I written home more often? Patricia was right after all—a woman's premonition.

'Have I waited long enough? Pull the ripcord. The 'chute opens with such a violence that I think my body will be split in half. I waited too long to pull the "D" ring. I swing once to the left and start to swing to the right. The ground is racing up towards me. The yellow farm house is just to my left and the ploughed field is below. I hit the ground like a rock and the 'chute starts dragging me down the furrows with the German family hot on my heels. I am pulling the bottom shroud lines to start collapsing the 'chute when rough hands assail me and grab the 'chute and my .45 from its shoulder holster. They are now sitting on my back and holding my legs and talking to themselves. I then hear in somewhat broken English a phrase that I shall live to hear hundreds and hundreds of times again: "For you the war is over." It was.'

William Klusmeyer, the pilot, Fred Wright, the co-pilot and Ferrell landed in Boppard, Germany near the same farmhouse. All were taken prisoner almost instantly. The rest of the parachutes were strung out over several miles (Millard C. Miller, the badly wounded second navigator, survived) and although one or two of the enlisted men managed to evade, they were all captured later.

Ferrell continues, 'We were held in a fire station and turned over to the 28th Wehrmacht Division who in turn gave us eventually to the Luftwaffe as flyer prisoners came under their domain. Eventually, we were taken to Frankfurt and Dulag Luft. My pilot, co-pilot and I were kept a night or two in a civilian jail in Frankfurt before going to Dulag Luft on 17 October with several other rounded-up crews.'

One of those who came in was Colonel James R. Luper, CO of the 457th Bomb Group who had been shot down on 7 October while leading his group to Politz. Ferrell recalls, 'We had been told never to fly with wallets or cigarette lighters or letters or anything of that nature; not even rank. And here was this very overbearing full Colonel wearing a leather flying jacket with his name over one breast pocket, his wings over the other breast pocket, his group insignia [the "Fireball Outfit"] sewn on his front above his right jacket pocket, his 8th Air Force insignia sewn on one shoulder and the USAAF patch painted on the other shoulder and the bombs painted on the back of his jacket showing the missions, dates and names of targets. He was wearing a round "wheel hat" when he had baled out. It blew away of course. So, he was hatless. He marched into the 'Kriegie' room I was in, looked around, saw my overseas cloth hat was the better looking and promptly commandeered it on the spot!' [Luper was killed in a B-26 flying accident in 1953].

Luper was sent to Stalag IIIA, Luckenwalde. Ferrell was to spend almost six months' imprisonment in the American (South) Compound at Stalag Luft III, 'Hauling dirt on the tunnel project, helping as a decoy for two men who crawled under the south-east rear gate for an escape as far as Vienna and studying Spanish and Aeronautical Engineering courses. Other than that my actions were just those of pure survival. I was no hero. Just a green 19-year-old lieutenant in the 8th Air Force who was shot up over Cologne and who parachuted out over Boppard, Germany.'

Rene III *leads the 457th Bomb Group over the English Channel. This B-17 (named after his wife) is the aircraft flown by Colonel Luper when he was shot down on the 7 October raid* (USAF).

Part 2
ESCAPE AND EVASION

6 'Shorty' Gordon

Allied bomber crews shot down in World War 2 often had to rely on their own devices to evade capture and escape. If they landed in Germany the task was well nigh impossible but devising an escape plan once they were en-route to PoW camps or even behind the wire, was another matter. Even so, only the most daring and resourceful of men could succeed. Staff Sergeant Lee Gordon, a B-17 ball-turret gunner in the 305th Bomb Group at Chelveston and nicknamed 'Shorty' by his comrades because of his 5 ft 2 in frame, was just such a man. His height, or lack of it, was ideal for the close confines of a Flying Fortress Sperry ball turret. 'Shorty' Gordon was among the few gunners who could, and did, wear a parachute while actually in a ball turret.

Before the war 'Shorty' had sought adventure and excitement on the flat desert tracks of his native California where he was a 'gow' driver, behind the wheel of a tuned-up Model A. He craved for more excitement and tried to enlist as a gunner in the RCAF but was rejected because he was one inch too short. Though America was still at peace 'Shorty' gambled on the USAAF and enlisted on 22 October 1940 at Fort MacArthur, California, joining the 7th Bombardment Group. When the 7th departed for Salt Lake City, prior to going overseas, 'Shorty' was left behind to do three months hard labour for being improperly dressed. On 7 December 1941, his sentence completed, he planned to ask for a transfer to the Philippines where he intended to hop to Burma and join the 'Flying Tigers' as a ground man. But the Japanese attack on Pearl Harbor changed all that and he threw up his job as armourer to take up gunnery.

'Shorty' was posted to the 305th Bomb Group commanded by Colonel (later General) Curtis E. LeMay. The General has written of 'Shorty', 'Maybe he was a Tech-Sergeant by the time we reached Europe: but we didn't have to wait any time at all until it was necessary to bust him back to Private. He would overstay his leave, sass some officer, take a swing at an MP, or not be at the proper place at the proper time—generally he wasn't shall we say, in a high state of discipline. He resented being bossed. In combat he was OK. Back on the base, No, no, no. Normally, I would leave disciplinary matters of this nature to squadron commanders but ''Shorty'' was a very special case. He was always being brought up to me and recurrently we found ourselves busting ''Shorty'' back to Private again.

'But we needed ''Shorty''. I lost half my crews before we started getting any replacements. We made up crews of anybody and everybody. We went around scratching the bottoms of barrels and bins. We took people out of offices. Bombardiers assumed navigator's chores. As for the gunners, if anyone wanted to go and shoot, we'd walk him once through the armoury shop and he was a gunner. That went for cooks, medical orderlies, supply people, truck drivers, anybody, everybody.

'''Shorty'' Gordon had been trained and was experienced in the air and we needed him for crew duty. So the way we'd work it was, when the time came for a mission, we would make him a buck Sergeant, send him on the mission: then take his stripes away from him when he came home. We did that a lot of times. What we were trying to do, of course, was to protect him and get better treatment for him, if the airplane happened to be shot down. In that case ''Shorty'' would be a non-com and get somewhat more preferential PoW treatment than he would have received as a Private. Also, of course, all the rest of the gunners on the combat crews were non-commissioned officers. The skill requires it, no matter which position is flown. I felt that it was highly unfair to send ''Shorty'' into battle as a buck Private.'

During the mission to Bremen on 26 February 1943 the 305th was forced to switch to the alternative target at Wilhelmshaven after cloud obscured the primary target. Gordon's pilot, Lieutenant George E. Stallman, followed the rest of the group to the German port. But about fifteen minutes from the target their Fortress was attacked by German fighters. Machine-gun fire and flak from the ground ultimately forced the crew to abandon ship.

Ralph S. Cohen, Gordon's armament and gunnery officer, was flying top-turret gunner in the Martini crew: 'We were leading the second element and on the right wing of the group lead. Stallman's plane was to the right and below our plane. Going into Bremerhaven, we met frontal attacks by the German fighters. I fired on some six fighters coming from directly in front. I know that of the six none of them fired on us as they turned and "Split S" out of the way before getting into firing range for their sights.

'During a breather, I saw one fighter come in below us and to the right. He was in a firing position on Stallman's aircraft: however, he was coming in too high for "Shorty" to fire on him. I didn't think at the time he had hit anything, but on looking a few seconds later I saw Stallman's plane going down and saw a parachute break out of the ball turret. I knew then it was Stallman's plane as "Shorty" was the only gunner I knew who could and did wear a 'chute in the ball turret. Most had to come up into the plane and snap on their 'chute and exit through the gun port window or door. I saw "Shorty's" 'chute open, but we turned north to go out some distance before turning back for England.'

It was the start of some of the most eventful experiences of any airman on the run in World War 2. Lee Gordon tells the story: 'Flak was bursting all around. A German fighter came towards me, turned up on one wing for a look and flew on. In the jerk of my parachute my flying boots, electric shoes and gloves dropped off. I was cold and had to beat my feet and hands together to keep warm. I felt foolish for opening the parachute so high.

'I must have been in the air half an hour, drifting over the bay south east of Wilhelmshaven. When I came through the clouds the ground looked far away. I saw a breakwater with stakes along the edge of the bay and thought that I was still high in the air. The next thing I knew I hit the ground with an awful jar. The parachute started to drag me over the stakes. I disentangled myself, walked a few feet in the mud and stopped to feel how I was.

'On the dyke I saw a girl and a small boy and walked toward them still half dazed. I hoped that somehow I might have drifted to Holland. When I asked the girl whether she was Dutch, she replied, "*Ja, Ja, ich bin Deutsch, und Sie sind in Deutchland.*" About forty men working down the dyke looked at me without coming towards me. Before I could do anything an old soldier, about seventy, with a rifle on his back, cycled up. He made me put up my hands, searched me for a pistol but missed the escape kit and purse in my trousers long pocket. A young soldier cycled up, followed shortly by six automobiles with officers in many different uniforms. A Luftwaffe officer asked me in good English what nationality I was. I replied that I was an American aviator. He asked me whether I was a Canadian and I repeated I was American.

"Was I flying with the RAF?"

"No, AAF."

He went into a huddle with the other officers. He asked me whether I was flying in a British plane.

"No, American."

He went into another huddle. He seemed to think I came from a Lancaster. Finally, he asked me if I was wounded. I replied that I was OK. A number of officers took out cameras and photographed me.

'A guard marched me in my stockinged feet about a mile and a half down a cobblestone road. An old woman asked the soldier if I was an Englander. When he said I was American she exclaimed, "American Devil!" The guard took me to a listening post. There the Germans said that they had heard us coming an hour before we arrived. All the Germans were laughing and were obviously happy at a good catch.

'A Corporal rushed out a book on aircraft identification, thumbed through silhouettes of Fortresses and Liberators, pointed to a picture of a B-17 and jabbered, "*Ja, Ja*". I opened my escape kit and ate some chocolate. I offered a guard some. He remarked, "*Nicht!*" and backed away. I smoked a cigarette and offered the German one. He looked around, took one and smoked it, muttering, "*Gut, Gut.*"

'Soon, a Luftwaffe officer in a chauffer-driven car picked me up, collected Sergeant William L. Jones, my waist gunner, at a barracks five miles away, and drove to a ferry. We rode down the river to Bremerhaven where I noticed a place which seemed to be repairing two-engined flying boats. I made a mental note of it.

'At dark we reached a collection of buildings outside the city and went in. A couple of officers and orderlies searched us and found my escape kit and purse. An officer saw that I had eaten the chocolate and had thrown some things away. They found my escape compass, counted the escape money and made out a receipt for it but did not give it back to me. One of the Germans looked curiously at the hacksaw and muttered something about "gangsters". The Colonel asked me for my dog tags. I had not bothered to wear them that day so I told him that I threw them in the sea. He blew up. The only identification I had was an American penny. We gave our name, rank and serial number and home address for the Red Cross.

'My tongue was swollen and my back and right foot hurt so I asked to see a doctor. I was fixed up and then taken to a cell. Two officers, Lieutenant Walter Ewing and a navigator from the 422nd Squadron, were there. Since I still did not have any shoes, Lieutenant Ewing gave me his flying boots.

'Early the next morning Ewing, myself and Sergeants Morse and Amterman from my crew, together with ten from another crew in my group, were put on a train for Frankfurt. We reached the Dulag Luft Interrogation Centre before dark. The camp Kommandant told us in English that we were not to talk to each other or smoke. Most of our group were put in cells in the lower camp. Two of us were taken up a hill to a two-storey barracks and I was placed alone in a room about 10 ft square. Its only furniture was a bed, a dresser, a chair and a table. Some coarse sheets were on the bed. I searched the whole room carefully for microphones, tapped all the walls and looked up the legs of the bed but I found nothing at all. It never occurred to me then that microphones might be in the electrical fixtures or bulbs.

'That afternoon an orderly dressed in civilian clothes came in with a Red Cross form and said that he was from Geneva. He told me to fill out this form, which was all in red on white paper with some Red Crosses and "Geneva" printed on it. I filled out the same information I had given previously. There were spaces for bomb squadron, group, command, air base, crew members and gun positions. I filled in only the names of my crew members who I knew were prisoners, thinking that others might be evading. The man told me that it could not go to the Red Cross unless it was complete. I said that was too bad. He got annoyed and walked out.

'Next day I stood at attention but did not salute when a Luftwaffe officer entered. "You're Sergeant Gordon," he said, offering me a cigarette. He brought out the same Red Cross form for me to fill out. I refused to complete it. He asked me what part of the country I came from.

I said, "California."

"What was my profession?"

"Professional soldier."

'Then he tried to draw me into conversation about the United States. He had been in Pittsburgh and New York it seemed.

"When did you enlist?"

I did not tell him. I also refused to tell him my squadron and group.

"Come now, don't be like that", he protested. He tried to insist that these were just little things which did not make any difference anyway.

"What base did I come from?"

I did not answer.

"What shot you down?"

"I don't know."

"You American Sergeants are pretty goddam dumb!", he exploded.

"Maybe we want to be dumb," I suggested.

"I'll keep you here until you rot," he shouted. Then he told me that as soon as I told him some of the little things he wanted to know, I could go down to the other part of the camp and see my friends and get good food.

'The next day no-one came to see me. While I was getting some fresh air at the window some RAF Sergeants walked by. I asked them to get me something to eat. They threw me some cigarettes, a piece of chocolate, some crackers and some cheese. I was famished and grateful but I was still a bit suspicious because an RAF lecturer had warned about possible stool pigeons.

'On the fourth day I had my photograph taken, profile and full view. I tried to distort my face so that I would not be easily recognizable later when I escaped.

'On the fifth day the German officer returned with a briefcase. He pulled out some papers and remarked, "Well, so you wouldn't fill out the Red Cross form. Now we've got everything here." He handed me a form with my squadron, group, bomber command and everyone on the crew; some of whom I had never even known. He asked me whether it was my crew. I said, "No." When he asked me to explain I told him that I was just flying with them that day and could not identify them. I asked him if he had found our plane. He did not reply. I remarked that it must have flown back to England. He became interested immediately and asked me if I wanted to fill out a form myself. I wrote down that I had previously filled out, added the crew as he had it listed, but refused to answer the rest. He remarked that I had better write down the crew or they would be shot as spies if they were caught. He asked me if some of the men were killed or missing. I decided that he was just trying to get me to talk.

'After I signed my name at the bottom, the officer settled down to questioning me. He seemed to want to get me talking and then to catch me up. "We know all about you," he began, and then told me every single move my squadron had made from the time we left Harlingen Engineers' School to our arrival at our base at Chelveston, complete with dates and commanding officers' names. I asked him how he got all this information.

"American newspapers," he replied. "They really fix us up. Every time a man goes to school or gets another rank they have a note about it. American newspapers are sure good friends of ours. They help us a lot."

'When he asked how our plane was shot down I replied that I did not know, that I was only the ball-turret gunner. He declared that I ought to know as I was a Sergeant. He seemed to want to get me angry so I would tell him everything I knew just to prove that I was not a dope. He talked about all sorts of subjects and finally declared that I would have to stay where I was for a few days longer.

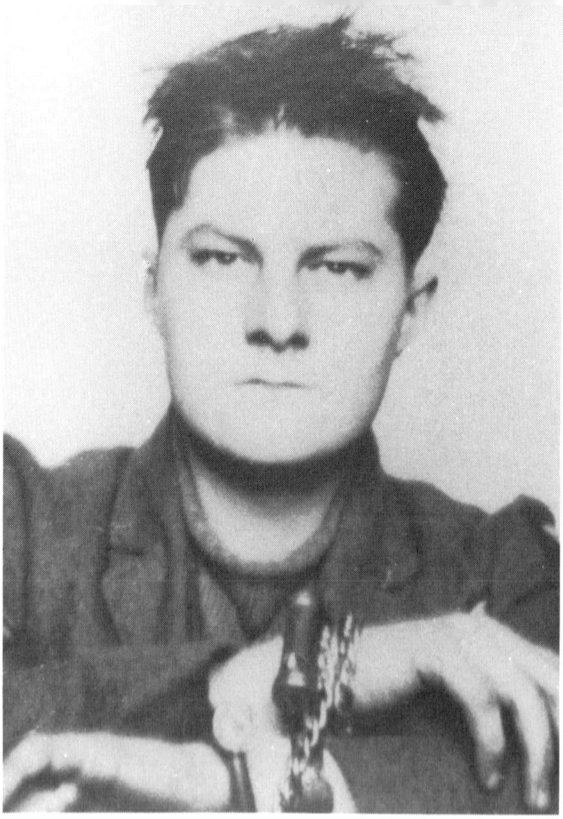
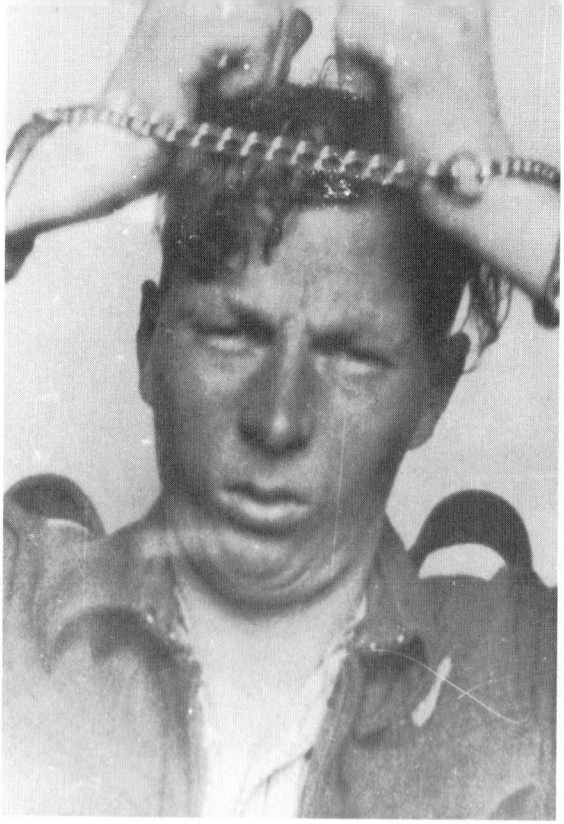

British PoWs at Lamsdorf manacled by the Germans following the raid on Dieppe (via Bruce).

"If you answer everything we ask, we could let you out sooner," he remarked, "You know how it is in solitary confinement." I did, I had been there five days.

'On the sixth day I was allowed a shower and a book. In the afternoon of the seventh day five others were moved down the section of the camp where we had first been. There was a large book there in which men who had been shot down wrote their names, the date they were shot down, how many crewmen were killed and how many were PoW. I looked through it and noticed names from nearly every bomb group in England.

'We were issued RAF uniforms. There was no American equipment but a few American Red Cross parcels were available. In general the food in this section of the camp was good and adequate. That evening we had a couple of kegs of beer and sang songs. Later, an air raid warning sounded and we saw flashes in the distance. A cheering sight.

'We could not figure out why our group stayed in the camp while others were leaving. Finally, on 11 March we were told that we were leaving for Lamsdorf. The camp Kommandant lined us up, said that we were fliers in the RAF and AAF and should act accordingly. He emphasized that any man who escaped would be shot immediately and he repeated his statement. At the station we had twelve Luftwaffe guards for the seventeen in our group, which included three British commandos. The Germans watched the commandos with particular care.

'We were on the train for four days. Our two cars, occupied by about 118 men, including about 42 Americans, were in the middle of freight trains. Sergeant Roy Livingstone of the 306th Bomb Group jumped off the train during the journey. On 15 March we reached Lamsdorf on the Silesian plain and were taken to the main camp of Stalag VIIIB, one of the largest British PoW camps. As we marched down from the train we all gave the V-sign while a German officer took our picture. We sang *Tipperary* to keep the morale of the fellows who were tired. I saw some RAF and other British soldiers walking around in handcuffs. As we marched in British and Canadian soldiers threw us cigarettes.

'We lined up and spread all our possessions out in front of us. The Germans made us give up our leather A-2 jackets and our flying boots. Over the next two days we had our clothes deloused, had our finger prints taken and given identity discs with our PoW numbers on them. After four days in quarantine we were allowed to walk around the camp. 28 Americans, were staying in the Indian and Arab barracks. Three American Rangers captured at Dieppe were there but unlike the British captured at

Scenes of PoW camp life at Lamsdorf (via Bruce).

Dieppe, they were not manacled. They told me they had been interrogated by high German officials in Berlin.

'On about 22 March we were told that all Americans would leave Lamsdorf. Before we went to the train we had to lay everything out in front of us but we were not stripped. The search was very slack. Then we marched to two filthy boxcars. Fifty of us sat tightly packed on little seats in one. Wounded men were in the other. Again we were warned that any man who tried to escape would be shot. On the first two days of the journey we were given water and were allowed out to relieve ourselves. The second two days we were neither allowed out or given water. We started yelling for "*Wasser*". At one station a guard took a prisoner out to get water. The train moved out and left them behind. While the guard ran around frantically, the prisoner chased after him to keep up as best he could!

'Since I expected to make an escape from the train I had secured from a Canadian at Luft VIIIB, a magnetized needle. The British at Lamsdorf had briefed two of our party on escape to Switzerland and told them that we had a great chance to get loose. Someone had detailed maps to follow our train route. There was a hole in the door through which a man could reach the latch. We unwrapped the barbed wire from the door handle and bolt and took off the wire which held the bolt in. We left a piece of barbed wire on the latch so that the door would look undisturbed.

'Eight of us made up our minds to escape. We had picked the area for our attempt, chiefly because we thought that we could head east from there into Austria. We figured that towards the end of the journey the Germans would become especially watchful, so after Chemnitz we knew that we would have to escape if we were going to. We had the wire off the door and waited for the train to slow down. When it was going up grade at about 30 kilometers an hour we opened the door. The first three men, Staff Sergeants Floyd B. Ammerman, William L. Jones and Sergeant Cassius E. Morse, all from the 305th, jumped off between Lamsdorf and Moosburg. About an hour later they hopped a freight train and hid in a boxcar. In Nuremburg the next day a German discovered them. They started to run but were caught. Ammerman and Morse had a fist fight but they were eventually overpowered, taken to a camp at Nuremburg and sent to Stalag VIIIA.

'Three more men, Staff Sergeant Darel W. Coats, Tech-Sergeant Earl B. Willis and Sergeant Arnold, jumped off the train together. They walked about 30 km and were caught near Regensburg. After three days in jail they were sent to Stalag VIIA and each given fourteen days confined to barracks. Around 10 May Coats and Willis escaped again with another prisoner. They walked for five nights, sleeping during the day and were picked up at a bridge at Ingolstadt. They were brought back to Stalag VIIA and given another eighteen days confined to barracks.

'Sergeant Bernard Saltz from the 305th Bomb Group and I were the last to jump from the train. I hit the ground. My feet caught in the signal wire along the tracks and I went head over heels down the bank in the darkness. I saw the lights on the back of the train and lay still. I was alone. In a few minutes I heard someone run and whistle. It was Saltz. We lay there a few minutes thinking over the situation and then found a stream to drink from. I later contracted dysentry, probably from that water. After a few minutes' rest we went through the brush, cut back across the railway tracks and hid on a hill until morning. Although we were wearing RAF overcoats it was extremely cold.

'We had agreed to try and hop a freight train, so we started down to the village where we saw one. Too many people were around for us to try the freight train so we went right on through the village. Sergeant Saltz, who could speak a little German, asked an old man for a glass of water and the man brought it. He also lit our cigarettes. We said "*Danke Schòn*", and walked on heading west by my needle compass. Some German soldiers passed us and in the next three villages we walked through we must have passed a hundred people.

'We stopped at a brook to clean up and shave. After 10 km or so we ran into a man and girl with an ox-cart. We discovered he was Polish and she Ukrainian. We said we were American aviators and asked for food. They gave us their one loaf of bread and told us that police and soldiers were in the town ahead. We went around it over a hill and walked through a large forest where some girls who looked like Ukrainians were working. They saw that we were in uniform and paid little attention to us. The forest was far from a good place to hide because it was too open. We passed a number of people without any trouble.

'When we finally got out of the forest we saw a railway track. We still wanted to board a freight train. When we crossed a road some people on bicycles saw us and rode away. We skirted a road and almost before we knew it police on bicycles and motorcycles had surrounded us. They took us in sidecars to a beer joint. They searched us, made us strip and looked through our clothes. Our map was found but not my magnetized needle which I had stuck in my lapel. Many more police came—we showed them our Stalag tags and told them that we were American PoWs. They looked at Saltz's dog tags and noticed that he was Jewish. One short German policeman started yelling. Saltz said he wanted to go to the lavatory. The policeman stuck a gun in him and marched him out but he was an American PoW and they could not do anything to him. We were taken to a filthy prison in another town, slept on wooden racks and ate poorly from very dirty dishes.

'In retrospect this was a pretty poor escape because we had no real plan, but at least it was good experience and gave me a lot more confidence for a successful break.

'I also tried to obtain information from men who had evaded. Staff Sergeant Kenneth Kurtenbach, a tail gunner in the 303rd Bomb Group, had been one of many loose in France for about a month after being shot down on the Romilly-sur-Seine raid on 12 December 1942. We later elected him our "man of confidence". He was a top notch man and did a wonderful job. He was most popular with the men and they especially appreciated his nightly report on Red Cross conditions. The man of confidence was primarily concerned with administering Red Cross affairs and activities for the PoWs but he also represented the men in any other relations with the camp authorities, such as voicing complaints or making requests.

'I knew a number of men who came into the camp had evaded in France. They seemed to have been taken to some place around Paris for interrogation about their evasion. About thirteen men who had been in prison there came into the camp. Among them was Staff Sergeant Charley L. Gilbert of the 305th Bomb Group and a ball-turret gunner on a crew that was shot down in a raid on St Nazaire on 16 February 1943. He was the first American evader to be caught in France when the Germans picked him up near Bordeaux. I got the impression from talking to the evaders that France was not the place to head for.

'From a Frenchman in prison I bought, for a can of coffee, a detailed map of the Swiss border showing Lake Constance, Singen and the Schaffhausen salient. From another I bought, for a can of coffee and two packs of cigarettes, a large well-detailed tourist map of southern Germany as far west as Ehingen. From another I got a map covering south Germany from Ulm to the Rhine and showing the towns from Ehingen to Singen. I was never searched in prison and I had no trouble keeping those escape articles. I studied my maps for hours on end, memorizing which way the rivers flowed, the names of towns and everything that I should know about the country in case I lost my maps. I had learned that I should know about the country in case I lost my maps. I had learned that it was bad to pull out your maps as one journeyed. I also got Frenchmen who had been in south Germany to brief me about the terrain.

'I learned that one could travel in Germany on slow trains and go short distances without any papers but that in other trains it was most dangerous to do so. I learned that it was fairly easy to travel by freight trains while German roads were well marked and that many had bicycle paths. I heard that it was best to keep off the Reichsautobahnen, the military roads on which walking and bicycling were not allowed. I learned that many had road blocks where anyone who looked suspicious was stopped and checked.

'It seemed fairly easy to get hold of a bicycle. At worst I could simply steal one so I decided to make the trip to the Swiss frontier by bicycle. I tried to find out why escapers who rode bicycles had been caught. I figured that if I looked younger than sixteen I would probably not be questioned about not being in the army, or not working. I decided to try and get hold of a Bavarian youth costume. I learned what kind of clothes Bavarian boys wore, how they wore them and everything I could about their actions and looks.

'I traded a pack of cigarettes for a pocket knife and got an excellent French military compass for a can of meat. For a can of lemon powder, two packs of cigarettes and a packet of tea, I got a civilian knapsack.

'Early in May I complained about being kept in the detention barracks so long. On 5 May I was moved to the American compound and from there I could circulate pretty much as I wished. I realized that I could not assemble all the clothing I wanted so I went to Sergeant Major W. O. Berry, the British man of confidence, told him that I had a good plan to escape and asked him to help me. I explained my plan to cycle to Switzerland and declared that I needed some *Lederhosen* (leather shorts). Berry had the Germans so well bribed that he could do anything he wanted, including going to Munich in a dinner suit and enjoying himself. He even sent tea to the camp Kommandant. But although he made things as comfortable for himself as he could, he would do everything within his power for anyone who was intent on escaping.

'Berry got in touch with a German who could get the shorts for 25 cans of coffee. The German took my measurements and arranged to get the Bavarian shorts on the black market. I collected eighteen cans of coffee by raffling off my Red Cross parcel. I sold part of my tourist map of Germany for two more cans. Then I took my twenty cans of coffee to Sergeant Major Berry and explained that I could not raise any more. From the Red Cross parcels which he controlled, he made up all the food necessary to purchase part of my escape equipment including a bicycle. He found that the German would get one for 1,000 cigarettes and ten cans of coffee; a price which he considered pretty steep. I explained that I did not have the asking price and he paid for it himself. He also arranged to get food for me; three or four tins of malted milk or Ovaltine from the hospital, six chocolate bars and some boxes of raisins.

'I thought that I might be cold wearing just the Bavarian youth costume, so I decided to get a set of German worker's clothes. First I got a regular black peaked cap. Then I traded some of my Army clothes for a civilian shirt and sweater. Since I still had no civilian trousers, a most helpful Frenchman had a French tailor make me a pair out of a grey blanket for two cans of coffee, a can of meat and a pack of cigarettes. The Frenchman got a hat from a German and arranged for a pair of shoes to be cut down to look like civilian ones.

'While I was still gathering equipment I had a long talk with Robert Cahin, a French Alsation who was interpreter for Barracks 36. He suggested that I go to a French *Arbeitskommando* (Labour detail) in Munich and have the French workers put me in a freight car for France. He suggested that if I could get to Alsace, it was possible to travel into France by river boats. At first Berry was as much attracted by this plan but we both concluded that, since I had gathered all the equipment for the escape to Switzerland, it might be best to follow my original plan.

'I had a simple system of getting out of the camp. Under three guards, a detail of thirty American infantrymen worked levelling ground for a town cemetery. When the party was returning at about 1700 hours the first three men in rank would jump over a bank on the road and hide in the bushes. During the day the men hid food around the cemetery. Between 5 May and 27 May 1943, fifteen men escaped this way without the Germans catching on. After a careful count by the Germans, thirty men went out in the morning; 27 came back in the evening. The Germans checked them in as the full thirty. I arranged with the American Private in charge of the detail to let me go with it and escape from it.

'Between 20 May and 31 May I went on the detail five times so the guards would get to know me and think that I was an infantryman. About 27 May the Germans caught on to this easy system and watched the work detail more carefully. The guards were warned that if any more men escaped they would be sent to the Russian Front.

'I kept my equipment in the barracks. We had no searches. By the end of May I had most of my equipment and was ready to set out for Switzerland. Berry arranged with a German on the camp staff to get my Lederhosen and the bicycle and to bring me these things outside the camp after I had escaped. I talked to the German and reviewed my plans with him. I had decided not to head directly for the Swiss frontier but to go west and then south.

'Berry shared all these discussions and I gave him my route almost down to the last tree. I planned to allow five days and nights with little moonlight to cross the frontier and I thought that I might have to crawl a large part of the last stretch. If I was successful, Berry would send other men by the same route. Just before I left he gave me the address in Switzerland of Mrs Jeb Scott. She had taken care of three men who escaped by train from Munich. Berry was, I believe, in code contact with her.

'On 31 May I went out with the work party to take a final look at the escape situation. That night I made my last arrangements with Berry. A French barber cut my hair very short; "*Egal au Boche*". Everyone agreed I could pass for sixteen. My equipment included a toilet kit so that I could keep close shaved and spruced up.

'The morning of 1 June 1943 I got up at 06.00, put on my Bavarian costume under an infantryman's uniform and lined up with the infantrymen for the work detail. Only eighteen of us went out this morning. Although only a couple of men knew that I was escaping, someone yelled, "Good luck, Shorty," as we marched out.

'I had arranged that men cover me while I made my break, so tall men were all around me. We picked up a wagon and some pushed, some pulled. A German rode by on a bicycle counting us three or four times. Two guards walked behind us. The detail marched up the road. I ran into the bushes to a small field of high oats and crossed it, making as wide a path as I could. When I reached solid ground I ran on about 100 yards. Then I back-tracked cautiously to the oat-fields, went into it and lay down carefully.

'Within five minutes I heard Germans yelling and shouting about thirty yards from me on the road. A car stopped. Germans got in and drove off. I lay in the oat-field all morning. I heard many Germans yelling and shouting. One German with dogs came close to me. The Germans followed my trail through the oat-field but my back-tracking fooled them. In the afternoon I was drenched in a downpour and decided that I had better find cover. I went to a forest. Near a road I heard somebody on a bicycle and dropped to the ground. A German soldier with a rifle on his back passed within eight feet of me. I dived into a swamp where I was well hidden. After an hour I went to a hillside in the forest and stayed there until night, cold and wet.

'At night I hid my infantry clothes in the forest and went to meet the German with the bicycle and my knapsack. When he came I put the civilian suit over my Bavarian costume. He reminded me not to go through Freising at night, wished me good luck and walked away. I adjusted the pack to look as small as possible and started off. Before I knew it I was in Freising. I turned quickly, found a place in the bushes outside of town and tried to go to sleep. It was still raining. In fact it rained on and off during my whole escape.

'At dawn I tried to spruce up, mounted my bicycle and rode right through Freising. A few people were going to work but no one stopped me. I rode straight to Munich on the main road. I did not locate the French *Arbeitskommando* until noon. When I finally found the right place I asked for the man I was supposed to see. He was not there. The French workers were suspicious of me because my disguise looked so German. I decided that I had better not look suspicious, so I bicycled toward Paysing. However, before I knew it, I had reached the north-east railroad station instead. My knapsack fell off the back of my bicycle. While I was fixing it a couple of German women came up laughing and talking. I gave an

A portrait of Lee 'Shorty' Gordon as it appeared in Air Force, *the official journal of the USAF in June 1943.*

occasional "*Ja, Ja*" and left as quickly as I could. I finally got on the road to Augsburg and saw road signs clearly marking the way.

'About 10 km west of Munich I changed into my Bavarian youth costume. At dark I was about ten kilometres from Augsburg. I hid my bicycle in a small haystack and crawled into another. The next morning I got up before dawn so as not to be seen getting on the road and continued my way to Augsburg. There I set out for Nuremberg and had to go back through the city to get on the road to Gunzburg. Going up a steep incline a truck passed me with a German hanging on the back. I hung on too. When the German yelled at me I replied with an occasional "*Ja, Ja,*" or "*Gut, Gut*". I let him drop off first so that I would not be drawn into a conversation.

'Just before I reached Gunsburg my bicycle chain broke. I fixed it with a piece of wire which I was carrying for picking locks but the chain broke again in the middle of a village. While I was working on it an old German started talking to me. I ignored him for the most part, keeping him off with a couple of "*Ja, Ja's*". A lot of Germans seemed to go around with a grouch on, so I just acted like one of them and grunted.

'While I was riding along between Leipheim and Ulm dressed in my Bavarian costume, I saw some boys in the middle of the road, some in *Lederhosen* like mine; others in cloth shorts and some in Hitlerjugand uniforms. A boy of about fourteen dressed in a black uniform was drilling them up and down and yelling at them. When I came close to the group he turned. I said. "*Heil Hitler,*" and gave the Hitler salute. The group came to attention and he snapped a reply.

'At Ulm it rained so hard that I took cover under a tree—a dangerous thing to do. At dusk just before I reached Ehingen, I saw some haystacks in an orchard and a shack on the side of the hill. I was very tired from riding since dawn and I wanted to go to sleep. I swung off the road, hid my bicycle and climbed into a haystack. I pulled out my maps and studied them, tearing up the one that went only to Ehingen, since I did not want anyone to check my route.

'About half an hour later I heard someone pick up my bicycle. Two men were talking. I raised my head and saw them standing nearby. I ducked quickly but they walked over to me, told me to come out and started questioning me. They asked me what I was doing and why I was not working. (I had my worker's clothes on over the Bavarian costume). I replied, "*Nichts Arbeit*". They started searching me and asked if I was Russian, French, Serb, Dutch or English. One of them pushed me. I said that I was an American aviator PoW and showed my Stalag tags. They made me pick up my bicycle and walk down the road. They explained that they had been watching the road with field glasses from a chateau. I should have been more careful in lying up that night. I had become over-confident. I should have waited until it was dark before I stopped but I was tired, and saw a good chance to sleep, so I took the chance and had lost.'

7 If at first you don't succeed. . .

'Shorty' Gordon was taken to the Burgomeister of a nearby town and put into civil prison. A German officer arrived later and snapped handcuffs on him and the would-be American escaper was taken to a military prison near Ulm.

Gordon continues, 'An interrogator in a room with several other Germans asked me where I was shot down and how much damage had been done in that area. When I told him that the damage was terrific he got very annoyed. He asked me when the war would be over and I said, "November". He said they were going to invade England next month. I laughed in their faces and said, "*Deutschland kaput; Allemagne kaput.*" They asked me if many American bombers were in England. I said there were thousands of them. At that they had a conference and concluded that I was a liar. I was taken to a cell where I received the best food I had ever had in any German prison.

'They had searched me fairly carefully but they did not feel my lapels, leg seams or back seams. I was in jail there from 3 June to the eleventh. On the eighth I ate two chocolate bars and some raisins in honour of my 21st birthday. I tried unsuccessfully to trade some chocolate for some cigarettes. I had no cigarettes in all that time, probably the worst punishment of all. I kept whistling to keep from going "Stalagy". The German guards tried to point that it was "*Strengt Verboten*" to sing or whistle in prison but I kept saying, "*Nichts Verstehen.*"

'On 12 June 1943 a tough looking Feldwebel who had been wounded on the Russian Front took me to the train with some Germans and some guards. I never was with any German guard who stuck so close. We went through Sigmaringen and Tuttlingen to Stalag VB at Villingen. There my Bavarian clothes were taken away from me. I was put in detention barracks where I slept in a large bed with seventeen Frenchmen. A number of men who had escaped were in the detention barracks and I tried to find out from them what their plan had been and what had gone wrong.

'I traded coffee and cigarettes with some Frenchmen for a 500 franc note, four 100 franc notes and a few small notes. I hid the 500 franc note in the cuff of my trousers, rolled up the 100 franc notes and hid them in cigarettes, carefully filling the cigarettes with tobacco again. The Frenchmen had played me a dirty trick. They knew when we moved to Stalag VA at Ludwigsburg we were going to be searched. I did not.

'When I arrived at Stalag VA I was taken to a large administration building and into a large office. I saluted the officer there and was left alone with him. The office walls were covered with maps and it seemed to be a headquarters for information about escapes from south Germany. On a large map were many different coloured flags which I took to mark places where men had tried to cross the frontier and also where guard posts and patrols were located. The officer tried to find out what route I was taking. In order to take his attention off the Swiss border, I told him that I was heading for France. The officer asked me the usual routine questions about when I was shot down, conditions in England and the United States and so on. Throughout the interview he was friendly.

'At Stalag VA I was given the most thorough search that I ever received. I was stripped and gone over by a German Sergeant. He looked through the food I was carrying and through my knapsack. In my shorts he found some small French notes that I had hidden in the top hem as a blind. He went through my undershirt, shirt and jacket, inch by inch, feeling every part and especially the seams. He went through my trousers and found the 500 francs in the cuff. He felt very confident and contented. The only part of my clothes that he did not look at carefully was my shoes. They were turned upside down and shaken but I could have hidden something in the toe. He looked at the cigarettes, shook them all out, looked in the package, examined a couple and gave the whole pack to me.

'Myself, Sergeant Coker of the 168th Infantry and Dorsey, another infantryman with whom he had escaped from Stalag VIIA about the time I did, were taken back to Stalag VIIA, Moosburg. There we were given a poor search. The three of us were put in one cell and given two blankets. My dysentry got so bad that I had to be taken to the hospital for treatment.

'For more than two hours one of the camp interpreters interrogated me to find out how I had escaped from the camp, where I was heading and what my plans were. He particularly wanted to find out how I had gotten the bicycle. He suspected that someone in the camp had helped me. I told him that I bought it from two Frenchmen in Munich for 500 marks. This was a mistake. I did not know how much a mark was worth and 500 marks was too much to pay for a bicycle. But I stuck to my story, giving a description of the Frenchmen which I would have no trouble remembering. The interpreter told me I was a liar but he could not break the story. He insisted that someone in the camp had helped me. They shouted at me but finally they gave up and had me sign a sheet with my version of the story on it. I was taken to Barracks 39, where my French friends welcomed me back. Thanks to my old British friend's arrangements, each of the three of us received a Red Cross parcel. At that time only eight parcels were left in the camp.

'I was soon taken up for trial. I walked in and saluted an elderly officer who with another officer, constituted the court. They had an orderly and an interpreter. The head of the court, looking at my papers, remarked, "Aha! You're the one we're after," and asked me a lot of questions: where I had been shot down; how long I had been a soldier; where I lived; how I liked the climate and so on. About the only thing he did not ask me was how the food was in England. He knew, because my British friend was keeping him supplied with Red Cross food.

'He sentenced me to eighteen days confined to Barracks 39, then knocked off eight days. I stepped back, saluted and walked out. I learned that the Germans gave less time for a good escape than they did for a bad one. Sergeant Coker was given 21 days for his escape and ten days for stealing a bicycle. The GI was given fourteen days for the escape and ten for stealing a bicycle. He was sent to 40B to do his time; a dark hole full of lice and a lot worse than 39. If I had not declared myself a Staff Sergeant I would have caught it worse. The Germans gave three graders better treatment.

'The plan for going to France was very much on my mind. I learned from Robert Cahin that his *Arbeitskommando* connections in Munich still worked. France seemed the best way out.

'During June the "graveyard detail" had been sent to Munich to work with the two *Arbeitskommandos* which were associated with the camp. Some 150-250 men were in these details. I think that they were rebuilding bombed buildings or doing some other construction work. Some were working with a tile and pottery concern, supposed to be putting on tile roofs. They had to carry tiles up four stories of scaffolding and they had some disagreements with the Germans about carrying more tiles and the safety of the scaffolding. Some men who were supposed to mix one part of cement to three parts of sand mixed one part of cement to every fourteen of sand. The same group kept reinforcing the cement with all the loose tools they could find.

'An American-Czech was camp leader of the *Arbeitskommando*. The Germans thought that he was trying to do too much for his fellows, sentenced him to 21 days in jail for "propaganda" and sent him back to camp. A number of men escaped from the *kommando* barracks and a number of men went there just to escape. In June eleven men crawled over the wire. One was caught on the fence, a couple were found close to the camp and some near Freising. All were caught within 24 hours. Two were caught on a flatcar in a railway yard near Regensburg. All were given fourteen days. Two infantry Sergeants who escaped walked toward Switzerland. They had already jumped off a train coming from Italy but had been picked up in the mountains by ski patrols. They bribed a German guard to get them out on a supply truck and were caught trying to go through Freising at night. They were put in prison and taken back to Stalag VIIA. En-route they escaped again, in a station, and made their way to Munich where they were recaught in the railway yards, still dressed in their uniforms.

'On 3 July I was moved to the American compound. I spent the next days lying in the sun, resting up for my next escape. Something went wrong with the American Red Cross parcels. Late in July the Canadians loaned us some 1,000 parcels and in August the Serbs loaned us some more but we had a pretty miserable time of it until the American supply flowed freely again late in August.

'We were getting the camp organized and we could not have learned better the need for good organization. Knowing our rights as NCOs, we had refused to work for the Germans. They tried to break our morale and get us to go on work parties by promises of better food and living conditions. Only a few men responded, and about half of them volunteered only for a chance to escape. We called a meeting and decided that all of the men could not escape and that any work party would be helping the Germans. We agreed we would all starve together. When the question of sending officers' batmen to Stalag Luft III came up, we held a meeting and ruled that only infantry Privates should go as they had to work for the Germans anyway.

'We developed our organization for welfare in a number of battles over food prices with the other nationalities in the camp. One result of our efforts was the development of an American post exchange in spite of many German objections. Another result was the election of a committee to welcome new men into the camp and tell them how conditions were. Unfortunately, our organization for annoying and resisting the Germans was much better than our organization for escape.

'In July some 500 Americans were made to stand in a violent rain storm without overcoats for five hours without moving. The pretext was that the Americans had not been falling out exactly at 08.00 hours. After the numerous American escapes, an additional fence was erected around the American compound. Barbed wire was piled between the fences and bells rigged up on the outer fence.

'During the first two weeks of August the camp discipline officer, Kruger, had us fall out for roll call at 21.00, midnight and 03.00 hours. We were so punished because many Americans had been escaping. We all tried not to grumble about this and showed such good morale that the Germans discontinued the annoyance. We could sleep all day, unlike the guards.

'In general, the German treatment was quite correct. A guard at the gate once kicked me but I was in French clothing at the time and my back was turned. My only real complaint was against the German who put handcuffs on me after my second escape. In April a Russian was shot on the compound wire and left hanging there wounded. A British airman went to pull him off the wire and was shot. He spent some time in the hospital but I believe he recovered.

'Meanwhile, I made plans for a new escape. I got another civilian suit from my French helper in return for a Red Cross parcel. About the middle of August I was interrogated on my last escape. The camp authorities had discovered my bicycle. I repeated the fiction of buying the bicycle from two Frenchmen in Munich for 500 marks. They could not break my story and had to give up. The Sergeant to whom the bicycle belonged tried to make friends with me later and learn who had helped me but I never told him anything.

'About a week later the Germans pulled off the first big search of the camp. Although we were tipped off in advance, they found just about everything, including my suit of civilian clothes which I had hidden under the ashes in a fire box in the latrine. I should have worn it. With six or eight men searching over a thousand one could get away with almost anything. Just stand in the line to be searched and then walk out at one point as if you had been searched. Or, watch closely for the German making the most careless search and stand at the end of his line. This last was one of the best ways for getting through a mass search. I also found I could hold small articles in closed hands which you raised while the German searched your body.

'The Germans gathered a great pile of maps, compasses, books without Stalag stamps, bottles, wires, pliers, picks, shovels, chisels, hammers, hacksaws and all kinds of tools. I was surprised to see how many things had been hidden around the compound. The Germans discovered the camp radio; an inheritance from the British. We thought that one of our men had betrayed the presence of this radio. One man was supposed to have told a German that he wanted to go out and have fun. A German called Karl (to whom the bicycle used in my escape belonged) took him to town and he slept with a couple of women. After that the Germans threatened to put him in prison for ten years unless he did everything they asked.

'After the loss of my suit of clothes I got a little discouraged about my next escape. I waited to see what would happen in Italy. Like some of the Germans a lot of us thought that the landing would take place in August or September and that Germany would collapse within a couple of months. During August and September there were relatively few escapes. The news of the Italian capitulation reinforced the general feeling that the war would probably be over by November. I spent much time studying maps and learning all that I could about German geogaphy.

'In September I had a case of beri-beri with nasty running sores. The British doctors got me back into pretty good shape. Except for many cases of beriberi, (there were 300 infections in August) Americans were generally healthy. We missed fresh vegetables and fruit.

'From the middle of September the camp was in a continual uproar. So many American, British and Australians were being sent through the camp from Italy that the place was completely overcrowded. Tents had to be pitched on our baseball field for the Italians, who made an awful mess of the compound.

'During the bombing of Munich in September we went out of the barracks to watch the fireworks. The Germans came into the compound with dogs. One dog jumped up into a window but was stabbed by a retreating American. During the Regensburg raid we were outside when we should not have been. A German fighter flying over the camp reported that someone in the American compound had been signalling with a mirror. After that we were told that anyone outside during an air raid would be shot. One night a Ju 88 with its lights on made two runs over the camp and dropped cement blocks. The Germans began talking about the Allies bombing camps containing their own prisoners.

'When some American officers were brought into the camp in September and October, the escape committee approached me to help get two of them out of the camp. I did not know what the escape committee actually knew or did. I did not think they questioned the other Allies to learn all they could from their escapes. I think they knew I was friendly with some Frenchmen and they guessed that I had some methods of getting out of the camp. I gave them all the methods I knew about getting out of the camp except for the one which I was planning shortly to use myself.

'On 9 October I asked the escape committee for some Red Cross supplies to help in escaping. They sent me to Kurtenbach who arranged to cover for some supplies from the Red Cross which were earmarked for a mass exodus of 1,300 American NCOs two days later to Stalag XVIIB. This was the first large movement of Americans and it was heavily guarded. A lot of men had been planning to jump off the train. By 11.00 hours all the Americans were moved, except some men in the hospital, a few Red Cross men and some infantrymen. I lined up with the Australians for their count.

'We heard that all American Air Force men were to be moved to Stalag XVIIB at Krems. The rumour began to circulate that we would have SS guards at the new camp. I had learned from the French, Serbs and Russians what the SS were and I feared that the chances of escape at Krems might be pretty slim. I decided to stay at VIIA and escape to France after all the Americans had been moved and so I changed identities with an Australian, Lloyd Ferguson, for the purpose. He had been captured at Ruin Ridge at El Alamein on 27 July 1942, had escaped in Italy and had been caught at the Swiss frontier. I gave him my prison tags and when I told him I had a plan to escape he gave me his complete civilian outfit.

'I made final preparations for my escape. I had learned from Robert Cahin that the coast was clear in Munich. Cahin arranged to get us out of the camp with the help of another Frenchman. I was leaving with Captain Richard Carr of the British Army, who knew French. We would head for Munich. There the French workers would take care of us until we could get a freight train to France.

'I packed my escape kit and my clothes in my old knapsack and arranged with an Australian to throw it over the compound fence when the guard's back was turned. I took no compass and no maps for I already knew the way to Munich. I bribed the guard at the gate with a couple of cigarettes, caught my knapsack from the Australian, and walked to the British and American officers' compound. On the night of the twelfth I slept in the compound with the British and American officers. The Australians had arranged to cover at the count.

'I was to meet Captain Carr in front of Barrack 36 the following night, 13 October. I put my civilian clothes on underneath a French uniform which I had traded from one of the French prisoners. At about 16.00 hours I went out of the compound past the guard with the usual story about going up the street for a moment. I went up to the main gate of the camp, saw two Sergeants whom I knew and ducked into the dispensary. When the coast was clear I walked by two German guards talking at the gate pretending I had regular business outside.

'When I got to Barracks 36 at 16.30 hours as arranged, Carr was not there. I thought he had gone so I walked into the office building and into a toilet where I locked the door. Carr turned up and a Frenchman from Barracks 35 came and let us out as arranged. He brought my knapsack with him. At 18.30 the German guard came to check the blackout and try the doors. The Frenchman helped us get into the women's toilet from which we were to escape. He gave us our equipment and left us with a "*Merde*" for good luck.

'The Frenchman helped us out of the administrative section of the camp and we jumped over the outer wooden fence while the watch tower guard's back was turned. At about 02.30 we ran around the corner of the office building and hid in the shrubbery. We jumped over the picket fence and started down the road in bright moonlight. Before we had gone far two men cycled towards us. Carr wanted to run into the woods but I grabbed him and told him to keep walking as if he belonged there. The assistant camp Kommandant and an interpreter rode by without bothering us.

'We went around Moosburg and took the main road to Freising and Munich. My idea was to get to Munich as fast as we could. Going through a village we ran into a German on a bicycle but we had no trouble. I was afraid that a bridge over the railway might be guarded so we circled and joined the road below it.

'At about 03.00 we lay up in a forest north of Freising. We had agreed that we would stay there all the next day and go on next night. Carr insisted that we should camouflage ourselves so we stuck some branches in the ground around us. It proved extremely effective. During the day, 14 October, we heard sirens blowing (for the second American raid on Schweinfurt). We enjoyed the sound. In the afternoon a boy and girl walked through the woods picking mushrooms and making love. They walked within three yards of us without seeing us. Soon, about five Germans in Bavarian shorts walked through the woods. One of them pointed toward us. We hugged the ground and they all went off without seeing us. I was thankful for our little camouflage.

'About 18.00 we left our French uniforms in the woods and started off in our civilian clothes. We walked through Freising and took the main road to

Munich at a good speed. Just before Dretershein, at a tiny village, we saw an armed German soldier and a dog. The dog barked and ran at our legs. The guard said nothing and we kept on walking. After about three steps he asked us for our papers. We kept right on walking. He kept shouting until we were about 100 yards away but he did not come after us. We were really sweating and Carr was angry at me for wanting to walk on the roads. From that time on we walked around all towns.

'My spiked shoes were too big for me and I was beginning to get blisters. Surprisingly quickly we neared the outskirts of Munich. We stopped at an irrigation ditch, washed and shaved. I thought that we should wait for daylight and then go right into Munich as if we were workers. About daylight we walked by the Baierische Motorworks where people were already going to work.

'We made our way to *Arbeitkommando* 2903 on Bayernstrasse west of Hoffmanstrasse and met our interpreter. We told him that Robert Cahin from Barrack 36 at Stalag Luft VIIA had sent us. He told us that Captain George Tsoucas and Captain Ralph Palm, a South African pilot, from Stalag VIIA had preceded us. We were told to stay in Munich acting like French civilian workers until we could leave by freight train. We were to rendezvous at cafés on the Hoffmanstrasse and live in the barracks where the French workers slept. That evening, 15 October, we rendezvoused in one of the cafés where we met the Frenchman who was to make the arrangements for sending us out in a freight car. Carr talked with him in French. We stayed that night in a barracks about two kilometres from the cafe and were introduced to a British captain and an American airman. Some Yugoslavs and Ukranians were in other parts of the barracks as well as French civilian workers.

'Carr was to meet Tsoucas every morning at 09.00 hours and see me at 10.00 to report whether there was any action. I spent twelve days in Munich. Each morning I met Carr to find out about our departure. The rest of the day I walked around trying to look like a regular worker about my business. My feet were getting very bad so I rode the streetcars and went to four or five movies. Once I made the mistake of sitting down on a park bench. I knew this was a bad idea, since a man not working was immediately suspected. A man sat down and asked me how it happened that I was not working; was I a medical case? I said, "*Oui*" and left as quickly as I could. Once I went with a Frenchman and a German to a good cafe where we ate ice cream and cake and drank coffee. We talked English in a low voice.

'I spent as much time as I could in cafes frequented by French workers but it was suspicious to spend too long a time in them. I tried to stay not more than an hour and preferably only half an hour. I went many times by myself and other times with Carr or with a Frenchman whom I had come to know quite well. All this period I lived on beer and "Stamm", a conglomerate food which was one of the few unrationed dishes available in restaurants.

'I spent the nights in the barracks of French workers from various *Arbeitskommandos*. I would come in late in the evening and leave before 07.00 in the morning, since the Germans were around in those hours. For the first time I was bitten by lice, bedbugs and fleas. My face got so swollen from bedbugs that I could hardly see. In one *Arbeitskommando*, French girls were living in the same room with the men. These girls had been brought to Germany to work in the factories at high wages. When they were not paid the promised wages they had refused to work and the SS guards forced them to scrub railway cars for twelve hours a day. The girls' spirit was broken and they went back to the factories.

'The French treated me well and did everything they could for me. A Frenchman who had been in the detention barracks with me at Moosburg gave me some money. A German girlfriend of a new French friend of mine gave him some money and he gave me half. The French also sold some chocolate on the black market for thirty marks, which they gave me.

'At the barracks I met Michel, a Frenchman who had been at Stalag VIIA. He had escaped from a *Kommando* and was living at various *Kommandos* or with his German girlfriend who worked at Gestapo headquarters. He wanted to go to France and on to Africa and he talked as if he knew about a plan for getting out of Germany. We met Michel's girlfriend right across the street from the Gestapo offices and went with her to a good café. She knew I was an American airman.

'When I met Carr on 20 October he said he thought we would leave the next day. We were supposed to go by train to Strasbourg and pick up a river boat there. I stressed that we would need food and water for the journey and suggested that it would be best to buy beer. The Frenchman sold some of our supplies to the black market for thirty Deutschmarks and we got some boiled potatoes from them.

'Next day I met Carr. He talked for some time to Tsoucas and Palm. I went to the cafe for a beer and Stamm, somewhat to Carr's annoyance. I saw Carr walking with Tsoucas and Palm and went to join them. As he passed me Carr threw at me the sack with the potatoes and shaving equipment and made some remark about teaching me not to make such stupid blunders with him. I could have dropped in line behind him but I would not follow him for anything. I had more pride than to go with him. Carr had already acted as if he wanted to get rid of me ever since we reached Munich. He said he could not spend four days cooped up in a freight car with me without going crazy so I separated.

'I met Michel and eventually he found the man who arranged the freightcars. He was the same man who had fixed up Carr, Palm and Tsoucas' escape. (The day after their escape the Gestapo raided one of the barracks near where I had been staying, looking for an English Captain and an American Sergeant). The Frenchman was persuaded to help both myself and Michel to escape and we were to go on the night of the 27th. I met Michel and his German girlfriend brought him some food. We got some bottles of beer to take with us. At dark we picked up four more Frenchmen and went to the railway yard. It was lighted and German police were around. Some were yelling. We stayed in the shadows as much as we could. Michel and I climbed into the guard section of a car with sides but no top. When the other Frenchmen climbed into the car they dropped our six bottles of beer. I was furious for I knew what a time we were going to have with nothing to drink. At least we had some bread, French crackers, cans of meat, margarine and string beans.

'After a couple of hours our cars where shunted to another yard. It was cold and the French, knowing there was a four-day ride ahead of them, talked about leaving. Two of them did.

'The next day the cars were taken to the main Munich yards. The night of the 28th we moved out. We went up through Augsburg and Ulm to Stuttgart. Next morning there we were shunted around. We had been warned that there were two guards on the train and we had to be careful not to make any noise when the train stopped in the yards. In the afternoon we moved again and reached Karlsruhe in daylight. As we passed under a bridge a couple of people looking down the tracks saw us. I was very worried, but they didn't give the alarm. Two men could have hidden successfully in the car but with four it was impossible. It was a cold and miserable ride. Two of the men in the car were getting sick and having fits of coughing. I was sure that we were going to be discovered.

'Most of the day of 30 October we spent in the yards at Strasbourg. At last we moved on but we stopped about midnight. I was getting worried because the Frenchmen were making so much noise coughing and because there seemed to be so much activity about the train. I jumped to the ground as carefully as I could to scout around. A German got out of the car ahead of ours. I dropped to the ground. He shone his torch and walked down the train. I saw about fifteen guards in the car from which he came. A train came down the tracks I was on. I moved and walked up the tracks some distance to a signal tower. I was so stiff, cramped and weak from riding the train that I fell down a number of times. At the signal tower I heard a voice say, "*Allo, Allo—Ca va. Heil Hitler*". I knew I was in France and probably in Alsace.

'Since the frontier was very carefully guarded and extremely hard to get through, I went back to the train. I saw about six Mark IV tanks on cars near ours and realized that we were on a military train. When the train started to move I swung back into my car. The Frenchmen were still coughing badly and we were all cold and shivering. I was sure that we would all be caught if we spent another day on the train.

'The morning of 1 November was foggy. The train stopped in some yards near Dombasle and I jumped off it. I had trouble getting out of the yards. I took a dirt road into the country. Two Frenchmen who seemed to be taking milk to the train passed me. I stopped one of them, told him I was an American aviator and asked him where I could find a place to eat and wash. He did not want to help and simply told me to go to St Nicholai where the policemen were all right.

'I walked down the road and picked some carrots in a field. On the outskirts of St Nicholai I told an old man that I was an American aviator and asked for a place to wash and eat. He would have nothing to do with me. I went to a cafe and had a beer. I told the proprietor that I was an American aviator. He seemed scared and I left immediately.

'A boy approached me on a bicycle and I told him who I was. He took me home and got some food for me. I went on to St Nicholai to a place where barges were loaded. I learned that the barges there only went to Nancy or to Strasbourg. By this time my feet were getting so bad that I could scarcely walk. I knew that I had to find help soon. I tried a number of people for help but without success. Finally, at a cafe I found help and my remaining journey was arranged. I was in France for a long time and started to get impatient but my helpers reminded me: "Patience! Courage! Confidence!" No advice is better for an escaper.'

8 Operation 'Bonoparte'

Lee Gordon was taken by a girl Resistance worker from the cafe to Nancy where he had his photograph taken for his ID card. For four days he lived with a French Alsatian family in a coal yard near the Marne-Rhine canal off Charles III Street. They wanted to have a message sent over the BBC when he returned to England: '*Petit Est Ca Va.*' Gordon met the brother of the woman of the house. He was deaf and spoke no English but he was a fisherman and sometimes took escaping and evading Allied airmen to waiting British ships. He told 'Shorty' he had taken two British officers to meet a ship of the Royal Navy and they had got back to England. He said he would take the American if he was not moved out within the next ten days.

However, on 11 November the organization began moving their growing band of evaders along their escape routes to a collection point in Nancy. Gordon was taken to an apartment in the centre of Nancy where he teamed up with Sergeant Mike Olynik of the 96th Bomb Group. Olynik, a waist gunner, had been shot down on the disastrous Schweinfurt raid of 14 October 1943. He had been taken in by the French Resistance in Sampigny and hidden in a room above a cheese factory run by Robert Collin for three weeks. They had to endure visits by the Germans as Olynik recalls, 'German officers came to the factory a couple of times. One of them said, "Upstairs would be a good place to hide someone". Collin asked if they would like to look, but they didn't bother. (On 8 February 1944 Collin was arrested by the Gestapo and spent time in prisons and forced labour in a Messerschmitt factory in Zwickau. He lost 74 pounds in captivity).'

Later, three Frenchmen visited Olynik and produced false identity papers which featured a photograph from his escape kit. Three weeks later he was moved to a house near a railway depot. On one occasion, when the lady of the house was shaking a rug from an upstairs window, a passing German asked if anyone was hiding up there. She asked him if he wanted to look but he moved on. A week later, on 11 November, escorted by a French girl, Olynik left by train for Nancy. En-route the Gestapo checked their papers but his false identity of 'Allen Louis LeFer', passed inspection.

The French group at the apartment in Nantes had a brand new RCA sending and receiving set and they asked for a message to be sent over the BBC; '*Bonjour Aù Clown Gangster.*' Within days Gordon and Olynik were on their way to Paris. They rode through the night and arrived in the French capital in the early morning. While their escort made a telephone call to his contact, the two airmen waited in a coffee shop. There were several German soldiers but there was no trouble. In Paris Olynik and Gordon came under the direction of the Reseau 'Shelburn', a French Underground network which specialized in getting escaping and evading Allied airmen back to England via Brittany.

Two French-Canadians from Ottawa and Montreal, Sergeant Major Lucien Dumais and Sergeant Ray LaBrosse, had been parachuted into France in November 1943 by British Military Intelligence to organize 'Shelburn'; named after a county in Canada. The escape network would try to help hundreds of Allied airmen who had been and continued to be shot down during the massive Allied raids on Germany and the occupied countries. Great numbers of airmen were holed up in Paris and Brittany, thus endangering the lives of hundreds of patriotic Frenchmen who were hiding them.

Both Dumais and LaBrosse had escaped from France earlier and had volunteered to go back to organize 'Shelburn'. Dumais had been captured at the ill-fated raid on Dieppe in August 1942: he escaped from a German PoW train and made his way to Marseilles from where he escaped by way of the famous 'Pat O'Leary' escape line. LaBrosse had parachuted into France in February 1943 to help organize a sea escape route but their group was infiltrated by the Gestapo and he was forced to escape to Spain when his leader, Val Williams, was arrested.

Taking advantage of the contacts that LaBrosse (code name 'Claude') and Williams had made in Brittany early in 1943, 'Claude' and Dumais went to work to build the most successful escape network of World War 2. Not one airman was ever lost once he was in the hands of 'Shelburn', nor was an agent or helper ever captured by the Gestapo. 'Operation Bonoparte' was the code name given to the 'escape by sea' mission of the 'Shelburn' network.

In Paris an organization had been set up to interrogate, make false papers, shelter and pass airmen to Brittany. This was under the direction of Paul Francois Campinchi, a French lawyer. Marcel Cola, a Ford Motor Company executive in Paris, recruited a nucleus of English-speaking agents to work with him in and around Paris and to do the preliminary interrogating.

Lee Gordon and Mike Olynik were escorted to a large building where they stayed with Mlle Germaine Roynec, a very nice French lady. Olynik recalls, 'During this week one man was shot by the Resistance people for being too friendly with the enemy. We next moved to the second-storey apartment of Dr and Mrs J. Gorjux and their daughter Pierette. (Later, Dr Gorjux and his wife were arrested and sent to different camps. His wife was killed but Dr Gorjux located his daughter.)

'Fleas in the building were plentiful. At one time there were six airmen with the Gorjux.' The doctor was a very good man and very busy with his medical work. He often brought meat home for the table. Mrs Gorjux, a remarkable woman, jumped with joy like a child when our bombers were over Paris. The doctor took Lee and I out on tours of Paris, including the Tomb of Bonoparte, where the caretakers were an old couple and their daughter Yvette. (Later in the war the man was killed by the SS and mother and daughter returned ill to Paris).'

Weeks passed into months and Gordon became impatient to get away. 'Early in January 1944 I was moved to an optician's shop and received new identity papers. On 25 January an elderly chief of detectives turned up at the opticians with an opening for one. Since I had been gone the longest I took it.' Gordon finally left Paris on the morning of 1 February and went by train to Quimper in Brittany. 'There I was met by a Frenchman named M. Fanfan who arrived in his fish truck to pick us up. In the back were a Fortress pilot named Davidson, an engineer called Krueger, a Canadian Mustang pilot and an Englishman who had been flying in a secret squadron dropping arms into France.'

Other evadees joined the group and that evening an attempt was made to sail from Quimper and rendezvous with a British torpedo boat. Unfortunately, the French boat sprung a leak and they were forced to return to Quimper. The Germans were waiting for them but Gordon and most of the others managed to evade capture. (Davidson and Krueger's story is described in Chapter 10.)

Gordon teamed up with the Canadian Mustang pilot and they walked to Pont Croix. A French family hid them in their farmhouse until contact was re-established. Gordon was eventually returned to Paris where he was reunited with Mike Olynik. On 23 February both men were sent along the 'Bonoparte' escape route to St Brieuc where they changed trains for Guingamp. On arrival at St Brieuc or Guingamp, the airmen were taken in charge by the Brittany organization under the direction of Francois LeCornac. Guides like Andre Chareton and Fernand Trochel met the trains and escorted airmen to homes in the area including their own. Airmen were usually kept in the area of Plouha for three days.

Timing was important and moving them out was part of Francois Kerambrun's responsibility. Owner of a garage in Guingamp, Francois carried supplies for the Germans by day and carried airmen by night. His truck was the main mode of transportation to the last rendezvous point at La Maison d'Alphonse; a primitive Breton dwelling belonging to a sailor named Jean Giguel and his family. This small stone house was about three quarters of a mile from the cliff and the beach where the airman would meet one of three MTB boats of the Royal Navy.

On the night of 26 February 1944 Gordon, Olynik and fourteen others, were taken in five rowing boats to rendezvous with an MTB. They boarded the boat without incident and arrived safely in England the following morning. Gordon was the first American airman to make a home run to England after an escape from a German PoW camp in World War 2. This incredible feat earned him the Silver Star.

Two men who joined Gordon and Olynik on the trip to England on 26 February were Milton L. Church and Kenneth O. Blye. Both had been part of a 94th Bomb Group crew, led by pilot Glenn B. Johnson, who were shot down over France on 5 January 1944 during a mission to a large German air base north-east of Bordeaux.

Church, Blye and the rest of the crew had no premonition of disaster as they boarded their B-17G but Ralph K. Patton, the co-pilot, had a feeling that it was 'going to be a rough one'. Patton might have had cause for nerves because the crew's usual ship, the *Horrible Hanks*, was out of commission with a cracked air intake. No crew liked flying a substitute aircraft—it was considered unlucky. Their replacement ship was a relatively new aircraft but it had been badly shot up and had only just managed to make it back to England on a previous mission.

Patton recalls, 'We had been briefed, and it wasn't very reassuring, that we could expect heavy flak. There was also an operational training group of young fighter pilots about sixty miles south of Bor-

Right *Ralph K. Patton, co-pilot, 94th Bomb Group* (Patton).

Below *Glen Johnson crew, 94th Bomb Group, 30 September 1943. Back row (L-R): Ralph Hall (engineer); Isadore Viola (gunner); James Stubblefield (ball-turret gunner); John Czwak (gunner); Kenneth Blye (radio operator); James Stone (gunner). Front row (L-R): Milton Church (navigator); Ralph Patton (co-pilot); Jack McGough (bomb aimer); Glen Johnson (pilot)* (Patton).

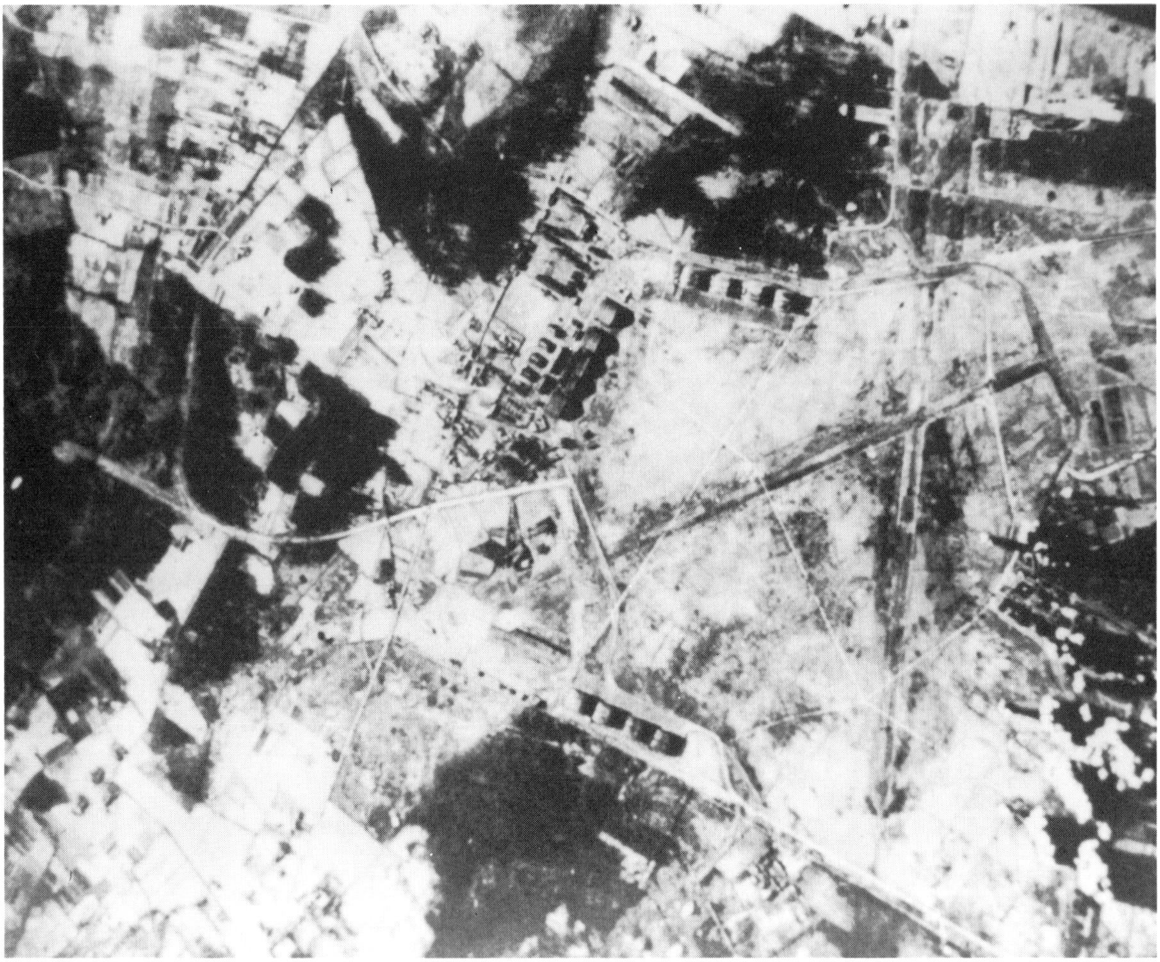

deaux and they had at least sixty fighters. Our fighter escort wouldn't be able to stay with us over the target because of fuel limitations. We could expect the 'schoolboys' to be there in force. About fifteen minutes from the target our fighters, already ten minutes over-extended, had to swing back and we were alone.

'We began our run, heading for pillars of smoke from the 'planes that had preceded us. Glenn Johnson, our 6 ft 4 in pilot, signalled he was taking over. Then I began the co-pilot's toughest job—sitting around with nothing to do but pray that the guns firing at us wouldn't find their mark. Just after we had dumped our bomb load a shock hit the 'plane. Johnson and I struggled to right it. Black anti-aircraft puffs were all around us. As we moved out of range the call came in over the intercom—"Bandits 12 o'clock high!" Then they came in at 3 o'clock and one o'clock. Suddenly, five Fw 190s in single file came in from one o'clock level. Orange puffs of 20-mm shells could be seen on the leading edges of their wings.

'We headed west to get out over the water and limit the distance they could follow. On the second pass we knocked one of them down. On the third pass they fired four cannon shots in the tail before turning and heading back. Looking around we saw several empty spaces in the formations and a few cripples were limping away from the mainstream but we had our own problems. Suddenly, the tail assembly began shuddering and we had to reduce our speed to 150 mph.

'Slowly the formation pulled ahead of us. When we reached the Breton coast the rest of the formation was almost eight to ten miles ahead of us. Suddenly, as anti-aircraft fire began to burst close to us and as we swerved to elude it, our gunners spotted two Fw 190s hiding in the glare of the sun. Our tail-gunner called out, "Here he comes!" As he released his microphone switch I could hear his guns open fire. Those

Left *Bordeaux-Merignac airfield east of Bordeaux feels the weight of bombs unloaded by the 94th Bomb Group on 5 January 1944* (via Patton).

CLASS OF SERVICE
This is a full-rate Telegram or Cablegram unless its deferred character is indicated by a suitable symbol above or preceding the address.

WESTERN UNION

1201

A. N. WILLIAMS, PRESIDENT — NEWCOMB CARLTON, CHAIRMAN OF THE BOARD — J. C. WILLEVER, FIRST VICE-PRESIDENT

SYMBOLS
DL = Day Letter
NL = Night Letter
LC = Deferred Cable
NLT = Cable Night Letter
Ship Radiogram

The filing time shown in the date line on telegrams and day letters is STANDARD TIME at point of origin. Time of receipt is STANDARD TIME at point of destination

WA2 43 GOVT=WMU WASHINGTON DC 18 1158P

MRS VIOLA M PATTON=

1417 MILL ST WILKINSBURG PENN=

1944 JAN 19 AM 12

THE SECRETARY OF WAR DESIRES ME TO EXPRESS HIS DEEP REGRET THAT YOUR SON SECOND LIEUTENANT RALPH K PATTON HAS BEEN REPORTED MISSING IN ACTION SINCE FIVE JANUARY OVER FRANCE IF FURTHER DETAILS OR OTHER INFORMATION ARE RECEIVED YOU WILL BE PROMPTLY NOTIFIED=

ULIO THE ADJUTANT GENERAL.

THE COMPANY WILL APPRECIATE SUGGESTIONS FROM ITS PATRONS CONCERNING ITS SERVICE

LSS/mrb

WAR DEPARTMENT
THE ADJUTANT GENERAL'S OFFICE
WASHINGTON

IN REPLY REFER TO
AG 201 Patton, Ralph K.
(15 Jan 44) PC-N 017062

22 January 1944.

Mrs. Viola M. Patton,
1417 Mill Street,
Wilkinsburg, Pennsylvania.

Dear Mrs. Patton:

This letter is to confirm my recent telegram in which you were regretfully informed that your son, Second Lieutenant Ralph K. Patton, 0-680,283, Air Corps, has been reported missing in action over France since 5 January 1944.

I know that added distress is caused by failure to receive more information or details. Therefore, I wish to assure you that at any time additional information is received it will be transmitted to you without delay, and, if in the meantime no additional information is received, I will again communicate with you at the expiration of three months. Also, it is the policy of the Commanding General of the Army Air Forces upon receipt of the "Missing Air Crew Report" to convey to you any details that might be contained in that report.

The term "missing in action" is used only to indicate that the whereabouts or status of an individual is not immediately known. It is not intended to convey the impression that the case is closed. I wish to emphasize that every effort is exerted continuously to clear up the status of our personnel. Under war conditions this is a difficult task as you must readily realize. Experience has shown that many persons reported missing in action are subsequently reported as being prisoners of war. However, since we are entirely dependent upon governments with which we are at war to forward this information, the War Department is helpless to expedite these reports.

In order to relieve financial worry on the part of the dependents of military personnel being carried in a missing status, Congress enacted legislation which continues the pay, allowances and allotments of such persons until their status is definitely established.

Permit me to extend to you my heartfelt sympathy during this period of uncertainty.

Sincerely yours,

J. A. ULIO
Major General,
The Adjutant General.

Above right and right *A telegram and a letter from the US War Department informing Mrs Viola Patton that her son had been MIA since the 5 January raid over France* (Patton).

were the last words I heard him speak.' The Fortress was raked by 20-mm cannon fire and the tail-gunner was killed. Jim Stewart, the ball-turret gunner, was also killed. Johnson felt the control pressures go limp as the nose shot up violently. By the time Johnson gave the order to bale-out, Patton was on his way to the escape hatch.

'Cannon shells were bursting in the waist, the radio room, the nose and the cockpit. There was a snap and the ship nosed straight up. We jammed the controls forward but there was no response. I was out of my seat and heading for the door when someone shouted, ''Bale-Out!'' I jumped and held off as long as I could before yanking the rip-cord. I watched the folds of silk billow up in front of my face as it opened. Suddenly, it was quiet. I began counting other 'chutes: six of them. The throb of the Fw 190's engine broke in and I saw one of the 'planes coming straight at me. I waited. I had heard stories about Luftwaffe pilots machine-gunning parachutists. But at about fifty yards he veered away. Out of ammunition? A nice guy perhaps? I don't know but he droned off into the distance and never returned.' (Sergeant William A. Munson, the waist-gunner, was killed on the way down.)

'I came in over a hedgerow, hit my heels and came down on the seat of my pants with a solid thud. I tried to collect my wits. My 'chute was draped in a large tree I had missed by a few feet. Forgetting all about concealing it, I left the 'chute hanging in the tree and ran to a group of peasants standing nearby. They seemed to be looking past me, and turning, I saw Jack McGough, the bombardier. We shook hands and faced the peasants together. Some were frightened, some were amazed, and a few were smiling warmly. Then the big figure of Glenn Johnson came lumbering across the field to join us and all three of us struck out along a winding pony trail. We soon stopped to figure out what had happened to the others while about ¾ of a mile behind us, a pillar of black smoke marked the end of the bad luck '212.

'We pushed on through a field of waist-high weeds. In a clearing in the centre we sat down to rest. I tore open our survival kit and found 2,000 French francs, silk maps of France and a compass. We decided to head for Spain. We thought we were somewhere near the village of Kegrist Melleou. At about 13.30 hours we headed out, first north, then east and on our way. About 16.00 hours we saw a man in his sixties and a boy about sixteen. After trying unsuccessfully to hide, we let them approach us. The old man pointed to the column of smoke from our ship still visible in the distance. We nodded and he smiled. He brought us some bread, butter, salt pork and cider. That night we found a farmhouse. A young man there pointed in the direction of the smoke and then held up four fingers, drawing his finger across his throat. We were shocked. We drank some hot concoction, ate some black bread and then followed one of them outside. It was a long walk and we passed a house where there were a number of German soldiers.

'Jack McGough, Glenn Johnson and myself were taken to a big, old farmhouse out in the middle of nowhere. That first night we slept in three beds on the second floor. We were smart enough at that point not to ask anyone their names. We had walked about nine miles over the fields during the day and were tired. We were naturally a little bit nervous but we were able to sleep about six hours. The next morning we got up at sunrise and were given a little breakfast by the couple who lived in the house.

'At about 9.00 am we started walking again. We had been pointed in the direction of where we thought we wanted to go, which was east. We hoped we could get out of the Brittany peninsular and head south toward Spain. We walked in bright sunshine across fields trying to steer a course with our compass. About half an hour or so after we left the farmhouse, a German plane went over and we scrambled to hide but he passed on and we took off again. We walked all through the day, finding a few turnips and potatoes in the fields for lunch.

'At about 15.00 hours we came across a road and met a gendarme on a bicycle. He was shaking his head. We thought he might turn us over to the Germans because he left us on the road and went back toward the town but we took off across the road and headed on our course. I was wearing a British battle jacket, Johnson had coveralls and a leather jacket and McGough looked weird in a blue electric flying suit with coveralls over the top.

'After about half an hour of walking a little Frenchman came up to us and indicated he wanted us to follow him. He told us he was a teacher. He knew a few words of English but not enough to really help. We were taken to a little farmhouse outside the village of Gourec and told we could stay in a haystack there. He brought a can of sardines and some black bread and we ate in the field. When it started to get dark we crawled into a hole in the haystack and tried to sleep. During the night a dog came out and started barking. The farmer followed, looked in and there the three of us were. All we could do was say we were American.

'He just smiled and went back into the farmhouse. Moments later he came out again, this time with a jug of Calvados and a loaf of bread. He brought two other people with him. They looked in at us and seemed quite pleased that three Americans were hiding in their haystack. Then they all went back, taking their dog with them. We dozed, although it was too cold to sleep.

'At dawn the teacher returned and brought us hard

boiled eggs and bread then took us back down a dirt path to the main paved road and we started down it toward the village of Gourec. He indicated he would go through the village and that Germans were guarding the bridges but at that hour of the morning we could get through all right. About a quarter of a mile down the road the Frenchman and Johnson, who were in front, stopped quickly. McGough and I froze, figuring there were Germans ahead. Just then two figures popped up out of the ditch on the right hand side of the road. Before I could grasp what was happening, one of them threw his arms around me and said, "Lieutenant Patton, you're still alive. I thought you were dead." It was our waist-gunner, Isadore Viola and Norman King, a navigator from another 'plane in our group that had been shot down the same day.

'We were now five Americans and one Frenchman. He had had enough trouble figuring out what to do with the three of us. He led us through town and we crossed a bridge over a canal. On the other side we followed the canal until we came to a thicket covered hillside where we were to hide during the day. It was shortly after dawn at this time. Our guide pointed out a German observation tower across the canal then left us, to return at noon with a tureen of hot soup and bread.

'Our teacher returned from classes at around seven o'clock in the evening. He took us further on, through another village in the pitch dark. All the houses had their lights shielded from the outside. About five miles outside the village he told us this was as far as he could go. He gave us a map and told us to go to the Abbey of Langonnet, a monastery, where the brothers would shelter us. We went on alone, ready to dive into the hedgerows at the slightest sound because we were conspicuous in our flying clothes.

'At about two o'clock in the morning, tired, we laid down and tried to sleep but it was too cold. In vain we tried building a fire. We rested for about an hour before carrying on to Millionec, marching through the town just after dawn. At about 11.30 am we came to Plouray. We knew we couldn't just walk through this town so we decided to circle it. A boy of about ten years of age spotted us and we tried unsuccessfully to lose him. This made the boy late for school and when his teacher asked why, he blurted out. "Teacher, I saw five Americans in the road." The teacher turned his class over to another teacher and she came out to find us.

'In the meantime, a Frenchman with a wounded knee (I knew him as Louis Caoueder) approached us. Judging by his expression he thought we were crazy to be on the road in the middle of the day. Caoueder indicated he had been wounded in the knee by the Germans and he had a grudge against them. He took

Ralph Patton photographed by the French in front of the schoolhouse door in Plourey, January 1944 (Patton).

us to a nearby house where we were given a large pot of soup, a roast and two monstrous barrels of wine. We ate and drank and after about an hour we didn't much care if there was a war or not.

'Caoueder took us out in a field, told us to hide and he would bring clothes. We heard voices and over the hill came the school teacher and with her a girlfriend who was also a teacher. We were asked if we knew Frank Green. Jack McGough said, "Yes." Apparently, he had been shot down a year ago and had lived with them until they had got him out safely to Spain. One can imagine our reaction to this piece of news. As darkness fell we marched back to the schoolhouse. It was like a parade and at every corner a Frenchman popped up. They had scouts out to reconnoitre our route back to the school.

'When we arrived at the school half the village

must have been there. It was a French country school with a room on each side and in the middle was Toni's living quarters which she shared with her brother. Toni was 31 and very attractive and her husband was a prisoner of the Germans. Toni's friend was Josephine Valy and she became known as "Joe". Her fiance, Marcel Pasco, lived across the street. Later in the war Marcel was sentenced to death and had dug his own grave before he was liberated by the American Army.

'Toni and Joe, together with another teacher, M. Daniel, whom we called "Mr Chips", were responsible for us. Two of us stayed at the school while the others were sent to other houses nearby. Toni had her hands full getting food for five American airmen. She was helped by local farmers who gave the schoolchildren food to give to their teachers. One day a pupil brought some butter for Toni and walked in on us. We passed ourselves off as cousins of hers from Paris.

'After five weeks everyone knew we were around and we bcame bolder. One night we went to the mayor's house and drank wine and cider and enjoyed crepes. Another night we ventured to the baker's house but the rest of the time we stayed in. During the daytime we played chess, cards and chequers and talked. Luckily, there were no Germans stationed in the village but a party came to the school on one occasion to ask directions. We hid in the attic although there was a special place hollowed out under the floor which had been made for Frank Green.

'Toni, meanwhile, had contacted the Underground and it was decided that our group should split up. We were given civilian clothes and false identity papers forged by M. Letoganek, a 61-year-old Frenchman who had two German officers billeted in his home at the time! Twice he cycled the forty miles to Plauray to bring us clothes and papers. When we were finally kitted out we split into groups. Norman King, the navigator from the other 'plane, and I, went to a bistro on the road to Lorient owned by Jean Violo. It was a little tavern and we were confined to one room all day, only venturing out for one evening during our two weeks there. Jean's wife, father-in-law and two sisters-in-law, also lived there.

'At the end of the fortnight King and I moved to the "Hotel Tournebride". We stayed with an older couple, the Garniers, who had been bombed out of their home in Lorient. The hotel was run by their nephew, Joseph Goulian. He had been a sailor in the French Navy and now, with his wife Alice, wanted to continue the fight. Joseph hid us for two weeks and every night we went for a walk. The Abbey of Langonnet was just across the street and the war seemed far away.

'However, we began to realize we were being guided by an organization ("Shelburn"). We were not being permitted to stay in one place longer than two weeks at a time. We suspected that somebody had taken over and that our friends in Plouray were now out of it. King and I were marched away in the middle of the night by a M. Germain, who had lived in the States, to a farmhouse a long way out in the country. There we stayed with Louis and Batiste Lanour and their 71-year-old mother. We spent four days there, playing football with rolled up newspapers at night because of the safe seclusion of the countryside. It was our first release of tension by physical activity.

'On the fourth day two Frenchmen burst into the house and shouted, "*Allez, vite, vite!*" We knew they meant "go fast" but we didn't know where. They were so excited and in such a hurry that it didn't seem to be the time or place to ask questions so we headed outside to be joined by Isadore and Glenn on the

Left *Members of the Resistance group in Guingcamp taken in 1954 (L-R): Georges Lecun; Francois Kerambrun; Fernand Trochel; Andre Charleton* (via Patton).

Above right *The home of M and Mme Desirè Laurant, Rue de l'Etang due Prieur, Guingcamp. Over thirty evadees were hidden here at various times. Mme Laurant died in 1954 and M Laurant died in 1960* (Patton).

Right *Wartime photo of the* camionette *owned by Francòis Kerambrun which he used to transport American airmen during 'Operation Bonoparte'* (via Patton).

road. One man said, "Hurry, we have a truck, we must go!" McGough was already in the truck. Now there were five Americans again, and three Frenchmen. We were surprised to learn that we had a train to catch. However, when we reached the station, the train had left! Our French guides had been delayed for one and a half hours looking for us at the wrong house.

'The leader of the group was Monsieur Lecren and his sons Desirè and Renè. They took us to their home for the night. Lecren was the town barber and all five of us received a haircut. At 2.30 we went to the station and caught the train for Guingamp with our diminutive French guide. The train stopped at every village, every house and every outhouse. During the stops at stations the Germans on the train got out and stretched their legs on the platforms. They sometimes looked in our compartment but noticed nothing amiss.

'We arrived in Guingamp after dark at about 7.00 pm. We split up and were told to follow different people. McGough and I followed the guide. There were no soldiers around so we walked about five blocks with another woman and her husband. We spent two nights with the Laurants and on the third a truck pulled up and two men entered. They tuned into the BBC. Greetings transmitted in French seemed unimportant to us but they were signals for the French Underground. They waited for a prearranged signal and then said, "Let's go". We left the house and got into the pick up truck, a charcoal burner. We were not sorry to leave the Laurants' house because one block away was the German headquarters. (In March 1944 Guingamp was in the coastal defence belt so it was heavily defended by its garrison). We travelled about twenty miles, picking up men en-route. There were now about a dozen of us and our final destination was another house, "La Maison D'Alphonse".

'It was now the night of 18 March and though we did not know it, this was to be our final rendezvous along our escape route: 24 of us gathered at La Maison D'Alphonse. We looked a motley group. Among us were French, English and Canadians but most of us were American. We were dressed in a wide variety of clothes and various items of military dress. There were a fortunate few with GI shoes but most wore ill-fitting civilian shoes of every description. We had all arrived at this particular part of France, a farmhouse, at this precise hour by virtue of one of the best organized and executed escape operations of the war. But not one of us had a clue as to who these people were or what made them tick. This was especially true of myself and McGough. We weren't sure whether we were going to England, our previous hiding place, or to Heaven or Hell.'

In only three hours, 24 airmen were brought from a radius of fifty kilometres to the Maison d'Alphonse. Unknown to them, the BBC had broadcast a code message at 19.30 and 21.30 hours. "*Bonjour tout le monde a la Maison d'Alphonse*" meant that a rescue ship was ready to leave Dartmouth to anchor two miles off Bonoparte Beach to pick up the airmen on signal.

Patton continues, 'We met the officers of "Shelburn" and the officers of the French Resistance group in the area. The leader of the operation was Captain Harrison (the alias of Sergeant-Major Lucien Dumais of the Canadian Fusiliers Mont Royal). He wanted to discover why two extra escapees had turned up at this secret rendezvous two kilometres from the Channel coast.' (Patton and McGough had originally been scheduled to depart on the mission set up two nights later, but someone had decided to move them out of hiding in Guingamp).

Dumais did not stand on protocol, firing questions at the two men in quick succession:

'When do you wear epaulets?'

'Do you wear anklets?'

'What was your last stopping point when you left the USA?'

'Where were you stationed in England?'

'Wait a minute,' shouted a voice from the rear. 'You don't have to answer those questions—you're an officer in the US Air Force; give only "name, rank, and serial number".'

'Shut up!' shot back the interrogator. 'I'm Captain Harrison of British Military Intelligence. It's my job to get you back to England. Some of you may have a hole in your belly, but you'll get back.'

'His GI issue .45 looked more like the famous French 75 as it pointed to our nervous bellies.'

Patton and McGough, the two uninvited guests at the escape party, managed to satisfy Captain Harrison that they were not spies by stumbling and fumbling through a series of questions that a true spy would have answered promptly and intelligently—and would probably have been shot for!

Just before midnight Captain Harrison issued his last instructions. 'This is the most dangerous part of your escape. Do exactly as you are told. When you leave here, follow the man in front of you very closely, don't deviate one step left or right. When you get to the cliff sit down and dig your heels and hands in tightly. Don't slip or you might take the whole line down with you. And above all, keep your damned mouth shut.'

Led by Pierre Huest, a former pilot with the French Fleet Air Arm, the apprehensive airmen headed out into the dark unknown. Patrols, mines coastal defences and weak hearts were a few of the hazards between La Maison d'Alphonse and Bonoparte Beach. Pierre had the mines located. LeCornec and his men had the patrols spotted and timed and Job Mainguy, a former sea Captain, had the German coastal defences well located. Since the airmen were young and fit, all hearts were strong enough to take the strain.

The escape party, now 35 strong, reached the beach without incident and Captain Harrison, from a spot halfway up the cliff, sent his Morse letter 'B' to the vessel anchored offshore. The signal was flashed every two minutes with a masked torch: below the signaller was a blue light hidden in a cove off of the beach to direct the small boats to the exact spot on the shore.

The minutes seemed like hours as the party on the shore waited for the boats. Impatience disappeared as the sky lit up bright as daylight, followed instantly by the loud roar of a giant coastal battery. The first surprising salvo was followed by a second and a third, then silence again. Ralph Patton recalls, 'We sat there wondering if they had hit our boat. Then at 3.00 am five little plywood rowboats came in on the tide, moonless, black. The leader told us to get in the boats, each of which was rowed by a sailor of the Royal Navy. I jumped in one quickly but there were too many of us and I had to get out. I ran up and down the beach trying to find a boat to get in and although they were all crowded I was finally allowed aboard one. The lead one had a little radio to home in on the mother ship, which was about two miles offshore. The shore batteries by now had quit—the little boats wouldn't come in until they had.'

As Captain Harrison and his band of courageous

Left *Panorama of the rugged Brittany coast: the evadees' point of embarkation is in the extreme left centre of the photo* (via Patton).

Right *MTB* 503 *of the Royal Navy which was used to take Ralph Patton, Lee Gordon and many others to England and freedom* (Patton).

French patriots waved adieu to the men they had risked their lives to help, they turned to climb back up the cliff to begin planning for the next mission two days hence.

In five minutes all the airmen were aboard and were heading out to meet the corvette. The men in the boats could make out the mother ship and Ralph Patton's sailor told him that it was a very fast diesel gunboat. 'We scurried aboard, the boats were hauled up and we went below. When the engines started up it sounded as if my ears were going to break because we had tried so hard to be quiet and now the noise was so loud we felt all the world would hear it. But I felt that we were now free.

'We had been underway about an hour when a British sailor came down below and asked us if we wanted to see some excitement. He said the gunboat had received a cable that six German E-boats were between us and the coast of England! We could make out their searchlights but no-one went up on deck. Somehow we eluded them. The gunboat could outgun the E-boats but they could outrun us.'

The British gunboat docked at Dartmouth around 8 o'clock. Ralph Patton and his compatriots disembarked and were given British uniforms, a meal and their first hot bath they had had in weeks. Later, six of the escapees left by truck for a rest and recuperation station. 'We looked like a bunch of raw recruits so no-one would have been the wiser when we went by train to London to be de-briefed. We were met by British Intelligence and the American section of Intelligence and interrogated for two days before we could cable home to the USA. Some RAF crewmen, including a navigator and engineer, were interested in the terrain of the part of France where we had been. Although we did not know it at the time they required this information for the coming invasion.

'Ralph Hall, our engineer, didn't get out until August (he crossed over the Pyrenees into Spain and home via Gibraltar). I later lectured to other fliers on escape tactics and eventually got home in April 1944.'

Two days after Patton's crew were shot down, another American airman who had need to use the 'Bonoparte' line was Staff Sergeant Robert H. Sweatt of the 389th Bomb Group. Sweatt's crew, led by Captain Wilhite, had returned to combat duty after being released from internment in Portugal in the summer of 1943. All went well until 7 January 1944 when Wilhite's B-24 was attacked by a rocket-firing Fw 190 near Paris. A rocket shell exploded in the cockpit and other hits signalled the end of the bomber.

Bob Sweatt, who was the only survivor, recalls: 'The Fw 190 knocked our right wing off at about 21,000 ft and by the time I got my 'chute on the 'plane was spinning and burning. I was half way out of the waist window when the B-24 exploded and I was blown out. Wendell Dailey, my co-pilot managed to get out but the Germans killed him when he landed on the ground. [The rest of the crew were never found.] I fell about a mile before I could get the 'chute open. My jugular vein was punctured and I had to pinch my neck to stop the flow of blood. Later, when I landed, I filled the hole with mud.'

Sweatt was unconscious when the French found him. Seriously ill from wounds and fever the French hid him in a secret medical facility for several weeks until he recovered. While in hospital Sweatt's watch, which had been attached to his steel helmet when he baled out, had been found, still running, and was

Captain Wilhite's crew, 389th Bomb Group. Back row (L-R): Sam Flatter; James McConnel; Lieutenant Harry; Captain Wilhite; Rudy Salties; Harold Saunders. Front row (L-R): Charles 'Denny' Dewett; Max Snyder; Roger Caplinger; Bob Sweatt. All the men in this photo except Sweatt; (Harry did not fly the 7 January mission) were killed (Russ Hayes).

returned to him! Sweatt was later transferred to Paris, sent along the 'Bonoparte' line and ultimately to England on 23 March 1944.

Altogether, the brave men and women of 'Operation Bonoparte' were responsible for the safe return of 128 airmen (94 of whom were US Air Force personnel) and seven agents to Britain during the Second World War. In addition, 'Reseau Shelburn' sent 98 men to Spain and another 74 in hiding were rescued from the forest of Freteval in August 1944. Altogether, 365 airmen and agents owe their freedom to 'Reseau Shelburn' and 'Bonoparte'.

9 Passport to the Pyrenees

Airmen such as Bob Sweatt and Ralph Patton were thankful that escape routes such as the 'Bonoparte' line existed. Allied airmen who were brought down over occupied Holland were equally grateful for the escape lines which ran into Belgium, through France and ultimately to the Pyrenees for the crossing into neutral Spain.

All this was far from the minds of most bomber crews even though they were briefed on what action to take if they were shot down over enemy territory. However, at Thorpe Abbotts, Suffolk, home of the 100th Bomb Group, escape and evasion lectures were probably more pertinent because the group sustained such heavy losses at intervals in the European Theatre of Operations that it was referred to as the 'Bloody Hundredth'.

It had all started early in the war, or so the story went, when a pilot of a badly shot up B-17 in the 100th Bomb Group knew he could not make it home. He had indicated surrender to incoming German fighters by lowering his wheels. However, as the German fighters closed in to escort the ailing bomber to a Luftwaffe airfield, his gunners had opened up and destroyed some of the German fighters. In revenge the other German fighters shot the B-17 down and from then on the 100th became known as a 'marked' group, to be singled out by the Luftwaffe at every available opportunity.

This story passed into legend and was told to every new crew who joined the 'Bloody Hundredth'. The story was so widespread that crews passing through replacement depots even got to hear about it before being assigned to combat duty. They prayed fervently that they would not be posted to the 'unlucky' 100th Bomb Group. Those that were sent to Thorpe Abbotts were usually greeted with the sardonic retort of 'You'll be sorry' or 'Fresh meat on the table'.

However, there were the lucky ones. In August 1943 Frank McGlinchey, at 23 years of age, was assigned to Bill MacDonald's crew in the 350th Bomb Squadron as bombardier. After surviving their first few missions the crew felt confident enough to name their B-17 *Salvo Sal* as Frank McGlinchey recalls. 'All the crew felt good. After finishing nine missions we felt we had a good chance of finishing our tour and being home for Christmas.'

But it was not to be, as Frank McGlinchey recalls: 'On 8 October 1943 we were called out at 2.30 am. It had never seemed so dark. With briefing in an hour we didn't have too much time to get dressed. Everyone was quite anxious as we sat down in the briefing room waiting for the white curtain to be drawn and reveal the target for the day. One could hear a few groans as we saw the line which marked our course heading straight to Bremen. Take-off was not for several hours but waiting around always seemed to make us very nervous. However, they made it

B-17 Flying Fortresses of the 388th Bomb Group crossing their target obscurred by German smoke pots at Bremen on 8 October 1943 (USAF).

tougher today as take-off was changed twice. We didn't actually leave the ground until 11.30. In the meantime I sneaked down to the Mess hall and had what proved to be my last meal in England. It was roast pork and it wasn't bad either.

'The raid was to be a major effort. Our group had little trouble forming up and it wasn't long before we were out over the Channel. P-47's had given us good support and things seemed rather quiet as we winged our way toward the target. Minutes passed and soon we were over the IP. With bomb bay doors open we turned on the target. The groups in front of us were enveloped in a huge black cloud as they passed over the target and dropped their payloads. It was the most intensive flak I had ever seen. We had a good run on the target and our bombs went away very well. Just after the bomb bay doors closed the ship jumped as we received a very bad hit just to the rear of number two engine. All three ships in the lead element were also hit. The two wingmen went down in flames. The leader, apparently partially out of control, fell out of formation. I looked for our two wingmen but saw no-one. Our whole squadron of nine ships had been knocked out. (I learned much later that only one ship made it back to England.)

'Although out of formation and heading back to England by ourselves, we seemed to be doing all right until a flight of German fighters bounced us. Suddenly, the intercom was alive with actions of fighters bearing in from all directions. All our guns, with the exception of the two nose guns, were knocked out in fifteen minutes. Our waist-gunner, Douglas Agee, was killed by a direct hit from a fighter about two minutes after the fighting started. All our left controls were shattered and we had to put out several fires. Our radio too was gone. One engine was "running away" and two more were about to go. We were losing altitude rapidly and it was apparent we would not make it back to England. Suddenly, fire shot out from the rear of number three engine. With the Zeider Zee directly in front of us, Bill MacDonald gave the order to bale-out.

'But things had got so bad in the ship he wasn't sure that everyone had got the message. So he asked Carl Spicer, the navigator, and myself, to jump from the rear of the ship so that we could check that everyone had got out. We went back along the catwalk along past the bomb bay section and into the radio shack. By now *Salvo Sal* was a rattling old airplane. Fire was coming out of the undercarriage and beneath the wing.

'Everybody except Agee, who lay slumped beneath his machine-gun, had gone, so I motioned to Carl Spicer to jump first. He jumped and I looked out to see if his 'chute had opened. It had. Then I went back to Bill MacDonald and informed him that everyone had gone. The enlisted men had been the first to go. All six were captured by German patrols shortly after landing. John James, the co-pilot, had jumped with a parachute that had been holed by a cannon shell and he broke his leg in a bumpy landing. He was taken prisoner by German soldiers and hospitalized.

'MacDonald said to me, "Now it's your turn and my turn right behind you so let's get out!" I went back to the bomb bay. I took one last look around and stepped onto a couple of brackets, saying goodbye to *Salvo Sal*, I took a long deep breath and jumped. Suddenly, everything went quiet. It was fantastic after such a hectic experience. This was my first jump and I couldn't get over the feeling of falling in space. I guess I fell about a thousand feet before pulling the ripcord. My 'chute opened at about 5,000 ft. Off to the right I could see Bill MacDonald's and Carl Spicer's 'chutes and our B-17 suddenly starting to circle around. It began to glide and eventually crashed on the Dutch countryside some miles away.

'It took me about five minutes to come down. Beneath me I could see a canal, which I was drifting towards. I suddenly realized I must activate something to avoid falling in it. I shifted pulls of the 'chute and managed to drift away from the canal but the ground was coming up pretty fast. As I was about to hit I suddenly realized that telephone wires were immediately beneath me. I fell past them but in doing so my 'chute got hung up in the wires and prevented me from hitting the ground. I stepped out of my 'chute harness and was met by a group of Dutch farmers. They welcomed me to occupied Europe. No-one spoke English but they seemed to understand it was important I should get out of the area. A motorcycle roared into the area and I thought all was lost. But it was a local Dutch policeman. He realized my problem and held back the crowd. In the meantime they had pulled my 'chute down from the wires and had hidden it. The policeman guided me across the field and waved me on. Using sign language he indicated good luck and goodbye.

'It was a very strange feeling to find oneself in a foreign land. We had not been briefed to any extent in England about evading or escaping. Things came naturally and I started to walk. I spotted Spicer, perhaps a mile away, running across the fields. I took after him and had quite a time catching the tall, gangling mid-westerner. He had seen me minutes after I started running and had mistaken me for a German. Eventually, I caught up with him and we hugged each other. Exhausted, we lay in the field deciding in a general way where we were and which way we should travel. (We had actually landed about ten miles due south of Drachten in Friesland near the town of Jubbega-Schwuega.)

'We decided to travel in a southern direction as we were quite sure that we were still east of the Zeider Zee. We had come down about 4 o'clock so we still had a number of hours of daylight left. We stayed off the roads because the traffic was most likely German vehicles carrying troops scouring the area for us. It was not until sunset that we stopped walking. We lay on a small hill in the Dutch countryside looking through our escape kits not really sure where to go.

'Suddenly, out of the farmland area came an old Dutch farmer carrying a brace of buckets on his shoulders. He had obviously been milking his cows. He smiled and offered us a drink of milk. Shortly thereafter out of the trees on a nearby road came a nurse on a bicycle. We assumed she was a nurse because she was all in white. She asked us in English if we were fallen fliers. We told her we were and she said she would try to get us some civilian clothes if we would wait for an hour or so. Several hours passed and she did not return. We grew uneasy. We did not want to lose an opportunity of securing help but to wait any longer might be dangerous so we started walking again. It was pretty damp and chilly. When we had stopped to rest the cold would shake us and make us walk again. We kept near to secondary roads and walked all night, about ten miles.

'As dawn approached Carl and I, pretty much exhausted by this time, realized we must decide on the next move. We were confronted with the problem of where to hide during the day. Finally, we decided to head for a nearby farmhouse and await the outcome when the farmers went out into the fields. It was not long before an elderly farmer ventured into the fields with his dog following closely behind. The dog picked up our scent and took off after us. As the farmer approached we stood up and raised our hands.

'Using sign language we indicated we had been shot down and needed help. He grasped the situation pretty quickly and took us to his farmhouse where his wife gave us breakfast. Using sign language again we indicated we would like to sleep. We were taken upstairs to a bedroom and we just fell onto the bed after taking off our shoes and a few other garments. We slept the entire day. Just as the sun was going down we were awakened by footsteps. There was a knock at the door and in walked a Dutchman who turned out to be a teacher. In English he asked us who we were and how we had got to the farm. He seemed satisfied with our answers and he listened patiently to our hopes of reaching either Switzerland or Spain. He told us he could not be of much help himself but he did know of an organization in Wolvega, Friesland where he could get help.

'We slept and relaxed for two days at the farm and the couple looked after us very well. On the evening of the second day our teacher friend returned, bringing two young men with him. After talking with us for some time in English they were satisfied we were *bona-fide* flyers. They explained that they were going to take us to a hiding place under the control of the underground. We said our goodbyes and cycled along the lane from the farm. I, having been warned and having forgotten, rode along the wrong side of the road and almost ran down some pedestrians!

'Our two young Dutch friends put us straight and we headed for the town of Meppel. We arrived that evening and were taken to a church. It was empty but we went in by the back door and were taken up to the loft and told to wait until someone arrived from the Underground. We were told it would probably take one or two days to make contact and determine what help could be afforded us.

'The rector of the church visited us during the evening hours and brought us some food. He talked to us briefly and said we should make ourselves at home, such as it was, beneath the belfry tower. We could see out into the town but we were very nervous. We could not be certain that somewhere along the line we would fall into the wrong hands and be turned over to the Germans. On the third day the rector appeared with a girl aged about 23. She introduced herself and chatted with us in quite good English and seemed friendly. She took some papers out of an envelope and told us it was very important to her and to the Dutch Underground that from this point on we must be certified as legitimate fallen fliers otherwise we would endanger their whole Underground set-up in the area. It took us quite a while to realize that if we did not co-operate we would not be vindicated.'

McGlinchey and Spicer were to discover later that her name was Tiny Mulder. She recalls: 'Screening new arrivals was a dangerous and complicated task. I gave Frank McGlinchey's and Carl Spicer's addresses and serial numbers to the central organization of the escape line and this information was then sent to London for reference. The central organization then arranged when they could be put on the escape line. All this was very necessary because sometimes German spies infiltrated the escape line by presenting themselves in American uniforms and speaking in a Texas drawl.

'It was sometimes hard to identify an airman. There was not always a crashed plane to account for the presence of one or more flyers as often they had walked for days. The Undergound asked airmen who were already in hiding for questions we could throw at the newcomers that could only be answered by an airman who had come from England, America or Canada recently. The awkward result was that sometimes the airmen suspected that I might be a German spy, which led to unhappy situations for us both. This happened later when Carl Spicer moved further along the Underground with Fred Boulter, a Canadian radio-operator. For a time I did not trust Boulter. One of my friends was behind the door with a pistol while I interrogated him. Fortunately, after a long time I found out he was alright but he remained suspicious until he realized he was not being turned in by Germans but was being given everything he needed to appear a normal Dutch citizen.'

Countless Allied airmen who were brought down in the skies over Friesland owe their lives to people like Tiny Mulder. She and her other brave members in the Underground movements were responsible for the escape lines out of Holland and into Belgium and France. But it was not always possible for downed crews to escape from Holland with the help of resistance workers. Up until late 1942 RAF aircrews were told that if they were shot down over Holland they were not to involve the population but to make the best of their own devices or wait for the Germans to make them prisoners of war. After 1942 this policy changed. Air crews were told to try to return to England with the assistance of the Dutch population and preferably with the help of the Underground. By that time London knew that in Holland escape lines to neutral countries had been organized. It was very dangerous work. Sometimes German agents succeeded in penetrating the escape organization and claimed quite a few victims.

The first escape line from Friesland started at Drachten. It had been organized by three men in charge of all underground work. From the outset they were only too aware of the risks downed airmen entailed. They endangered other resistance work, like sabotage. Therefore, escape work was not only kept secret from the rest of the population but even from other members. Mr R. C. Vermeulen was placed in overall chrage of the escape line. He later went into hiding in Leeuwarden but Drachten remained a major centre in the escape network.

Mr Vermeulen continued organizing the escape line to England through Belgium, France and Spain. But until airmen could begin their journey along the line they had to be hidden in 'safe houses' and provided with false identification papers, clothes and food. This part of the organization required a lot of time and energy. Tiny Mulder had been working for the Dutch Underground since the spring of 1942. She spoke English and had been freed from the task of hiding Jews and other people in danger and placed in charge of helping downed airmen.

Frank McGlinchey takes up the story again. 'Tiny Mulder explained that the Underground had radioed London who had informed them that the two Americans were genuine airmen. She added that the Dutch Underground would do what it could for us. Tiny and a companion ushered us out of the church and into a large van. We were amazed but assured that there would be no problem in transporting us this way. After about three quarters of an hour we arrived in Drockden where we were to hide out at the Mulders' house. The family welcomed us and Tiny introduced Carl and I to a young Jewish girl the Mulders had adopted. The Germans frequently checked out families very methodicially but she was safe with the Mulders. Her parents had disappeared from the area many months before'.

Frank McGlinchey was full of admiration for the risks the Dutch Underground were taking. 'Though a delicate operation this group of Dutch patriots had dedicated themselves to help fallen fliers evade and escape. We talked of several schemes during the next two days. We were told that there was an opportunity, if the proper signal could be made, for the Royal Navy to pick us up. But this could not be done and so we were to remain in hiding for a time. Later, a route would be developed to move us out of Holland by train, car and bus, through Belgium and France through to the Spanish border area'.

Carl Spicer was later taken to the Sieberen van Velden's little farm near Drachten. Tiny Mulder told Frank McGlinchey, to his surprise and happiness, that Bill MacDonald had also evaded capture and was being hidden in the house of M. J. Peper, a sports teacher in Drachten.

Frank McGlinchey waited patiently at the Mulders' house until an escape route could be arranged. During the day he kept out of sight and tried to stay quiet in the rear of the small and unpretentious house. It was located just outside Drachten on a canal road. Tiny's thirteen-year-old brother was also in hiding in the outlying farmlands during the day. Occasionally, he would venture into the house at night but Frank McGlinchey saw little of him because of the danger it presented.

Tiny and Mrs Mulder arranged for some paperback books to be given to Frank McGlinchey and many an hour was passed in thoughtful solitude. Mrs Mulder could not speak English so communication had to be made using sign language. Mr Mulder, a car mechanic and salesman, was usually at work in town. However, on his return home he would often teach McGlinchey the very difficult Freisian dialect. Frank McGlinchey reciprocated by teaching Mr Mulder American slang. He also helped Mrs Mulder with some of the household chores and even turned his hand to churning butter. In the evening he slept in a small alcove off the front parlour. In the dark shadows he watched German soldiers patrol the town. The proximity of these patrols and their frightening implication if the house was searched, served to increase the admiration the American flyer felt for his Dutch hosts.

During the darker evenings Tiny and Alle walked with Frank McGlinchey across the farmland. Equally gratifying were the occasional visits of Bill MacDonald and Carl Spicer. These visits were very dangerous and could only be attempted under the very best conditions. One over-confident move could have brought certain death to the Dutch organizers, the Mulder family and possibly to the American airmen themselves. Outwardly, the Dutch Resistance did not seem to consider the outcome of the risks they were taking. It was even suggested that the airmen stay in the Drachten area and fight with the Dutch Resistance movement. But they understood that the Americans' mission at that time was to try and get back to England.

The Underground activity continued unabated while the American and other Allied aircrews were sheltered by Dutch families. One dark night several young Dutchmen entered the Mulder household by the back entrance. They sat down at the table looking nervous and depressed. Mrs Mulder offered them coffee while Tiny tried to console them. They had been on a very difficult assignment against a Dutch 'Quisling' farmer and his family. It was very evident that the incident had left them drained. No Dutchman or woman liked fighting against their own countryfolk but it was a question of survival. The young men of the Underground movement were fearless and daring and carried out hit-and-run missions against the Germans at all times.

During the second week of November 1943 Tiny Mulder informed Frank McGlinchey that plans for moving the American airmen from Drachten on the first stage of the escape route were nearing completion. The airmen were to move in pairs with guides in the daylight hours. Each pair plus a guide would move several days apart. McGlinchey asked to pair off with his pilot, Bill MacDonald.

It had always been intended that the Americans would dress in suitable civilian clothing to avoid suspicion. Throughout their concealment the Underground had meticulously collected enough clothing for them. However, the clothes were only part of the operation. The Dutch Underground had prepared cards which identified the escapees as Dutch students travelling on the continent. On 19 November Frank McGlinchey and Bill MacDonald boarded a train at Drachten with Tiny Mulder as their guide. She had instructed the two Americans not to talk if questioned. It would not arouse suspicion because Dutch people always refused to talk to the Germans or answer their questions unless it was absolutely necessary.

The train journey lasted several hours. Nearing their station Tiny gave a pre-determined signal to indicate that they must leave the train. The two men followed her down the platform, handed in their tickets and went out into the street. Without any parting formalities Tiny gave the two Americans farewell glances, turned, and headed back into the station for the return train to Drachten. MacDonald and McGlinchey were sad to see her leave but Nel Estes, a young woman who was to be their next guide, was waiting to meet them. She had bicycles waiting further down the street. McGlinchey and MacDonald mounted their machines and followed Nel along the road for seven miles to a large house in the country which turned out to be the home of Nel and her husband Dick. Both were doctors, having graduated from Amsterdam University during the German invasion of their country. They had immediately gone into hiding and were taken in by the Underground. They had married and had two children.

The Estes' home was small and cramped but the two airmen were made to feel very welcome. Dick was away most of the day and evenings, working for the Dutch Underground radio network. Nel, meanwhile, scoured the area for food for themselves, their two children and now two extra mouths. She was also actively engaged in resistance activities during the two weeks the two Americans were in her care. Despite the dangerous risks they were taking the Estes were delighted to shelter two downed airmen of the 8th Air Force. It was unusual how peace-loving Dutchmen and women could suddenly become involved in resistance work and help Allied airmen avoid capture. Sadly, Dick was shot by retreating German forces on the very day their area was liberated by Allied forces.

Early in December McGlinchey and MacDonald were turned over to 'Uncle Joe', a Dutch surgeon, whose real name was Doctor J. P. Kummel. 'Uncle Joe' escorted them to Amersfoort, a stopover en-route to the Dutch-Belgian border to the south. But the news that the Underground movement in the area had been discovered by the Gestapo effectively closed that part of the escape route. 'Uncle Joe' was very distressed but the resistance members were never downheartened for long. It was decided that they would head east to Stavenden instead. 'Uncle Joe' escorted McGlinchey and MacDonald to a pig farm and introduced them to the farm owner, part of 'Uncle Joe's' big, happy family. All through Christmas 1943 and New Year's 1944, the two airmen remained at the farm. Occasionally they were housed in safe homes in the area to help minimize the risk the local people were taking.

'Uncle Joe' was always in evidence behind the scenes and was the perfect host. 'He was quite a daredevil,' recalls McGlinchey, 'and delighted in taking us for rides on bicycles through the countryside. He knew the area very well and even at night he had us out. One evening we had a narrow escape. We were almost killed by a crashing bomber which ploughed in only a few hundred yards from our cycle path. Fortunately, we were able to leave the area quickly and were not discovered. But it was this kind of escapade that really frightened Bill and I.'

Early in January 1944 'Uncle Joe' advised the two airmen that a new Underground route had been established for their escape. Bill MacDonald and Frank McGlinchey travelled by cycle and train to Utrecht. They bade farewell to 'Uncle Joe' and continued through several small villages to what appeared to McGlinchey, 'the smallest village of all,' at Erp. Their new hosts were the Otten family and the two airmen stayed at their lovely home for five days. Although retired both the Ottens were very active in the Underground movement. Special hiding places were built into the walls of the Otten's home for any eventuality such as a search by the Gestapo. Frank McGlinchey recalls, 'This was a wonderful family. They were very gracious towards us and they took us upstairs to a beautiful old fashioned bedroom and put us to bed. Bill got into bed and disappeared into the soft mattress. We laughed at each other!'

The two men waited in their room. It looked out to the rear of the house across a typical lovely Dutch farmland scene. For a few days arrangements were made for the safe transfer to the next stage of their journey. It was still a constant source of amazement to McGlinchey and MacDonald that their Dutch hosts throughout the 'line' and especially the Ottens, continually put their lives in jeopardy by caring for downed airmen. Like all the other people in the escape line, the Ottens became the 'finest people' McGlinchey has known in his lifetime.

Orders came for the two Americans to move on quickly. A car collected them and took them to the station where they boarded a train for Maastricht at the very tip of Holland. They walked from the station and stayed several days with another Dutch family in a big town house. MacDonald and McGlinchey were quartered on the third floor while plans were made for their successful escape across the Dutch border into Belgium. New identity cards were forged. This time they showed that two students were travelling between colleges in Holland and Belgium. No difficulties were anticipated because this was a common practice among students in Holland at that time.

During the night of 21 January a guide collected the two Americans. They walked through the town to the border area and waited nervously in the shadows. A young woman in the distance brought refreshment to the German border guards. After a short time the two airmen were led quietly along a dark path around the control house and through a gate into Belgium. It was difficult to believe that after so many weeks of waiting patiently, it had all been so easy.

Now the Belgian guides took over. They kept McGlinchey and MacDonald quietly hidden in an area near a railway station until early morning when they boarded a train for Brussels. By now both men were highly excited. It was heightened by the sudden arrival of truckloads of German soldiers. They disembarked, boarded the train and searched it, asking for identification as they did so. In a heart stopping moment a German soldier asked for McGlinchey's pass but the fake identity card stood the test. He glanced at it and walked on.

The train quickly became very crowded and continued to Brussels without further incident. It steamed into Brussels station around late morning. McGlinchey and MacDonald were met by another link in the Underground chain and were whisked away to a house in the middle of the city. The excitement they had felt at the border overwhelmed them in the beautiful but occupied capital. The impact was so great that McGlinchey had only a fleeting recollection of his visit. He and MacDonald were quickly taken to an upstairs room where they remained for 24 hours. Fake identity cards were produced and the two men were told they would travel the next night on the International Express to Paris. McGlinchey and MacDonald were unable to contain their delight. Their nervousness and anxiety showed and their Belgian hosts had to continually reassure them that all would be well.

'Their enthusiasm must have been infectious,' recalls McGlinchey, because I was carrying a letter from the Dutch Underground to Queen Wilhemina in London and it no longer seemed to bother me. It had been given to me by some Dutch patriots in the understanding that I was to present it to her Majesty personally. I was also told that if I was captured en-route I was to destroy it.'

When night fell on 23 January McGlinchey and MacDonald left with their guide for the railway station. It seemed unusually dark. Both men carried bits of clothing and a few toilet articles in small bags. The station was crowded and so too was the train. Undeterred, their Belgian guide shoed them to their seats and sat down beside them. There were a number of German soldiers travelling on the train: a fact which seemed to delight their guide.

The train arrived at the Franco-Belgian border and everyone had to leave their seats and queue at the border control checkpoint. It was a very anxious moment for the two escapers. Their bags were inspected, their train tickets checked and their identity cards scrutinized. But all went smoothly and they were quickly through the control onto French soil. A little bewildered, MacDonald and

McGlinchey looked at each other while the train was shunted along the tracks. It had taken the two men only two days to reach France; a marvellous achievement which, without the help of the resistance movements, would have been impossible.

The train soon filled to capacity again. It pulled out of the station and headed for Paris. On the afternoon of 24 January it steamed into one of the capital's stations. Once again the two airmen were met by resistance members, this time French. They took them by metro to another part of the city and to a large housing complex. Once more Frank McGlinchey was too overwhelmed to notice much of the beautiful city he now found himself in. Only four months earlier he and MacDonald had dropped bombs on this very city from their Flying Fortress; now they were hiding in it.

The two evadees were led downstairs to the basement where several other men were clustered in dimly-lit rooms. Altogether, there were about two dozen would-be escapers, who, their guide explained, were being assembled for movement to southern France and the Spanish border. But the movement did not begin at once and time passed slowly. Despite the resistance members' forebodings about unnecessary talking the escapees bided their time comparing stories. An eerie atmosphere pervaded the basement.

It seemed days before events began to gain momentum. French identity cards were issued and food rations were distributed for the journey. Food was scarce and Frank McGlinchey's rations included only sugar and cheese. Train tickets were issued for the first part of the journey through France. The first stop was to be Toulouse, a large industrial city about sixty miles from the Pyrenees.

Twenty-four escapees and four French guides left during the night. Twelve of the escapees were Allied servicemen, mostly fallen fliers. The other twelve were civilians fleeing from the Germans. The party split into groups of four and departed to the metro station. Frank McGlinchey descended the stairs to the platform and was singled out by a French policeman and asked to produce his papers. McGlinchey nervously showed him his card. The policeman read it but did not seem to be entirely satisfied. He glanced at McGlinchey's bag, prodded it and asked to see its contents. The cheese and sugar seemed to interest him and then he turned his attention to the owner. He studied McGlinchey for a moment and then placed his arm on his shoulder. With a wink of his eye he told McGlinchey to go on.

Utterly relieved, McGlinchey carried on down to the train but his companions had gone. Fortunately, he had been told how many stops it would take to reach the train terminal. He counted them off on the short ride and reached the terminal without further incident. But once there doubt began to set in and he realized he was lost. In despair he walked down a street and into a bicycle shop. Using his train ticket and some sign language he asked the woman proprietor the way to the terminal. She shied him away but an elderly man, who sensed his predicament, took him by the arm and escorted the lost American several blocks to the terminal. An incredible sense of relief and elation pulsated through McGlinchey's body.

McGlinchey was spotted by the French guide as he made his way to the terminal. The Frenchman ran over and hugged and patted him as only Frenchmen can. McGlinchey was equally overjoyed to see him. The two men walked through the doors into the heart of the terminal building. It seemed to McGlinchey one of the nicest he had ever seen; at least that is how it appeared to him at that moment. Bill MacDonald greeted his long lost crew member and shook his head in disbelief as McGlinchey poured out his story.

Without further ado the group boarded the train. It seemed that trains were always crowded and this one was no exception. McGlinchey did not want any more setbacks but there were no more incidents on the long journey. On the afternoon of 30 January the train pulled into Toulouse. It was a very tired group of evadees and their guide who boarded the bus for the foothills of the Pyrenees. They drove for several hours before the beautiful mountains loomed before them. All the evadees were excited and noisy. Although weary they were happy to have come so far without being detected. All knew that freedom lay the other side of the mountains in neutral Spain but despite their impatience, the crossing could not be attempted immediately. Instead the group were taken to a large hotel more acquainted with tourists in the summer. It was now closed and had probably not seen tourists since before the war.

The evadees were like excited schoolchildren on a winters' holiday. Their French guide supervised and tended to their needs but showed concern for the older members who arrived to join the group, worried they would not be able to make it across the mountainous slopes.

Several days passed and finally on Saturday 15 February the bus reappeared. It picked up as many of the evadees as it could and the driver headed for a mountain pass. The Pyrenees were silhouetted against a starlit evening sky and it was difficult to imagine that war was raging in Europe. The bus driver drove the party as far up the mountain sides as he could. The escapees and guides alighted and walked single file through the mountain pass. They walked for hours, stopping periodically for short rests. After midnight a sudden storm enveloped the area and it began snowing. It quickly turned into a blizzard and although walking became very treacherous the guides urged everyone to keep going.

Finally, in the early hours of the morning the column came to a halt near some huts close to the Spanish border. The men took shelter and rested in the huts before moving on down the sides of the mountain led by their guides. Suddenly, shots rang out! Dogs chased the evadees to the ground. Some bullets found their mark and men fell dying. It had all happened so quickly there was no escape although McGlinchey had the presence of mind to destroy the letter he was carrying to Queen Wilhemina and dispose of it. Although the guides knew the mountain terrain very well they had overlooked the possibility of German border guards being in the area on Sunday mornings at a different hour to those during the rest of the week. It was their undoing.

In despair the cold and bitterly disappointed survivors were herded onto an army truck and transported to the German outpost at St Groiuns. They were held in the small village for a day before being taken to St Michael prison in Toulouse. McGlinchey and the others were questioned but only name, rank and serial numbers were given freely. The Germans confiscated McGlinchey's dog tags and reminded him he was a political prisoner, captured in civilian clothes. McGlinchey, MacDonald and the other survivors were turned over to the Gestapo and taken to Fresnes prison in Paris. All the captured men were separated and put into cells with civilian prisoners. McGlinchey was questioned repeatedly, threatened but never mistreated.

On 24 March the prisoners were transported to Frankfurt, arriving in the city during a daylight raid. Fires were raging and the city was in chaos. The prisoners were marched through a part of it and only came through unharmed through divine providence. Their captors were furious. McGlinchey was sent to a prison in Mainz and placed in solitary confinement but it was not long before the warden called him forward to answer for the 'many crimes committed by the '*terrorfliegers*' of the American Air Force'.

He threatened McGlinchey with all kinds of punishment but finally sent him back to his cell for ten days' solitary. The civilian prisoners gave him their rations and constantly reassured him that all would be well. They were right. Unexpectedly, the Gestapo collected all the airmen prisoners and took them on a tour of Weisbaden to sing the praises of their pretty town. 'Indeed it was despite the bombing,' thought McGlinchey.

However, the end of the ride was even more unexpected. It culminated at Dulag Luft Interrogation Centre at Oberusel where Luftwaffe interrogators put the prisoners through very intense and frightening periods of questioning. 'It was name, rank and serial number all over again,' says McGlinchey, 'They accused me of everything and threw all kinds of data at me. Surprisingly, some of it was quite accurate.'

In between the interrogations McGlinchey was declared a PoW and subsequently transferred to Stalag Luft I at Barth in Pomerania with Bill MacDonald. They arrived at the camp on 14 April 1944. Two weeks later they located John James, their co-pilot. He had broken his leg when he landed but had received good medical attention. Early in May they learned from an airman in a new intake that Carl Spicer had made it home to England via France and Spain. Spicer and Fred Boulter had left Drachten a little later than MacDonald and McGlinchey. They went through many adventures (a pub where they were staying in Brussels burned down) and arrived in Spain where they spent some days in prison before being set free by a British officer. They arrived home on Christmas Eve 1943.

Just how many airmen were returned to England from Friesland is unknown but their number must be well over two hundred. After the war Tiny Mulder was among those presented with the American Medal of Freedom with silver palm and from Britain, the King's Medal for Courage in the cause of freedom. Her citations state that she helped and assisted almost one hundred downed airmen in World War 2. After D-Day and the Allied breakthrough at Avranches no more downed airmen were sent along the escape lines out of Friesland. Some 100 men had nothing more they could do but sit it out and wait for liberation.

10 Return from Schweinfurt

Bill MacDonad's ship, *Salvo Sal* was one of seven 100th Bomb Group B-17s lost on 8 October and one of 88 American bombers lost on three successive days from 8-10 October 1943. In that same period the 100th Bomb Group alone had lost a staggering twenty Fortresses, including twelve on the 10 October mission to Munster.

Although morale was low and the loss of aircraft and aircrews high, the 8th Air Force had sufficient reserves of men and machines to make good the losses for a large-scale strike on the German aircraft industry four days' later.

On the afternoon of Wednesday 13 October plans were finalized for a large-scale heavy bomber strike on ball-bearing factories at Schweinfurt which the 8th had failed to knock-out completely three months earlier. On 17 August 1943 the 8th Air Force had lost sixty Fortresses in an attempt to destroy the manufacturing plants, with some groups flying a shuttle mission to landing fields in North Africa. It had been a disaster and the lesson was not lost on the young B-17 and B-24 crews. They knew that despite escorting RAF and 8th Air Force fighter forces, 370 miles of the 923 mile round-trip would be without friendly fighter cover.

Brigadier General Anderson, CO of 8th Bomber Command, and his senior staff officers at High Wycombe, were informed that good weather was expected for the 'morrow. It was the signal for Anderson to alert his three bomb divisions throughout Eastern England and the spark that sent ground crews out to their waiting Liberators and Fortresses to prepare them for Mission 115; Schweinfurt. Anderson hoped to send 460 B-17s and B-24s into Germany in three task forces; the Fortress groups of the First and Third Bomb Division flying thirty miles apart while the sixty Liberators of the Second Bomb Division brought up the rear, flying to the south on a parallel course to the B-17s.

During the evening of 13 October and the early hours of 14 October, all the necessary information for the raid was tele-taped to all nineteen bomb groups in the 8th Air Force based in East Anglia. Shortly after 6.30 pm instructions for bomb loading were passed to the bomb groups and ground crews began working feverishly throughout the dark, cold night and early morning, bombing-up and filling the mighty bombers with enough fuel to last the seven hour flight. They cursed and panted under the weight of the 6,000 lb bombs which had to be hoisted into the belly of every available bomber dispersed on the windswept and far flung hardstands of every airfield. Meanwhile, the fight crews slept fitfully. Most of the 8th Air Force had been stood down for three days now and crews knew that a mission was imminent. During the night rain could be heard on the roofs of their Nissen huts and they hoped that the weather would intervene once more. It meant another day to live.

On the bases only a handful of officers knew Schweinfurt was the target. Those in operations found out just after 11.30 pm when the first tele-typed field orders came through from headquarters giving the flight plans and details of the mission. Having got over the initial shock that the scheduled second deep penetration to Schweinfurt was only hours away, the group operations' staff melted away into the night to plan the mission. For the air crews their shock would come at briefing when the curtains were dramatically pulled back to reveal their target.

At Bury St Edmunds (Rougham) flight crews in the 94th Bomb Group were awakened early. Outside, the countryside was shrouded in fog. Second Lieutenant Roy G. Davidson Jr, a pilot in the 333rd Bomb Squadron, recalls, 'I was caging for a three day pass on 14 October but being a 2nd Lieutenant I was outranked by a Captain who wanted to leave the same day. He took his leave and I had to fly the mission.'

Davidson and his crew had flown to England in August 1943, 'eager and excited' to get into combat. 'Being young men we were prepared to believe all the propaganda we had heard. We believed we had superior training and superior aircraft and it never crossed our minds that we would be shot down.' The crew were sent to Bovingdon and given an indoctrination course before being assigned to the 94th Bomb Group. Despite their eagerness to enter combat they had to learn new techniques in flying and also attend ground school classes.

'One class', recalls Davidson, 'taught us what to do if a crew was shot down over enemy territory. We were told that an escaping airman, according to the Geneva Convention, was allowed to wear civilian clothes as long as he retained his dog tags. Our photographs were taken so that we had identification cards ready if we ever got shot down.' Davidson and his crew packed these photographs in their escape kits in the early hours of 14 October, unaware that the quality was so good the French Underground would never be able to use them.

The rude awakening on the morning of 14 October was followed by a short walk to the latrines. Davidson recalls, 'Some ingenious person in the 333rd squadron had rigged up a method of heating water with used aircraft engine oil so we always had hot shower water—something the other squadrons didn't have. Two days before Schweinfurt, Stan Chochester, my co-pilot, came back from the showers excited, saying he had seen a woman taking a shower! Apparently, a Captain who had not allowed anyone in his hut for the past two weeks had a woman in with him. She had been living on 'K' rations and she needed a bath.'

After a wash and shave the crews headed for the mess halls. One of the advantages of being on combat crew status was a breakfast of fresh eggs instead of the 'greenish-yellow' powdered variety. A good breakfast helped as the men talked among themselves or silently stared at each other over cups of hot black GI coffee. For many it would be their last breakfast on English soil. Davidson looked forward to the candy bars that were issued to crews to take on missions. 'Because of bad weather many missions were started or were aborted and all the crew would make sure they ate their candy bars for fear of having to turn them over.'

After breakfast the airmen crossed mud-splattered paths to the briefing room. Davidson recalls, 'We did all our travelling around the base on bicycles. They were handed down from crew to crew after they were shot down.' Crews assembled in the briefing room and Colonel Fred W. Castle, the Group CO, and his senior officers, entered and outlined the mission. The pulling of the curtain covering the wall map shocked the aircrews into silence. Crewmen who had flown only a few missions noticed that even the veteran crews appeared to be a state of shock. Davidson had already flown some rough missions, including the 8 October raid on Bremen, when his B-17 had only just made it back to Rougham before his fuel tank had run dry, and the 10 October mission to Munster.

There were few who did not at least have 'butterflies' in their stomachs despite some officers' platitudes that Schweinfurt was going to be a 'milk run'. The briefing officer talked of routes where the flak was minimum, areas where fighters were not expected and spoke in glowing terms of the friendly fighter cover.

Most crews were not taken in as Davidson remembers: 'When the covers were drawn on the route map, it showed that the fighter escort only went a short way with us to the target. We would have a long way from France onwards without fighter cover and on the way back too. We knew that we were in for a pretty rough time but we had no idea just how rough it was going to be. We had not been on the first Schweinfurt raid and didn't realize how bad Schweinfurt was. Despite this I really looked forward to the mission because I thought the accomplishment would be great. It never crossed the minds of the crew that we would not complete our 25 missions. A telegram was read out telling us that this was one of the most important missions of the war. When we had knocked out the ball bearing plants the war would come to a halt. We felt we were really going to contribute a lot towards winning the war.'

Roy Davidson's engineer, Fred Krueger, declined the B-17 assigned to the crew. (This ship, 42-3453, was flown on the Schweinfurt raid by Lieutenant Silas Nettles' crew in the 96th BG and a windmilling engine contributed to their demise near the IP). Davidson's crew was allocated *Wolf Pack* instead. The 333rd Bomb Squadron was used at Rougham as a fill-in squadron. This meant that crews were usually given the tail-end positions as Davidson confirms. 'I was flying in the low squadron as last man; the most vulnerable spot in the entire formation. But we felt safe because even though we were the last 'plane in a string of over 200 bombers, there were going to be a whole lot of Liberators following right behind us. This would really put us right in the middle of the whole string which seemed to be a pretty good spot to be in.'

Unfortunately for Davidson and the mission as a whole, the unpredictable weather intervened before take-off and hampered the Liberators' assembly and only 24 of the 49 B-24s which had taken off, arrived at the rendezvous point. The remainder managed to find their escorts but after circling around for half an hour, the small force was redirected on a diversionary sweep over the North Sea to draw enemy fighters away from the B-17 spearhead.

The 94th Bomb Group, part of the 4th Combat Wing, also had difficulty in forming. Major Charles Birdsall led the 24 B-17s of the 94th off from Rougham and soon disappeared into cloud at only 2,000 ft. Crews cursed the weather forecasters who had predicted cloud at 6,500 ft. Birdsall managed to get his B-17s into the correct slot in the wing formation and they headed for the coast.

The Third Bomb Division departed the coast of England over the Naze and headed for the Belgian coast. Soon there was an opportunity for the gunners to test fire their .50 calibre machine-guns. In the waist section aboard Davidson's B-17 Claude Page and Arthur Howell fired off a few rounds. Page had asked Davidson to keep the $600 he had won at a crap game. He was afraid to go to bed with all this money. Page had promised himself 'I'll send it home tomorrow'.

Ever since leaving the States, Davidson had promised himself that he would visit a dentist to have two teeth filled. He had got as far as the base dispensary at Rougham but had been put off by screams coming from the room. After this Davidson decided he would have his teeth filled when he returned to the States. Little did he know how much of an effect this decision would have on his life.

The Third Bomb Division crossed the coast of Belgium near Knocke at 12.55 hours and proceeded on a converging course with the First Bomb Division towards Aachen. The escorting P-47 Thunderbolts departed and the Fortresses carried on alone to Schweinfurt. Most of the First Division groups were torn to shreds in the ensuing battle with the Luftwaffe en-route to the target area but the Third Division groups came through relatively unscathed.

The First Division bombed Schweinfurt and then it was the turn of the Third Division groups. The 4th Combat Wing was the second wing to cross Schweinfurt and they headed for the VKF plant. Roy Davidson recalls: 'My position in the group formation as 'tail end charlie' really put us in the centre of the whole shooting match. We went into the target amid very heavy flak and fighter attacks. The fighters continued to attack us right through to the target area. They even flew through their own flak with no let up at all. But we were able to fight them off all the way to the target and out. Carl F. 'Hoot' Gibson, the ball-turret gunner, shot down a Bf 109 and the boys were really excited about this. But pretty soon the fighters came in thick and fast and everyone was getting to do a lot of shooting. By the time the fight was over I think most of the gunners aboard were out of ammunition. Fred Krueger, in the top turret, ran out and never did get to reload.'

It was after the target that the Third Bomb Division met their stiffest opposition. Davidson recalls, 'We had gone into the target, dropped our bombs and had started back out, when the fighters made passes through the middle of the formation. They continued to attack the last group [385th] until they ran out of fuel and were forced to seek land. Maybe the fighters would make one pass at one group and then keep zig-zagging through the formation until they got to the last group where they would continue attacking.

'We outfought the fighters but Richard Mungenast, the tail gunner, shouted that an Me 110 behind us out of range was firing something at us and it was leaving a black stream of smoke. We didn't know what it was at the time but we discovered later that it was a rocket. We had never been told of the existence of such a device. The first shot burst way behind us. The Me 110 pulled up closer and fired another one. It still burst short.

'Mungenast cried out, "Here comes another black stream of smoke!" Right after that the missile exploded right under our plane. It felt as if we were on an elevator; it lifted us up and did all kinds of damage. The plane felt as if it was trying to turn a loop. Chochester and I had to apply full forward pressure with both hands and our knees on the wheels to keep the plane straight and level. Right after the explosion there was an awful lot of excitement on board. All the men in the back of the 'plane were wounded and screams of, "I'm hit, I'm hit!" filled the intercom. I presume the explosion had also knocked off or damaged the flaps. The cable must have been broken because I could not adjust the trim tabs.

'We continued fighting the wheels and then we noticed that two of our engines were gone. One was feathered but the other would not and it began windmilling. About this time a call came in over the intercom that we were on fire and I was asked if I wanted the crew to bale out. I said, "No. Put the fire out." This was the last I heard from the rear for a while. In all the excitement of trying to maintain control and put out the fire we lost touch with our group. We looked around but they were nowhere to be seen. We found another group and pulled up under them to obtain mutual protection, even though we were fifty feet below them. We flew along with them but were unable to maintain their speed with only two engines.

'Mungenast called over the intercom, "All our oxygen has gone in the back of the plane. The rear door is off." Carl Gibson had a bullet right through his knee. Without oxygen, he got out of the ball turret unassisted. He saw that radio operator Louis W. Koth had lost an arm. He assisted Koth and then passed out. Both the waist gunners and Louis Koth baled out. I sent Al Faudie, the navigator, back with a walk around oxygen bottle to administer first aid and see if he could help with the oxygen. However, when he got to the rear of the plane he found that his bottle had a defective valve and the 45-minute supply had leaked out in about thirty seconds. He got the only other walk around bottle and had the same experience again. There was now no oxygen left for the men in the back of the plane.

'With no oxygen for the wounded, I decided to hit the deck and fly just above what I thought was low cloud cover, but turned out to be a layer of thick haze.

There were no fighters around at this time so down we went. Al Faudie wasn't sure of his position and so we headed in the general direction. It wasn't long before we had a Bf 109 off each wing about fifty yards out. We had no ammunition left and anyway, three men had baled out and Mungenast was wounded. The only guns we had left were in the nose. The Bf 109s were so close we could distinguish the pilots' facial features. I figured they were talking to each other to decide who would finish us off. They took it in turns to shoot at us, turning in directly from 3 o'clock. Whenever I saw his wings light up with cannon fire I took evasive action and turned towards him, like I was trying to ram him. Somehow or other, neither fighter succeeded in hitting us. I'll never know how in the world they missed us at such short range. We really gave it violent evasive action during each of their two or three passes and the manoeuvering worked.

'But it wasn't long, apparently after we had crossed into France, that we flew right over, what I learned later, to be the only anti-aircraft school in the whole of France. It was frightening but in a way amusing because we witnessed all these cadets running around to their guns, shooting at a real plane instead of a slow target. We got over them so fast they didn't even come close to hitting us.

'The two Bf 109s were still with us and not long after the flak school our third engine cut out. We knew we had to hit the deck. We were too low to bale out and couldn't if we had wanted to with my wounded tail gunner aboard. I began looking for a place to make a belly landing but everywhere was wooded and hilly. The area turned out to be the champagne district of France. We flew right over the village of La Chappele sur Orbais. Finally, Chochester spotted a clearing over at 11 o'clock and we headed for it with a lot of speed. We chopped our throttles in an attempt to slow down but the area was not large enough to land a B-17. It turned out to be a cow pasture, not much more than three to four American football pitch lengths from one side to the other. We had no choice but to make a wheels-up landing although at the time I didn't know that the machine-guns in the ball turret were still sticking straight down.

'Just as we got right over the last tree I noticed a whole herd of cattle in the pasture right in our path. I had to decide whether to hit them or hit the trees on the other side. Without too much delay I opted for the field. We made a pretty smooth belly landing, finding out later that the machine-guns protruding from the ball turret caused the B-17 to crack in the centre and bent the middle and tail sections upwards. I jockeyed my rudder so that no cow would come up through the cabin. We hit some of the cows with a little thud but it did not slow the plane up. (The French were pleased because they had more beef on the black market the following day than since the war started!) We skidded along the field and we were still going quite fast when we hit the trees on the other side and came to an abrupt halt. Everyone was alright because most of the crew had time to put their seats back and get into their crash positions. I did not have time to push my seat back and suffered a cut on my head and on the knuckles of my right hand.

'We scrambled out and the two Bf 109s made a couple of victory rolls on their passes over us. One of the German pilots delighted in making a couple of strafing runs. Fortunately, none of the crew was hit. We got the wounded out and gave Gibson a shot of morphine since he couldn't walk. I had an awful time finding a place to give him a jab since he had so much heavy clothing on. We dragged him away from the plane to a safe distance and I finally gave him a jab on the top of his hand.

'Before we cleared the plane we were supposed to destroy the Norden bombsight and the Gee set. We had never been told how this worked but to just punch a button. The bombardier was supposed to destroy the bombsight and the pilot had a button in front of him to destroy the Gee set. I pushed it and there was an explosion in the navigator's room that nearly scared Al Faudie to death because he was leaning over it at the time! Then we took a fire bomb and put it over a wing to set the plane on fire.

'This done we scattered in groups of twos and threes and started walking. We did not know where we were at the time. Fred Krueger, Richard Mungenast and I, headed in one direction while Charlie Breuer, the bombardier, and Stan Chochester, headed in another. Al Faudie took off on his own. That was the last we all saw of one another.' (Faudie made contact with the French Underground and lived with them for almost a year and a half until liberation. Louis Koth, Claude Page, Arthur Howell and Carl Gibson were all captured and though they spent some time in German Lazarets (PoW hospitals), all survived the war.)

Chochester and Breuer ran from the scene of the crash and carried on until they were exhausted. They made contact with the French Underground and hid for three weeks at a farm in La Chapelle sur Orbais. The Underground escorted them to Epernay and then to Rheims, where they stayed with a middle-aged couple who were terrified that the Gestapo was going to knock on their door. From Rheims the two evadees travelled by train to the west coast of France where, after a few days, they were put aboard an RAF Lysander and flown to England. Breuer was very worried about his pregnant wife getting word that he had been shot down because she was expecting a baby in two weeks' time but both men were back in England about 35 days from the time they were shot down. They arrived in the USA in December.

Davidson continues, 'We wanted to get us much distance between us and the airplane as we could and then we would hide until dark. But after a distance of only a few city blocks we came to a paved road and people were already coming down it. We hid in some bushes and it wasn't too long before some German soldiers arrived on the scene with dogs. We laid low and Mungenast, who was wounded in the shoulder, had a towel which we applied to stop the bleeding. We didn't want to risk being caught crossing the road so we laid low. While we were waiting the airplane caught fire and we heard the ammunition popping off and exploding. It seemed like a battle was going on. I began to worry if we had pulled Gibson far enough from the plane but it was too late now to go back and find out. There were too many people around.

'After it got dark we started our trek. We had been instructed to stay off all roads so we did, heading west and walking all night through the fields. After two hours or so Mungenast got so weak from his wounds that he could not carry on. We had to leave him by the side of a Frenchman's house so he could get help the following morning. Krueger and I continued walking all night. In the middle of the night a bull took after us in the middle of a field we crossed. We beat him to the next fence by about ten feet and it was more frightening than the air battle we had gone through.

'We saw a French street sign and realized we were not in Germany at least. It got pretty cold that night and around 5 o'clock we stopped to sleep. But it was so cold we couldn't get to sleep. We carried on walking until we came to a large stone farm house built in a rectangle. We looked through an open window of a barn and it turned out to be a storage room where bales of hay were kept. We crawled in and slept.

'At about 6.30 in the morning we heard the cheerful, happy voice of a sixteen-year-old girl who was coming to get the eggs. It so happened that the haystack where we were hiding was where the chickens laid their eggs. The young lady threw her egg basket in, almost hitting us and not knowing we were there. She crawled up the bales of hay to collect the eggs and what should she see but us two raunchy looking men! We must have looked a terrible sight. I had dried blood all down my face and we had been walking all night. It was quite a surprise for her and she let out the worst scream I had ever heard. In no time at all her father came out with a shotgun in his hands. He pointed it at us and we had a hard time making him understand since he spoke no English. Finally, he was convinced we were American pilots.

'The family physician was called out and he had connections with the French Underground. They came and got us and it started an interesting series of adventures with the Resistance for three months. We later had three attempts to escape. The first was when we went to Paris in civilian clothes and were supposed to go Spain. But there was only room for three people and three British boys were selected because the British government at that time was paying $600 per flyer and the American government, only $500. We were outbid and went back to the farm. Our second attempt came when we tried to get to Quimper and catch a fishing boat to meet a British submarine out at sea. There were about 35 of us: flyers, spies and Frenchmen going to join De Gaulle. But that night we received a message over the BBC that it was cancelled. We went back to the farm and shortly thereafter the Gestapo started rounding up the Underground. My helpers managed to get us away before they were taken.

'I was out of touch with the Underground for about a month until another trip was arranged to take the same fishing boat from Quimper. This time we were to rendezvous with a British MTB at 6.30 am.' On 1 February 1944 about 27 evaders were taken down to the beach in single file, piled into three small rowing boats, nine men per boat, and rowed out about half a mile to a 60 ft fishing boat with a petrol engine.

Davidson recalls 'It was about twenty years old . . . It was a pitch black night, cold and the waves were about twenty feet high. The old boat pitched and rolled. Everything was going fine except that everyone was sea sick but we were all so happy with the thought that we would soon be in England. We even composed a cable to send home to the States. But at about 3.30 am our plans changed abruptly when the engines suddenly quit. The crew went below to discover that the tossing about had caused a leak and water had flooded the engine room. The Frenchmen gave up and got down with their beads and started praying.'

The wind blew down the jib and the waves started to tear the planking loose. At about 5.00 am the water was two feet deep in the bilge and the men had to take turns operating the pumps. The Frenchmen were unwilling to work them. Davidson remembers that, 'Krueger, myself and a British pilot bailed water with a bucket for hours but we couldn't stop the boat from flooding.' Nearing the Isle of Sein the Frenchmen saw that they were shipping water faster than they could bail. They fired pistols and signalled to the island with lights. There were some sails and these were put up but unfortunately, the wind was blowing back towards land.

At daylight they were in sight of the coast but by 8.00 am the boat was only about six inches out of the water. M. Fanfan, their French guide, said they would have to crash on the rocks and the evaders would have to take their chances. He said he was sorry this had happened but it was simply fate. Fanfan pulled out a roll of money and gave some to Krueger, telling him to get away and get in contact with him at Quimper. (Fanfan and his brother were later taken away by the Gestapo.) The Captain looked for a place to crash the boat, saw a small cove with conrete steps going up from the beach, and headed towards it. The boat hit some rocks and the boom on the main sail hit a Canadian Intelligence man on the head, stunning him. Men jumped out and extended a mast from the rocks to the beach.

Krueger, Davidson and two others started up the coast on a path. At least three German soldiers were seen on the cliff above the spot where the boat crashed and six of the evaders were caught. Among them were Davidson and Krueger. Davidson recalls, 'Krueger and I were held by the Gestapo in Rennes and Paris. For three months we were constantly interrogated and threatened because we had been captured wearing civilian clothes. Finally, in April 1944, we were recognized as airmen and sent to Stalag Luft III.'

For Davidson and Krueger, the rest of the war would be spent behind barbed wire. In Stalag Luft III Roy Davidson got the feeling the war would never be over. 'I also worried about the two teeth I should have had filled. There were two dentists in the camp. A British and a New Zealand dentist were captured in North Africa. They took care of the dental needs for about 5,000 men. I had my teeth done and was so full of admiration for them I got to thinking that it might be a good profession to follow. I made up my mind that if the war ever did end that was what I would become. If it hadn't have been for that GI screaming back at Bury St Edmunds and the dentists at Luft III, I would never have become one!'

11 The 'Marathon' Line

As we have already seen, not all American airmen brought down in Germany and enemy occupied territory were captured and made PoW. Many managed to evade capture and some managed to complete their escape and make a 'home run' to England via the occupied countries, across the Pyrenees into Spain and home via Gibraltar or plucked from enemy hands by a fast launch from the coasts of occupied France.

During the Second World War these escaping and evading airmen relied heavily upon various resistance groups in Holland, Belgium and France. Patriots put their lives at risk organizing escape routes to neutral Switzerland and Spain and some of the most highly organized were in Belgium. It all began towards the end of 1940 when some ex-officers of the Belgian Army who were not incarcerated in PoW camps, formed groups called, '*Mouvements de resistance*'. The existence of such groups was later admitted by the Belgian government in exile in London. Some, like the '*Front de l'independence*' (FI), was very active but its members were predominantly communist. Their leader was Fernand Demany. Two other large groups, the '*Milices Nationales Belges*' (MNB) and the '*Mouvement Nationaliste Royaliste*' (MNR), also gave the German occupation forces many headaches.

All these groups were known collectively as the '*Armee Belge Secrete*' (ABS). It was perhaps better known as the 'AS' or 'Secret Army'. Its leader was Lieutenant-General Pire and his orders for sabotage and resistance came from London via special radio contacts and coded BBC transmissions.

Apart from carrying out acts of sabotage, the resistance movement in Belgium had a very efficient escape line for downed Allied airmen. By July 1941 stricken RAF crews were parachuting over the low countries in ever increasing numbers. As a result, the 'Comete Line' came into existence. Patriots set up safe houses along a route which led from Holland and Belgium through France to neutral Spain. Crews brought down in the Brussels area who were rescued by the Belgian Resistance were sent on to Paris where they came under the wing of M. Frederic De Jonge. He and M. Walthere Dewe were responsible for the functioning of the 'Comete Line,' originally called the 'Renau D-D' after Dewe and De Jonge. The British Secret Service referred to it as the 'Comet

Stakes' crew, 337th Bomb Squadron, 96th Bomb Group: Back row (L-R): Staff Sergeant Herbert Ruud; Sergeant Elton Aldridge; Sergeant Charles Robinson; Sergeant Humberto Rocha; Sergeant Paul Farmer; Sergeant Wilson. Front row (L-R): Lieutenant Richard Stakes; Lieutenant William Foley; Second Lieutenant Larry Grauerholz; Lieutenant J. M. Edmundson (later replaced by Lieutenant Tennyson) (Grauerholz).

Line' after the asteroid in the heavens.

M. Dewe was a brilliant engineer in civilian life and had been a founder member of the Dewe-Blauche resistance movement during the First World War. In the months preceding 1940 he was in charge of a special information service called, 'Cleveland'. After the Belgian surrender in 1940, General Dewe was removed to Germany and made a prisoner of war. But he was soon released when the Germans discovered that he held high technical qualifications. At the end of 1940 he joined the German controlled Telegraph and Telephone Service.

M. Dewe operated 'Clarence' Resau during this time, trying, unsuccessfully, to make contact with the British. It was not until 29 January 1941, when a British parachutist was dropped into Belgium, that contact was finally established. During this period M. Dewe left his job and devoted all his time to the 'Clarence' operation. On 7 January M. Dewe's wife and two daughters were arrested by the '*Geheius Feldpolizei*' (GFP). Seven days later M. Dewe himself was arrested and killed. His death effectively ended the 'Comete' line but 'Marathon' took over and the flow of evadees through Belgium and France was maintained. Secret camps, set up in the forests of the Ardennes, collected groups of airmen ready for transit across France to the Pyrenees and into Spain, for safe passage to England via Gibraltar.

One American airman who used part of the route in the winter of 1944 was Lieutenant Larry Grauerholz, a navigator in the 337th Bomb Squadron of the 96th Bomb Group stationed at Snetterton Heath, located midway between Cambridge and Norwich. Twenty-one crews were hustled from their beds as 5 January dawned bright and clear. They clambered into their clothes and headed for the Mess halls. The young American airmen looked at the two eggs on their plates and knew it would be no 'milk run'. Briefing confirmed it. The wall map was uncovered and the red ribbon stretched all the way from East Anglia to just west of Bordeaux in southern France: a round trip of almost 1,000 miles and well beyond the range of fighter escort.

Larry Grauerholz boarded his Fortress *Lucky Lady* at dispersal. Lieutenant Richard Stakes, a devil-may-care type of pilot, seemingly afraid of nothing, gunned the Wright Cyclone engines of his B-17 and taxied out behind the emerging line of bombers. After completing take off and assembly the 96th Bomb Group formation joined the bomber stream of the Third Bomb Division and headed out towards the coast of France.

After about two hours into the mission the escorting fighters peeled off with a farewell wing-dip and headed back to England. The flight over France was uneventful and crews began to feel as if they were on a practice mission. But as Bordeaux came into view ugly black puffs of flak enveloped the formation. Crews took evasive action but the German batteries had found their mark. Here and there an engine began to smoke and some B-17's began to lose formation.

Over the target the 96th flew straight and level as bombardiers took over the Automatic Flight Control Equipment to guide their B-17s to the aiming point. Crouched over their bombsights they seemed oblivious to the flak bursts going on around them. A flak burst exploded near *Lucky Lady* and thousands of steel splinters hurtled through the air. One of the starboard engines took a hit and began to lose manifold pressure. Stakes feathered the propeller. As the 337th Squadron turned off the target and out to sea, *Lucky Lady* began to lag behind, unable to maintain full speed on only three engines. German fighters spotted the ailing Fortress and closed in for the kill. They raked the Fortress, destroying the oxygen system and wounding one of the gunners.

Stakes realized the situation was hopeless and lowered his wheels to indicate surrender. By this time *Lucky Lady* was well out over the Atlantic so Stakes decided he would turn back and ditch in the sea or crashland on the shoreline. He brought the bomber in over the coast, threaded it through some trees and finally bellied in on a mudbank near the point where the River Gironde empties into the Atlantic. German fighters buzzed the scene, radioing the position of the crashed bomber as the crew scrambled out of the hatches and waist windows to safety.

The crew tried to set fire to *Lucky Lady* but when it is half submerged in a marsh it is not easy. After several unsuccessful attempts to ignite it, the crew finally dipped their parachutes into the fuel tanks and standing as far away as possible, threw a lighted cigarette lighter into it. Ammunition exploded in the heat and soon a column of smoke and flame rose into the sky. A German seaplane circled the scene and landed within a few minutes of the crash to capture the survivors.

Meanwhile, two of the crew had gone to a farmhouse nearby to get help for Charles Robinson, the wounded gunner who was suffering from a flak wound in his stomach. He was left where the Germans could pick him up and administer medical care. Robinson received medical attention but it was not until after the war that the crew learned that he had died in a prison hospital.

The rest of the crew struggled through the marsh and headed in the general direction of the Spanish border. They soon contacted a family of French farmers who gave them peasant clothes and wooden sabots (shoes) in exchange for their GI uniforms and weapons. Richard Stakes found an abandoned schoolhouse a mile or two away from the site of the crashed B-17 where the crew spent their first night in France. The next morning Stakes told the crew to split up into twos and threes and make for the Spanish border.

Larry Grauerholz paired off with Lieutenant William Foley, the co-pilot. Foley knew a little high school French which came in useful in their days of travel. Their second night was a nightmare of fear and cold. They made their way into Bordeaux but with no place to go and curfew falling, they hid out in alleys, huddling together to keep warm. Once they were certain someone shot at them as they ducked behind some junk. Listening to the bullet ricochet down the alley, they decided to stay put the rest of the night.

The following evening, after several vain attempts to enlist help, (French farmers told them, 'Don't try to find the Underground, they will find you') a farmer they begged food from invited Grauerholz and Foley into his home. They talked for a while and drank a little wine before the farmer sent for a 'friend'. Grauerholz recalls: 'We figured the odds were about 50-50 that the "friend" would be a German patrol but we had little choice if we were ever to make contact. Eventually, we were put in contact with a British agent by the French Underground, spent two weeks with the Maquis and began a complicated shuttle towards the Pyrenees and Spain.

'One of the first Frenchmen we encountered told us, "No problem about getting you back to England. They land a plane near here at night quite often to pick up fliers like you. You'll be back in Piccadilly in a few days.' We were chagrined later to learn the bit about the plane was true. Also true was the fact that a plane and crew were risked only to evacuate Majors or better in rank. Lieutenants like us walked.

'The Maquis raided German supply trains and depots during the night and slept during the day. Intermittently, they shuttled escaping American and British airmen towards the Spanish border. A large pot of stew-soup-or-what-have-you, was kept boiling on the open fire at all times. Each day the Maquis threw in a few potatoes, turnips, meat or whatever they happened to have, or could bring in on a raid. Toward the end of the week with several escaping airmen and one prisoner also to be fed, the pot of soup got low. Scraping the bottom of the pot for a few choice bits of vegetables and meat, one of the Resistance members dipped up a sock; no-one knew how long it had been seasoning the soup!

'By foot, by bicycle, by car, by train, we zig-zagged across southern France to near the Mediterranean Sea. From Bordeaux we were shuttled to Bergerac, Perigueux, to Limoges where we caught the Paris train south to Toulouse, a collection point for escaping Allied airmen. In Toulouse, we were in the command of a little old lady type known as 'Madame Francois'. She made arrangements for us to be taken to Carcassonne, the famous walled city and to Perpignan, the jumping off point for our walk across the mountains of Spain.

'An early disappointment was that false identity papers carried in our escape kits were useless. The forms were obsolete and new papers had to be prepared so we could clear checkpoints. My fake identity card which identified me as 'Laurent Grosdebois', a stone mason living in Montpelier, was prepared in Perigueux by our British agent friend, who had quite an array of forms, rubber stamps, appropriate seals and photographic equipment.

'At one stop our train was soon to depart when a German troop train pulled up on an adjacent track. Soldiers began to unload and sure enough, transferred to our train. They were Wehrmacht troops, bearing weapons, gas masks and all the gear of a soldier. They filled up the compartment we had carefully chosen with an elderly French couple. German enlisted men knew less of the French language than we did and had little to do with peasants. But it was an anxious trip as we huddled in the corner with our newspapers and feigned sleep.

'For the crossing into Spain we were in the care of two guides, men for whom the fortunes of war had created a bonanza. After pre-war careers of small time smuggling between France and Spain, they were now smuggling downed airmen across the mountains for fees that made us feel important.

'After three nights and two days dodging border patrols, getting lost and re-lost by following trails or near trails, we finally heard the welcome words. '*Ici Espana*!' (This is Spain!). We were on neutral soil. The next night, our group that included Americans, British, French and South Africans, was sardined into a Ford station wagon for a midnight ride to the British Consulate at Barcelona. From there it was by limousine (with the "Union Jack" on the side wing) to Madrid, where a trainload of escapees was made up for the trip to Algercias and Gibraltar. At Gib' we were "returned to military control", issued uniforms, surrendered what was left of our French "play money" and flown back to England in a few days by the RAF.'

12 The saga of *Squat N' Droppit*

In the summer of 1944 all eyes were on the inevitable invasion of '*Festung Europa*'. Fortress and Liberator crews of the 8th Air Force based in England flew relentless missions across the Channel and pounded the coastal regions of France and Holland. Losses among the young American air crews rose steadily with the upsurge in missions and new crews were sent to East Anglia as replacements.

One such crew which flew their Liberator from the USA to England via the southern ferry route in the early summer of 1944 was commanded by Second Lieutenant William Bailey. Once in Europe the crew spent two weeks' theatre indoctrination training in Northern Ireland. After that the crew headed for the 8th Air Force reception centre at Stone, England. Then it was back to Northern Ireland for some ground school and escape and evasion lectures.

George Cooksey, the co-pilot, recalls, 'We were told if we were shot down in France we were to approach only one person at a time. We were not to go near a house with electric lights or a house with a car or car tracks. "Be alert for collaborators," our lecturers warned. "I don't think I would jeopardize my chances by drinking anything alcoholic if I was shot down," I told Ben Isgrig, our bombardier—I didn't know the French!'

Bailey's crew were posted to the 448th Bomb Group stationed at Seething, Norfolk. The crew was needed immediately and they flew their first mission together, to Merseberg, on 28 May 1944. By D-Day, 6 June, they had flown a total of five missions without incident. Two more missions followed but it was not until 10 June that they could chalk up their eighth mission, to an aerodrome just east of Everuex, France.

Ben Isgrig recalls: 'There were supposed to be some Me 410s down there and we were dropping 100 lb GP bombs to make the 'field unusable. This was by far our worst mission. We were hit by flak before we got into the target area, several bursts hitting between the fuselage and the right wing tip. The ship directly behind us caught fire in the bomb bay and fell apart just as it dropped its bombs. Seven 'chutes were seen over the target—a hell of a place to have to bale out. Our left wing ship had its right waist window shot out and some men wounded. We dropped our bombs through clouds. The weather had been terrible since the invasion started.'

Two days later, on 12 June, Bailey's crew started on their ninth mission when the Second Bomb Division despatched its Liberators to targets in France again. The 20th Combat Wing, of which the 448th Bomb Group was a part, was assigned a railway bridge about twelve miles south of Rennes. Durwood B. Stanley, the regular ball turret gunner, was withdrawn and the crew reduced to nine members.

The mission began badly for Bailey's crew. It seemed as if their ninth mission might have to wait when, just prior to take off, their B-24 developed electrical trouble. Leslie Fischer, the engineer, got the auxiliary generator running and everything seemed fine until the crew got ready to swing onto the runway. Then the entire electrical system gave out. There was very little time to check the cause so a ground crew was called for to tow the Liberator off the runway. Bailey's crew were given a replacement ship called, *Squat 'N Droppit.* Air crews are normally superstitious and the change in aircraft brought mixed reactions from the nine men. George Cooksey exclaimed, 'What a name for a B-24!' He thought it was a bad omen. The rest of the crew laughed at him. Ben Isgrig was undeterred; he thought the mission would be another 'milk run'.

Squat N' Droppit finally took off from Seething but Bailey had a lot of catching up to do if they were to depart the coast of England in formation. *Squat N' Droppit* carried four 2,000 lb bombs in her belly and when they finally reached altitude it became obvious they would not make it. Bailey had to tag onto the 446th Bomb Group from nearby Bungay as number three aircraft in the low lead element.

At the IP the mission turned to a disaster as Ben Isgrig recalls: 'We started our bomb run but instead of dropping our bombs, the lead ship closed its bomb bay doors and headed towards England. Nearing the French coast we turned and headed towards the target again but once more we did not drop our bombs. By this time other groups in the same area had started home, leaving us on our own. We made a third run with the same results. Bailey said that we were getting low on gas and would have to leave formation and go home. He changed his mind and stayed with the 446th as it started its fourth and final bombing run. As we dropped our bombs we were flying on the right of the formation.'

George Cooksey was also horrified by the actions of the lead ship. 'I'll never know what happened to the lead crew but they really screwed it up. Four times over the target! The turns caused the formation to spread. We were low on the inside and just barely able to remain above stalling speed during the left turns. By the fourth time over the target the Germans had our altitude and must have even had the serial number of our aircraft. The flak was everywhere. How demoralizing those black puffs were—getting closer and closer.'

Ben Isgrig continues, 'We had been briefed to make a sharp left turn after crossing the target but instead of doing this, we waited too long and the lead ship led us directly over Rennes before beginning his turn. As we were flying on the right side of the formation we were in the position to catch the most flak, which we did. It was the most accurate flak I had ever seen, or hoped to see. The Germans had our airspeed and altitude exactly. We didn't have a chance. We cut sharply to the left and began doing individual evasive action. Over the interphone I guided Bailey away from where the flak was thickest as I had a good view of it from the nose turret; a much better view than anyone else on the ship. It seemed no matter which way we turned, the flak still hit us. To me it sounded like someone throwing gravel on a tin roof.

Right Squat 'N Droppit, *448th Bomb Group B-24H pictured at Watton in 1944* (Isgrig).

Left *Ben Isgrig pictured in October 1944 at the time of his marriage* (Isgrig).

Bailey's crew, 448th Bomb Group. Back row (L-R): Bailey; Cooksey; Fleishman; Isgrig; Fischer. Front row (L-R): Stanley; Zeirdt; Kovalchick; Buck; Van Horssen (Isgrig).

There was an occasional shudder as a larger piece would tear into the ship. I don't think I was scared; I don't know. I just wanted to get out of it as soon as possible. I wasn't wearing my flak suit as I hadn't thought I would need it, so I crouched down as far as possible in my turret and got as much protection as possible from my gun mounts and armour plating.

'After what seemed an eternity we were in clear air again and I breathed a sigh of relief. I relaxed and started looking for holes in my turret. Over the interphone I heard Bailey ask if everyone was alright but I don't remember hearing any replies. Our interphone was not working very well and my connection in my turret was not working at all. I had opened the turret doors and was plugged into a connection in the nose.

'After leaving the flak area we were slightly behind the formation but no further behind than we had been on several other occasions. We were gradually catching up when suddenly, I looked out and saw a stream of tracer bullets coming from the direction of the tail and crossing directly in front of me at about one hundred yards. I don't believe the tracers were more than ten yards from me as they passed my turret. For a second I was so stunned I couldn't move, then I yelled, "Enemy Fighters!" I don't know whether anyone heard me. At the same time I turned on my trigger switch and waited for the fighter to pass the nose but he evidently pulled off to the side because I never saw him. I heard the 20-mm shells explode, four of them, and our 'plane shuddered as they ripped into her guts. I don't know how many planes made passes at us, or how many times, but I believe it was three planes and I know that we were out on the first pass.

'A few jumbled words came over the interphone. I couldn't make them out. Then I heard Ken Zierdt, the radio operator, repeat over and over in a steady voice, "Fire in the bomb bay, Fire in the bomb bay!" In a few more seconds someone said, "Get the hell out of here" and I saw Vic Fleishman, the navigator, take off his oxygen mask and put on his 'chute. I pulled my oxygen mask and interphone connection loose as the alarm bell rang and climbed out of the turret. Meanwhile, Vic opened the escape hatch. A thousand thoughts ran through my mind but I wasn't afraid; I didn't have time. By the time I had my parachute on, Vic was baling out and Fischer had crawled up the passageway and was waiting to jump. I don't know what Fischer was doing there; he was supposed to go out through the bomb bay.'

George Cooksey was in turmoil. He thought, 'We're hit!' Those next few seconds trying to assess the damage seemed endless. The oxygen was gone and so was the intercom. 'How were the guys in the waist and tail? Number three engine gone. Right vertical stabilizer gone. Fire in the bomb bay. We were losing altitude. Bailey sounded the bale-out alarm. Where's Fischer? He's not on the flight deck. Zierdt said Fischer had gone through the tunnel to the nose. Why didn't he open the bomb bay door? How about the guys in the nose and rear? Are they still there? Are they out? How long can we maintain control?'

Isgrig and Cooksey both wondered why Fischer had left through the nose. Fischer explains, 'A round had gone through the bomb bay and set the ship on fire and I did not want to open the bomb bay doors and fan the flames. My interphone was inoperative and I couldn't communicate with the rest of the crew. Zierdt was pulling my leg to come down out of the top turret above his radio compartment. I had a little jump seat so I pulled the release and fell out onto the flight deck. Zierdt handed me a fire extinguisher. It looked as if the hydraulic tank was on fire.

'Either the fire extinguisher was inoperative or Zierdt had already used it because it did not work. I stepped back onto the flight deck and I told Zierdt, "Come on let's go!" Vic Fleishman was squatting over the escape hatch when I got there and as soon as he baled out I followed him.

'I didn't follow instructions like I should have. We were supposed to delay opening our parachutes until we could make out objects on the ground but I wanted to try mine out in a hurry. I must have opened my 'chute around 15,000 ft.'

Isgrig watched as the slipstream whipped Fischer past the Liberator, then jumped head first himself into the torrent of rushing air. 'In a fraction of a second I was falling on my back toward the earth, 19,000 ft below me. I began to spiral like a cartwheel. It seemed to me that I had been falling for an hour and I still could not see the ground. I thought of all the times I had been told by instructors that a person had perfect control over his body as he fell and decided they were mistaken. I couldn't stop cartwheeling or turn over and I was getting dizzy. I was scared of hitting the ground before pulling the rip cord so I pulled it at about 15,000 ft and the 'chute opened. I didn't experience any shock. One second I was falling free and the next I was floating.

Meanwhile, Cooksey and Zierdt had opened the bomb bay doors and had baled out. Zierdt had to be helped into a spare parachute because his had been burned in the attack. Cooksey recalls, "We were down to about 4,000 ft. The nose was beginning to head down. Out we went. Clear the plane. Pull the ripcord. Will the 'chute open? Then that tremendous jerk. Such a quiet sensation. I looked up. The canopy had billowed. I noticed that one leg strap was unfastened. The jolt caused me to lose my left flying boot and one of the GI shoes wired to my 'chute. How peaceful; how quiet.

'Did the guys in the nose and rear get out? I looked down. What pleasant looking country. Smoke was rising from the chimneys of a few scattered farm-houses. Occupied France! Only a few hours earlier I had been with friends in a warm and friendly country. Who will get my hat? It was from Oviatts in Beverley Hills. Who will want my A-2 jacket? How about all the Gillette Blue blades I had just received from home?'

Isgrig looked around and saw three fighter planes above him. 'I immediately thought they must be German. The nearest one, a Bf 109, turned and started diving at me. I thought he was going to machine-gun me and I prayed feverishly to God to help me. I pulled the shroud lines to start my body swinging; it was all I could do to help myself.

Kenneth Zierdt, the radio operator, was hit by machine-gun fire from the Bf 109 as he descended by parachute. Zierdt landed in a ploughed field and was alive for some time. Two Germans stood over him and would not allow the French to attend to him. After he died, the Germans cut out his zippers and took his watch and wedding ring.

Isgrig continues, 'The other two planes were Mustangs. One of them circled lazily above me while the other followed the German down. The Bf 109 cut to the left; passing within fifty yards of me, and began to climb. The P-51 was right on his tail and I never wanted anything in my life as much as I wanted him to kill the German who had shot us down. I was hysterical by this time and I screamed and cursed the German, waving and offering all my moral support to the American as he passed. The German didn't have a chance. Within ten seconds his ship began to fall apart and burn. The German baled out and he landed 300 yards from me.'

The P-51 climbed toward Fischer after shooting down the Bf 109, circled him and waggled his wings before roaring away. (Long after the war Isgrig and Fischer discovered that their saviour had been Major George Preddy of the 352nd Fighter Group. Preddy, who was killed on Christmas Day 1944 was the number two American air ace of the Second World War in Europe.)

A young French girl, Margaret Lecotteley, had witnessed the shooting down of the Liberator and the subsequent fighter combat above her home in Romille. During the air battle, which had taken place at a relatively low altitude, the villagers had cursed as the German fired at the helpless American airmen and then had cheered as the P-51 had finished off the German fighter.

Margaret was the first to reach the German pilot, who landed in a yard in Romille. He handed her a knife and asked the young French girl to cut away the boot on his wounded leg. As Margaret stood over him with the knife German soldiers ran to the scene and prepared to shoot her. They thought she was attacking the pilot but fortunately he stopped them from firing. The pilot was not seriously hurt and probably flew again.

As Fischer descended he could make out two German soldiers coming out of Romille toward him on bicycles. 'For a while it seemed I was going to land right on top of them. As it turned out, I flew across the road and came down in a field. I rolled under the cover of a small tree, pulled my 'chute down and discarded my bright yellow Mae West. I had lost a boot so I decided to get rid of the other one. I started running across to a tree line nearby and climbed up one of the trees about 30 ft high. It wasn't difficult to climb and I went up it like a squirrel.

'I sat down on a fork in the branches and hugged the trunk. Everything was quiet until all of a sudden, I heard dogs barking. I thought they must have bloodhounds after me. A little later I could hear talking. I peered through the foliage and saw two German soldiers. They had dismounted their bicycles and had circled around to the tree line. They were each armed with a rifle and were standing right underneath my tree. Amazingly, they walked on by. However, I wasn't taking any chances so I remained in the tree until darkness and spent the night in a haystack. I ate a candy bar but saved an orange for later.

Squat N' Droppit had gone down at about 10.00 hours. Vladimir Kovalchek, one of the waist-gunners, was wounded and captured but before the day was out most of the crew had avoided capture and were safely in the hands of the French Resistance.

Next morning Fischer knew he had to move. 'I walked down the side of a hedgerow to a sunken road. I had a compass and knew that the Allied beachhead was about 75 miles away but I had to have clothing and food before I could even contemplate such a distance. I walked several hundred yards until I saw a farmhouse. I crouched by the fence and saw a young Frenchman driving some cows from the road into a pasture just ahead of me. I stood up and made sure he saw me. He did not indicate he had seen me but walked on back into the farmhouse.

'In a short while an elderly white-haired lady (Madame Felix) walked across the road and asked me questions in French. I could only say, "*Non compri*". She used sign language and determined I was an American airman who had landed by parachute. She brought me some pancakes and told me to stay low until she returned. (I learned after the war that there was another house even closer than Madame Felix's. I had missed it because it was hidden by trees. Had I gone there things would have been different because a girl who lived there slept with Germans.)

'Madame Felix returned in no time at all and three men drove up to the farmhouse in a car. She pointed me out to them and they came over and talked to me. M. Dumay, was a travelling salesman who could speak English. The other two were Diney Morel and Roje Rhode. They questioned me and asked where I came from. All I could offer as proof of identity were my dog tags. They brought some civilian clothes and I tried on some shoes. I changed my clothes on the spot and walked into with Roje. We went a little way and hid my uniform.

'Roje and I took an indirect route to Geveze and I was taken through a small alley to a granary. The door was jerked open and I jumped in among the grain sacks. About an hour later all three men returned. I was told that Diney Morel owned the granary and Roje and his wife Evonne were staying there.

'I assured them I was not hurt and finally convinced them I wanted something to drink. They went through beer, champagne and cognac before I finally got to water. It tasted real good because it was the first drink I'd had for a day and a half. Then we really had a good supper and afterwards I was shown to the hayloft where a cot had been placed.

'Diney Morel was a baker and his wife worked with him. They had two children. Petit Diney or "Little Diney", as they called him, was four and their daughter Leon was nine. M. Morel sometimes brought little Diney to visit me but Leon was not told about me. Roje was about thirty and had served in the French Navy in submarines. He was hiding at the granary to avoid being sent to a slave labour camp. Evonne rode a bicycle to their home town of Rennes every day where she was a hairdresser. Evonne picked up some English books for me in Rennes and covered the fact by saying she had a very smart child who could read English. I don't believe she was afraid of the Devil himself!

'The granary was so situated that I could put my cheek against the window and look down the side of the house. I could see two German sentries on the church steeple which was used as an observation post. When the Morels learned that I had a birthday on 9 June, Evonne baked me a cake and we all had a little birthday party. Back in England we had been told not to eat too much because food was scarce in the occupied countries. However, I was assured by my French hosts that food was plentiful. This was apple country and the French seemed to drink cider more than water. I did the same because I noticed that the water came from a well adjacent to several outhouses!

'My French hosts were very good to me and seemed to have very little outward fear of the Germans whom they absolutely detested. Roje told me of instances when they stuck pins and needles in the Germans' bicycles. If they came across any German vehicles they would short out the batteries. They would do anything to aggravate their German occupiers. M. Morel told me that about the time I arrived the Germans might use his car to get out of the area when they withdrew. He knew he could not prevent the Germans from taking it so he drained all the oil from the sump. When the Germans did confiscate his car they only got as far as the outskirts of Geveze before they burned the rods out of it. M. Morel rode out on his horse and towed it back to the granary and had it repaired!

Leslie Fischer was to stay with the Morels for 57 days. 'My days were pleasant, the food good and the hospitality marvellous. My French hosts had everything at stake and if they had been caught the Germans would have executed the whole family. You do not run across people like them every day.'

Just as Leslie Fischer had landed in a tree after baling out of the doomed *Squat N' Droppit*, so too did Ben Isgrig, the bombardier. Several French people looked up at him slowly descending, practically falling out of control with his back towards the way he was drifting. The airman looked around for a likely place to hide after landing but almost immediately he had to kick his way through the upper branches of a tree that rudely welcomed him to France. Isgrig finally came to rest in a smaller tree as his parachute shrouds became enmeshed in the branches of the larger tree above him. It seemed hours before he finally escaped from his parachute harness and jumped to the ground.

'I used the phrase sheet in my escape kit and with the help of the French spectators who had gathered under "my tree", I discovered the precise location of the Germans. Then I ran in the opposite direction, down a slope and through a shallow pond. (I did this to throw any dogs off my scent). One of my boots had come off during my parachute descent and my unshod foot became quite sore. A barn nearby was burning and I could see some scattered pieces of Liberator wreckage. I assumed that it was our Liberator and that the rest of the crew must have been killed in the crash.' (The wreckage Isgrig saw was a 446th Bomb Group Liberator shot down on the same raid. *Squat N' Droppit* had been cleaved in two by the German fighter attack and had crashed on the Delacroix farm at Brieux and set it on fire.)

'After stopping to look at the burning wreckage I carried on running. I had not run very far when my foot began to hurt very badly. I was tired of running so when I spotted a house nearby I decided to try and rest there a while. A woman came to the door but when I told her I was American, she became very frightened and waved me away. For a short time I walked along the road until I heard men's voices. I stepped back into a field of barley and waited. Two young Frenchmen came into view, talking excitedly. I assumed they were talking about the air battle.

'I stepped out in front of them and said, "American!" They became very excited and one of them led me back into the field, taking great care not to leave a trail of bent barley behind us. He sat me down and motioned me to stay there until he returned. I stayed, not knowing whether the next face would be friend or foe. After a while I heard people approaching. I held my breath and said a prayer. A middle-aged man and a beautiful girl appeared. The girl spoke English and asked if I was American. I said, "Yeah". The man thought I had answered, "Ja" and pulled out a pistol. I figured that this was it but the girl caught his hand and said, "No, No!" (from then on I always said "Yes"). The girl's name was Michelle LeHuede and the man was her father, the local schoolmaster in Romille.

'After some more conversation and their assurances that they would help me, they left. A short time later Michelle and a man I had not seen before, returned, bringing Vic Fleishman with them. Needless to say we were most happy to see each other. The Frenchman, seeing that I had a bare foot, sat down, took off his own shoes and gave them to me. They were a little tight but okay. I didn't know until later that leather shoes were extremely scarce. I tried to pay him with some of my escape money but he would not take it. (None of these people would ever take money). When we left weeks later, Vic and I hid the money in a spot where we knew our French hosts would find it after we had gone.

'My spot was now getting crowded so we moved a short distance to another barley field and under an apple tree. They questioned us about our other crew members as they were trying to find them. They left and Michelle returned with a loaf of black bread and two bottles of red wine. The sun was shining and the day was warm and after a few bites of bread and drinks of wine the war seemed far, far away. Michelle left us again and returned later that afternoon with her father. They had found two more of our crew and asked us to go with them to meet them. Robert Buck, our tail gunner, and Van Horssen, our third engineer, had been found hiding in a garden in Romille. All four of us were taken to a large wood where we spent the next three days. Michelle came to visit us often, sometimes alone, sometimes with various Frenchmen. Once her mother came with her to meet the Americans. Michelle was eighteen and beautiful. We were young warriors that were trying to liberate her country. To us she was a heroine. We all fell in love with her and she with us. (After the war Michelle married Captain Marty of the French Army.)

'We spent the days in the woods eating the food that was brought to us. Each night after dark we moved to a barn loft filled with hay were we slept. We had to be out of the barn by dawn. In June the nights are very short in Brittany and although we got little sleep, we made up for it during the day because we had nothing else to do.

'During this time the LeHuede family were the only people we knew by name. Michelle was the only person we met who could speak English. Vic could speak a little French; the others none at all. We did not want to know names in case we were caught. If you did not know you couldn't tell. During our entire stay in France we never wrote down a name or address or anything that might be a danger to our benefactors if we were caught.

'Events began to move rather rapidly. We were told we were being moved and were walked to a back road where a lorry was waiting. We bid a tearful goodbye to Michelle and climbed in. We were told to get behind some boxes inside if we were stopped, and off we went. We were stopped twice at German road blocks but no-one looked into the back of the lorry. After about an hour we pulled into the courtyard of a rather isolated inn. We entered and met the man who was to take us by boat to England. We went to bed with the expectation of being gone from France the next night but the Germans were moving many troops through the area to the Normandy area so the plans were changed. Our escape photos were taken from us and later in the day we were presented with French identity cards. I was now "Paul Masson", a medical student from Brittany. If I was caught I could supposedly get by without speaking French as I was supposed to know only the Breton language.

'We realized we would not be escaping to England in the near future so we stayed at the inn for two days. We watched German troop movements from our upstairs window but no-one bothered us. The night we left Vic and I went with several Frenchmen and Buck and Van Horssen went with some others. We were re-billeted at the home of Grandmere Guillot. It was a two-storey stone house and Vic and I were taken to a second floor room. In the apartment below Grandmere lived with her orphaned granddaughter, Yvonne. This was more or less our permanent home for the remainder of our stay in France.

'About a quarter of a mile away lived M. Rene Guillot, his wife and three children. M. Guillot, who was about fifty, had fought in the First World War and had been wounded and gassed. He had spent some time in an American hospital and still used the US Army Gillette razor he had been given. He stood about 5 ft 10 in tall with a slender build and had a fierce moustache and usually a home made cigarette between his lips. An old cap was tilted over his right eye at all times. We could not communicate with the Guillots and we did not know where we were. The Guillots were rather isolated. I can now say we were at Plousane, Cotes de Nord. In 1944 I never saw Plousane.'

Apart from the crew of *Squat N' Droppit* other airmen were also hiding in the area. Some of them, like Blaine Barrett, came from the 446th Liberator which was shot down on the same day as the 448th ship. Barrett was the bombardier and had been trapped in his nose turret. The navigator had baled out and left him. It was almost impossible to get out of the nose turret of a B-24 without someone in the nose to open the doors.

By the time Barrett got out the Liberator was heading earthward and the nose was on fire. Barrett found his chest 'chute, snapped it on, and jumped. Badly burned and wounded in the leg he remained in a field administering morphine to kill the pain. After a few hours he was unable to see and it was two days before the French found him. They tried to talk him into giving himself up so he could get proper medical attention but Barrett refused. A French doctor later attended him and when Isgrig and Fleishman met him a week later scars were visible around his eyes but he could see and his hands and wounded leg were usable.

Another American in the area was First Lieutenant James Irwin of the 82nd Airborne Division. He had

(L-R): Isgrig; Blaine Barrett; Mme Petit; Fleishman and Jim Irwin. Barrett was from another B-24 shot down in France and Irwin of the 82nd Airborne Division was wounded and captured on D-Day only to escape later (Isgrig).

been wounded and captured on D-Day but later escaped. An underground courier arrived at the Guillotts and tried to persuade the Americans to join one of the resistance groups in the area. M. Guillott told the courier the Americans would not be going. Later, Isgrig and his fellow airmen learned that the group had been betrayed and all were killed by the Germans.

At that time M. Freville, leader of the Resistance movement in Brittany, had finalized plans for uprisings and sabotage to take place once the Allies broke out of the Normandy beachhead. Complete secrecy was needed if the plans were to succeed but eighteen American airmen had literally 'dropped in' on these plans and placed them in jeopardy. Their presence meant that more Germans would be drafted into the area to search for them. There was no communication between Freville's men and the rural resistance groups so the vicar of Romille acted as a go-between and communications between the two groups were established. The Americans were, by their very presence, responsible for the formation of Freville's mainline resistance group.

To pass the time before liberation, Isgrig and Fleishman helped with the harvest. For security reasons and probably because the Guillotts needed some relief from feeding the two airmen, Isgrig and Fleishman were moved for short periods of time. The amazingly brave truth is that nearly everyone in Romille knew where at least one of the eighteen Americans were hidden and not a single word was told to German searchers of their whereabouts. One man was held by the Gestapo and tortured. Once he was hung by his heels for twelve hours and since that time had been unable to speak and barely able to walk.

M. Rene Guillot and his wife (Isgrig).

It was under the constant shadow of threats like this that the brave French men and women continued to hide the American fugitives. On 9 August 1944 there was no hint that the day would be any different to the other 57 Isgrig and Fleishman had spent since being shot down over occupied France. However, that night they could hear the unmistakable thunder-like rolling sounds of big guns being fired in the distance. Next day rumours abounded in the village and Grandmere told her Americans, 'The Americans are coming and the Germans are leaving the village!'

Isgrig recalls: 'M. Guillot came running in at noon, highly excited about the events of the morning. Yes the Germans were retreating. The mighty Wermacht were throwing away their guns and helmets as they ran. They had the look of haunted beasts in their eyes, looking back over their shoulders every few steps as if fearing the devil himself was behind them.

'There were still Germans in the vicinity as we went out to meet the Americans so we had to be careful. We walked the back paths and through the fields. Vic and I didn't want to chance capture after waiting this long for liberation. All along the way the Guillots picked red poppies, white daisies and blue cornflowers. By the time we reached the main highway everyone had a corsage of "*blu, blanc and rouge*".

French people lined the road on both sides as far as we could see in either direction. Many flags were being waved, mostly French but a few American flags could be seen among the crowd. We didn't have long to wait and soon heard the rumble of tanks and the mounting cheers of the people as the convoy approached. The first big white star we saw on a tank was a sight I shall never forget. The stirring words of the *Marseillaise* could be heard among the shouts of the wildly cheering, laughing, crying crowd. The narrow highway was covered by a mantle of red, white and blue flowers as the begrimed but smiling tankmen passed slowly by, ever alert for any enemy still in the area. The gallant French had waited four long years for this day.

'As soon as possible Vic and I stopped a Jeep and identified ourselves as Americans; explaining that we were Air Force men shot down eight weeks previously. The soldiers were most surprised to see American airmen in enemy territory dressed as French peasants. They gave us cigarettes, which tasted most delightful after smoking strong French tobacco and plied us with questions. We were so happy we could hardly talk. If only the other members of our crew were alive and well, our happiness would have been complete.

'Later, watching the trucks pass by, I noticed familiar faces in the back of one of them. They were the faces of our pilot, Bill Bailey and our co-pilot, George Cooksey! "George, George!" I screamed. He looked up and saw us and in an instant he was off the truck and running towards us. I don't know whether we laughed or cried; we were so deliriously happy. We made our way to the nearest cafe, where with much free wine, we spent several hours exchanging our stories.

'Cooksey had been met by some helpful Frenchmen after landing in a wheat-field and had lived with Maurice and Lilly Chauvier and their family for several weeks. Bailey joined them and together they remained out of sight of the Germans. Their escape and evasion photographs were used by their French helpers to make French identity cards. At Pauley's Island, South Carolina in 1942 Cooksey had met a lovely girl from Columbia, South Carolina, called Justin Derrieux. She had worn her name proudly and Cooksey decided to use it on his ID card. He became 'Georges Derrieux—wine merchant from Dinard.'

The Germans had searched the Chauviers' home so it was decided that Bailey and Cooksey must be moved to the home of Lilly Chauvier's parents. For thirteen days they had nothing to eat but potatoes. While they were there Cooksey and Bailey survived a bombing raid by 36 A-20 medium bombers. Bombs burst close by and several windows and dishes were broken in the house. They were trying to bomb a railway bridge about a quarter of a mile away but the nearest bomb landed 140 ft from the bridge. The French Underground thought it must be important so that night they blew it up.

The two American pilots worked in the fields like Frenchmen but the time moved slowly. Their French helpers discouraged escape through Spain and recommended that they stay in the area. It was to pay off because on 31 July they heard the same guns Isgrig and Fleishman had heard. Next day Bailey and Cooksey hurried to a road about a mile away and met the long American column of tanks and trucks. Cooksey had a few tears in his eyes. He recalls, 'The French were cheering the troops along. There were many tears and laughing and crying. I had waited only weeks; the French had been waiting for five years. Flowers were tossed to the troops and wine appeared. "*Vive La France! Vive L'Amerique!*"

'The column stopped and GI's were tossing candy. I asked for a pack of cigarettes and was pitched a pack of "Chesterfields". The GI looked back startled and said, "You speak English pretty well." I told him I used to live in America. Within a matter of minutes I was taken to a Lieutenant Colonel riding in a Jeep. I identified myself and he asked about Germans in the area. I gave him what information I had picked up from the Underground and he asked us to join him. We looked like two of the French Resistance.

'We had joined the 6th Armoured Division of the Third Army. About noon we stopped to shell an area and then waited as troops picked up a few German stragglers. About two hours later I saw a half-track. A man was in it with a shiny helmet and three stars. There were two ivory pistols. The General was standing and holding a tommy-gun. It was General George Patton. About fifteen minutes later I saw another general calmly riding in the right of a Jeep. It was General Omar Bradley.'

The excitement continued as Bailey and Cooksey passed through several small villages. More flowers were tossed and French girls kissed their liberators. With dusk approaching Cooksey spotted two figures in the distance waving "V" for Victory. They looked familiar. It was Isgrig and Fleishman. Cooksey didn't even know if they had made it!

Instead of joining the American troops and making their way out of France and back to England as they were supposed to do, all four decided to spend one more night with the Guillots. Isgrig recalls: 'We returned to the Guillots by way of a number of French cafes and homes where we were toasted most royally. That night we had a farewell party that none of the participants would ever forget. The only English M. Guillot knew was, "*It's a Long Way to Tipperary*", learned in World War One. We sang it quite often during the course of the evening. Finally, exhaustion overcame happiness and we retired to our last night in French feather beds.

'The next morning we said goodbye to our wonderful friends, the French people who had sheltered us from the Germans and risked their lives many times for us. If we had been caught in the Guillot or Chauvier homes the members of the families would have been killed on the spot. These French people had gone barefoot so that we could have shoes; hungry so that we could eat and had slept without blankets so that we could be warm. They had loved us as if we had been their own sons.

'Yes, it was hard to say goodbye. There were tears in our eyes. We had to leave though. We still had a war to fight and we did not know what the future held for us after we returned to England. My last memory of these courageous people is watching Madame Guillot, tears streaming down her cheeks, disappear in the distance as we rode away in a GI truck.

'Not knowing what to do with us we were sent back to Omaha Beach along with German PoWs. On the

Ben Isgrig (L) and George Cooksey photographed in their French clothes at Little Rock, Arkansas on their return to the USA. The rifles are German (Isgrig).

way we stopped to pick up Van Horssen and Buck, after we convinced them they had to leave the village before the Germans retook it. Along the way we saw some French women collaborators with their heads shaved.'

At Omaha Beach Isgrig, Fleishman, Van Horssen, Cooksey, Bailey and Buck were put on an LST with a boat load of prisoners for Southampton. Meanwhile, Leslie Fischer had said a tearful goodbye to his helpers, the Morels, and had contacted the American Army in Rennes. 'I was returned to the beachhead in a Jeep with a couple of Intelligence officers and was interrogated officially at a PoW cage full of German prisoners. For the first time I learned something of the rest of my crew. According to the GI's at the cage they said some airmen had passed through two days before. They described one as being a 'blond, curly-headed Second Lieutenant'—which had to be Ben Isgrig.'

Isgrig and his fellow crew members had no money and found great difficulty getting to London from Southampton. Eventually, they were given food and rail tickets at a transit camp. They arrived in the 'spit and polish' capital feeling very shabby, dressed as they were in a mixture of GI uniforms and French peasant clothes. Ben Isgrig was wearing a blue beret, black shoes and an olive drab shirt and trousers with no insignia. Equally incongruously, he carried a souvenir German Mauser rifle. ''All my companions looked about the same as I did. Some had rifles and others, pistols. We were wandering around when a Jeep filled with MPs spotted us and arrested us for being out of uniform and having no ID cards. The ''paddy wagon'' was called and we were taken to jail. Some homecoming!

'Finally, we convinced the Captain in charge that we were *bona fide* ex-evadees and he apologized. Released, we eventually found our way to the Army Intelligence Unit at 23 Brook Street. After identification and interrogation we were quartered at the Red Cross hostel in Jermyn Street near Piccadilly Circus.'

Leslie Fischer, meanwhile, had been flown across the Channel to southern England. He telephoned his base at Seething and they flew down to pick him up. Later, he travelled to London and was reunited with the rest of his crew. Ben Isgrig continues, 'Young airmen and their money are soon parted so after two weeks Cooksey and I took a week's tour to Northern Ireland to give lectures on escape and evasion. Our clothes still hadn't arrived when we returned to London. We were told that they were at Seething. After reporting to Colonel Mason, the Commanding Officer, and our squadron CO, we discovered that most of our belongings had disappeared. Salvaging what we could find, we visited the few friends we had left among the many strange faces and returned to London.'

In September 1944 the crew flew home to the USA via the Azores, arriving in Maine because of a hurricane along the mid-Atlantic states. The crew travelled on to New York by train for more interrogation and were home for Christmas 1944. Crew celebrations took place and on New Years' Eve a toast was proposed: '*Vive La France! Vive L'Amerique!*'

13 The long walk

The crew of *Squat N' Droppit* had come to revere their French hosts after being hidden in various French homes following their shooting down on 12 June 1944. Many other American airmen also had to rely on the French civilian population after landing in occupied France. One of them was Staff Sergeant Robert J. Starzynski, who was shot down five days after *Squat N' Droppit*, on 17 June 1944.

In the summer of 1943 Starzynski had been assigned to the 4th Station Complement which was attached to the 306th Bomb Group equipped with B-17 Flying Fortresses at Thurleigh, near Bedford. When the 306th needed replacements to make up losses sustained on bombing raids, it was to the 4th Station Complement that squadron commanders turned. After repeated requests to transfer to a bomb squadron, Starzynski was sent to gunnery school on the Wash and sent to the 367th 'Clay Pigeon' Squadron in January 1944 as a gunner. The 367th were known as the 'Clay Pigeons' because of the heavy losses sustained throughout the war.

Robert Starzynski at Thurleigh.

His first mission, on 6 March, was a 'real rough one': the first American bomber raid on Berlin when Starzynski flew tail-gunner. Although there was a lot of flak en-route and on the homeward flight, Starzynski's crew came through the baptism safely. He flew several more missions filling in as a replacement gunner before being assigned to Lieutenant V. W. Dingman whose tail-gunner had been killed on the crew's first mission. Starzynski recalls, 'The crew had trained together in the States so it was a little rough getting acquainted but I fitted in and on 17 June we were briefed for an early morning mission to France.'

However, the mission was scrubbed just before briefing due to last minute changes. A 'hurry-up' mission was organized with a briefing at 09.00 and take off scheduled for 09.45. Although forty aircraft got off from Thurleigh, seven were forced to return to base after failing to rendezvous with the rest of the formation. Weather conditions deteriorated and cloud covered the primary target. The group was forced to select a visual target of opportunity, a bridge at Noyen, after the PFF equipment failed.

Starzynski continues: 'We encountered several bursts of flak just as we hit the coast of France. Our B-17 took a direct hit in the number three engine, which started to burn. We dropped out of formation and Dingham asked Lieutenant George Clements, the navigator, for their position. He asked which would be the better action to take; fly back across the Channel or head for the Allied lines in France. Clements replied that they were both the same distance. Several minutes passed and the number three engine was getting worse. Flames were leaping over the nacelle and the slipstream was carrying the fire back towards the tail.

'Dingman ordered us to bale out. In the bale-out procedure the tail-gunner is always the first to go so I shouted over the intercom that I was jumping. I reached behind me to pick up my chest 'chute but it wasn't there! It had apparently slipped down the fuselage to the rear landing wheel compartment. I took off my oxygen mask and crawled back to retrieve my parachute. It was fortunate it was there because there were no spares on board. I crawled to the emergency escape hatch and after a little difficulty, finally got it open. The door blew away and I put my feet out into the slipstream. Hooking on my parachute I got ready to jump. Luckily, I noticed that one of the hooks was not properly attached. I quickly remedied the situation and put my hands up to grab the top of the escape hatch. As I did so one of the gunners standing in the waist was also getting ready to jump.' [All of the crew survived but seven went to PoW camp.]

'The next thing I was floating down. I had baled out at about 22,000 ft and by the time I had got my oxygen mask off and my 'chute on, I had almost passed out. Apparently, the jerk of the parachute opening made me regain consciousness. I floated down and looked around for the aircraft and any other parachutes. The area was very cloudy and I couldn't make out either. After the roar of the B-17 the stillness was something I will never forget. Only the endless swishing of my white silk parachute disturbed the still, calm air as I continued my steady descent toward the ground with the words, "Pilot to crew, bale out, bale out!" still ringing in my ears and the vision of the fire melting the wing still before me. It seemed like a nightmare. I thought of Petersen's crew and how, on an earlier mission, only two of them got out before the ship exploded.

'It was as if I was suspended; nothing seemed to move. After what seemed to be minutes or so but which were probably seconds, a P-51 Mustang appeared and circled several times. I waved to the pilot and he dipped his wings in recognition. He continued on his way, I should think reporting my position as he did so. I kept looking around but I could see no-one. As I came through the cloud layers I could at last make out a large farmhouse. What had earlier appeared as flecks of greenery in the distance now emerged as clusters of symetrically formed trees and hedgerows. I was coming down pretty fast now; probably because my 'chute was the smaller, emergency type.

Top right *B-17F* Fightin' Bitin *and the artist, M. Kermit, of the 369th Bomb Squadron* (Richards).

Above right *B-17F 42-30727 of the 306th Bomb Group, 367th Bomb Squadron taking off from Thurleigh, Beds* (Richards).

Right *Staff Sergeant Robert Starzynski, 367th Bomb Squadron, 306th Bomb Group, Thurleigh, England in January 1944* (Starzynski).

'It was only a matter of seconds now. I desperately attempted to manoeuvre my 'chute but it was too late. I hurtled towards the ground at an alarming speed. Snap! Crack! Through the branches I crashed, picking up my feet to miss some hedges. By the time I could straighten out again, I was flat on my back on the ground. Fortunately, the ground was soft. I gathered up my 'chute and made for the hedges. I hid my Mae West and parachute under some leaves and rocks so they would not blow away. It was now around 11.15 am and I decided to stay in the area. I knew that my escape kit contained French francs, maps, a compass, benzerdrine tablets and chocolate. I took stock of these and went through my personal effects, tearing out all addresses; not that any were important. Under the concealment of overhanging foliage, I studied the cloth cap from my escape kit. It was still quiet so I decided to stay a little longer, at least until dark.

'For nine hours I remained hidden not knowing if the German Army had spotted my descent and were, at this moment, searching for me. Now, at about 11.30 pm, I decided it was dark enough to start walking. Checking my compass, I decided to walk south. All I had were my flying boots. I had slung my civilian shoes over my shoulder when I had left the plane but they had been whisked away. I began to feel very conspicuous because I was still wearing my flying jacket and suit and my heated flight shoes. I took my clumsy flying boots off and carefully looking about, I crept across a road and cautiously made my way to a farmhouse with carefully tended grounds. I knocked twice on the door. It was quite late and I assumed, that the occupants must be asleep. Eventually though someone answered. "*Aviateur Americane*', I called.

'Two men looked me up and down and I showed them my dog tags. They let me in and began talking rapidly in French, of which I understood nothing. After checking to see if anyone else was outside, one of the men drew the curtains while the other lit a candle. I pointed to my French phrase card and asked if the enemy was nearby. One of the men, using my map, pointed to the town of Buschy, north-east of Rouen and said that the Germans were everywhere in the vicinity. Again, I pointed to the card and asked if I might have civilian clothes and something to eat. They responded with cider, ham and hard brown bread. The clothes they brought looked as if they had been worn in the last war but I was in no position to refuse them. They also gave me a pair of shoes which were exceptionally tight but I put them on. I offered them all the money I had for the shoes but the offer was refused. I guess they were worth more money than I could offer.

'There were too many Germans nearby for the French family to risk hiding me or contacting the Resistance. Pointing again to my map, he indicated that Le Havre, seventy kilometres to the west, was a safe place to hide. I might be able to make contact with the Underground and slip across the Channel in a boat. I said goodbye to my benefactors wearing an old sweater, cotton jacket, a striped pair of trousers and a pair of shoes two sizes too small.

'It was Sunday 18 June when I left the farmhouse and strode out into the night. I headed for Buschy, pausing several times after hearing voices. Several German units were camped in the woods by the sides of the road so I did not stop. It was shortly after midnight when I arrived in Buschy. I heard the heavy clump-thump-thump of boots approaching and ducked into a doorway losing myself in the shadows. Only a moment later two Germans came around the corner and walked right by me. I could have reached out and touched them, they were that close. It was then that I decided to discount earlier Intelligence information provided at pre-mission briefings and walk during the daylight hours rather than at night.

'Scouting for a place to hide until dawn, I looked around and noticed a large house, a courtyard and smaller sheds nearby. Upon closer investigation, the shed, containing a hayloft, seemed the safest hideaway. The loft however, proved inaccessible and I returned to the courtyard. I ducked inside and sat behind a large stone wall. Before I could decide what to do next, I heard heavy footsteps grinding into the gravel path. Were the German soldiers returning? Had I been discovered?

'The door to the nearest shed was partially open. I plunged inside and crouched low in the shadows of a makeshift garage near a camouflaged German staff car. This should have tipped me off where I was but I looked around and discovered a very large barrel of cider. I helped myself. Then I heard the soldiers again so I just sat on the floor, not even daring to look up. The footsteps slowed and then stopped just outside the door. My heart beat faster and faster with each laboured breath sounding like thunder in my ears. Suddenly, two voices—the soldiers had returned. My only hope was to fade into the shadows keeping deathly quiet until dawn. An uneasy silence prevailed throughout the long night.

'Sunlight filtering through narrow slits in the wall announced the break of a new day. Had the Germans left? Recalling a bombed-out house across the courtyard, I decided to make a run for it. I had to take the risk.

'The house was a scene of destruction. Stairs leading to the second floor were a mass of crumpled brick and wood. Using the rubble as a ladder, I hoisted myself to the second floor. The two rooms upstairs had nothing in them. All that remained was an empty shell. Being uninhabited for some time, the house offered little chance of discovery. Some of the bricks in the wall had been knocked out allowing me a commanding view of the courtyard.

'Lying on the floor, I heard voices of German soldiers once again. Cautiously, I crept nearer the opening. In the courtyard below I could see one soldier showing his rifle to another. I was more fascinated than alarmed. I drew back slowly from the opening fearing they would sense someone watching them. Later I was to discover that the sanctuary I had chosen actually adjoined a German barracks!

'It was still too dangerous to leave because the German soldiers were coming out of the barracks and people were beginning to stir in the streets. Anxiety and restlessness began to mount within me so I left my hide-out and headed towards Rouen. My progress would be slow. Lack of rain had made the road dry and dusty. Blazing sun beat down incessantly. The enemy was everywhere.

'Not until late in the afternoon did I dare stop in a cafe for a drink of cider. Dusk found me near the town of Barantin where I decided to spend the night in an open field. By now my feet were really bothering me. The tight shoes were causing my feet to blister. Removing my shoes, I cringed with pain. Blood oozed from my torn flesh and sweat and dirt added to my discomfort. Mindful of the impending swelling, I carefully eased on my shoes. Overturning a few sheaves of wheat, I laid on the ground and scattered them over me for cover. I was awakened several times during the night by field mice rustling in the coarse grain. Morning, however, brought other visitors. Sharp stinging bites could signify only one thing: lice.

'It seemed like ages that I was on the road and as I limped along each step produced twin bonfires under my painful feet. I had to sit and rest. It must have been my lucky day. An old German guard of about sixty pedalled past me on a bicycle. He was wearing a large leather holster which probably contained a Luger and seemed to be supervizing some Frenchmen who were digging trenches alongside the road. Thankfully, he didn't pay me much attention as he cycled past me. Shortly up the road I met him again. Suddenly, I seemed to command all his attention. He came over to me and asked in French where I was going. I answered, ''Bolbec, Bolbec'' and pointed repeatedly to a road sign indicating the town of Bolbec straight ahead. From what I understood, he said it was a long walk.

'Abruptly, he asked me for my papers. I shook my head. He glared at me once again and looked me over, paying great attention to my old shoes and my clothes. Incredibly, he told me to walk on. Face unshaven, clothes smelly and filthy; he must have taken me for a tramp. I got away quickly although he should really have taken me in. Had he tried, he would have had a fight because I was ready to attack him. I didn't have any weapons because we were not issued any for flying. (Some of the boys carried .45 automatics but apparently there was a shortage and we never got any.)

'Shortly thereafter, dusk fell over the countryside. According to my map, I was nearly half the way to Le Havre. How much longer could I continue? Sharp stabs of pain from inflamed feet tormented my sleep. Oh, if only I could reach Le Havre, then cross the Channel to England.

'By the fifth day my bedraggled appearance was beginning to draw people's attention. A short distance from Bolbec, I asked a woman the directions to a barber shop. She understood when I pointed to my hair and used my fingers to imitate the movement of scissors. ''Two kilometres,'' she said, pointing up the road.

Staff Sergeant Robert Starzynski with the French Underground in July 1944.

'I arrived at the little barber shop and looked in. There was only a mother, a young girl and a young boy of about twelve years old. An old barber was giving the girl a haircut as I entered. The younger barber, who was about sixteen years of age, directed me to a chair. I removed my jacket and made myself comfortable. As one might expect, halfway through the shave, he nicked me. No sooner had he finished shaving me, than he walked toward the door. I paid little attention, but as I glanced in the mirror to see where he had nicked me, I saw that he was talking with a German soldier. I didn't know what they were saying as they spoke in a muffled tone. Ideas began spinning through my mind. Did the barber know I was American? If he did suspect me, could I escape in any way? Looking about the room for another exit, I noticed their curious glances directed towards me. The soldier mumbled something to the barber and he said something to me in French. Apparently, the German was in a hurry and wanted to know if he could get a haircut before me. I said "*Oui*" and with that the German soldier left.

'When the barber had finished with the girl the soldier had still not returned, so he motioned me to sit in the chair and began cutting. Almost at once the soldier returned with three other German soldiers. Scowling at me with displeasure they all sat down a short distance away and I thought, "Boy this is really something". The German who I had promised could go in front of me kept giving me dirty looks.

'About half way through my haircut the old barber asked me how I wanted my hair cut. I didn't really know what to say so I just motioned him to carry on. In the meantime, I could see in the mirror that the German was looking at me. He was also sitting on the chair where I had left my jacket. In it were all my maps and papers! All he had to do was look down but I didn't give him the chance. I leaped out of the chair, taking the largest Franc note I had and gave it to the barber. My haircut and shave cost me sixteen francs but the experience cost me sixteen grey hairs. The barber gave me change and I gave him a tip. I think he was relieved I was finished because he did not want any problems with the Germans. I thankfully grabbed my jacket, left the shop and headed up the road.

'At twilight I was only 16 km from Le Havre. My feet were badly blistered and I had to find a place to hide. I selected a neat, medium-sized farm just off the road. My head was reeling with excitement as I approached the house knowing I had somehow overcome tremendous risks. The farmer and his family listened to my story in disbelief. With the help of an English-French dictionary and broken phrases, I told them I received the clothes from a farmer near Buschy not far from the spot where I had baled out. My festered, swollen feet gave evidence of the truth. After providing me with some food, they insisted I bathe my feet.

'Only after resting for a short time was I informed that the German army had a road block ahead. My long walk had been in vain. I needed identification papers to gain entrance to Le Havre but there was nothing more I could do that night. Taking into consideration my poor physical appearance, they invited me to share one of their beds rather than a hayloft in the barn. After sleeping in fields and haylofts for the past five days, I was most grateful.

'The next morning I bade a reluctant farewell. Dejectedly, I began retracing my steps. I decided, after checking my map, to return to Bolbec and then head south to Lillebonne.

'Later that morning, after informing some Frenchmen at one cafe in Lillebonne that I was an American aviator, I was refused sanctuary. At another a woman who came to serve me asked me in French what I wanted to order. I could not understand her so I just said, "Jes Swei, Aviateur American." She looked at me oddly and started laughing. She called out to someone in the back room. Everyone thought it was a big joke so I left hurriedly and starting walking down the road towards the Seine.

'Just south of Lillebonne I came upon a junk peddler pushing a cart. He was a ragged Brazilian, who had been stranded in France before the war and had never accumulated enough money to return to Latin America. He was able to speak a few words of English and told me that the Germans had taken over the ferry boat which was the only way to cross the river. He added that there was a rowing boat which was operated by the French. He took me to the Frenchmen and told them I was an American airman. What he said must have sounded convincing, for my passage was free. The Frenchmen took me on board the boat and rowed me across the Seine.

'Reaching the opposite shore, we all entered a cafe for sandwiches and beer. We were in Quillebeuf. One of the passengers told me to remain at the cafe. I waited for three hours and nothing happened. I bought some postcards from a stand for some reason, probably to pass the time. Nothing happened and I got up and walked out. Just south of the river I hit the dirt. A sudden burst of machine-gun fire and several explosions erupted as two P-38s began their strafing and bombing run in the vicinity of the ferry boat. The ground shook with the bursting of exploding shells. Minutes later it was over.

'Gradually rising to my feet, I hobbled to an abandoned farmhouse. Once inside, I sat down and removed my shoes. My feet were very bad. Unexpectedly, a German soldier walked in and spoke to me. I just muttered, "*Oui*". He walked over to a

Right *Joseph Szumanski and son at Quillebouf, France in 1944. Szumanski was a Pole who settled in France after World War One. He looked after Starzynski for a time* (Starzynski).

Below right *Jacqueline Isvy; a good friend in France* (Starzynski).

wall and took away a home-made ladder. I assume he needed it to repair some of the damage to the telephone lines caused by the bombing. I figured that this was not the greatest place in the world to be so I got ready to leave.

'Before I could get far a voice called out, "What are you doing there?" Of course I didn't understand French so I replied in my best accent, "*Oui*". A blue-eyed blond civilian repeated the question and again I answered "*Oui*". Making little progress in our conversation, he enquired if I spoke English. I confirmed that I did. We conversed for a time and I told him I was an aviator. He looked so much like a German that I thought I had had it. By this time I no longer cared anyway.

'The blond Frenchman, who turned out to be called Charles Lamour, took me outside to an orchard and told me to wait. I thought he must be leaving to get reinforcements but when he returned an hour later he brought with him a woman who had some food for me. The woman kept asking for assurances that I was an American. They were ultimately convinced I was telling the truth when I kept answering nonchantly, "Sure I am, what do you want?"

'Later, I was to learn that my crossing of the Seine had been well timed. Apparently, the Gestapo had been enquiring about someone fitting my description. The boatman, who was a member of the Resistance, had told them that I had continued walking along the river and had not taken the boat across. Within an hour, they were searching everywhere for me.

'Charles Lamour contacted the French Resistance and they hid me from the Germans. I was taken to another farmhouse in Quillebeuf and only allowed out at night. I stayed in Quillebeuf for ten weeks, hiding in every place imaginable—barns, houses and air-raid shelters.

'During my time in hiding we would carry out some limited acts of sabotage like cutting down telephone lines. Twice we stole a cow from the Germans for food and on other nights we stole beans from the fields. The American Air Force tried repeatedly to blow up the ferry boat. Each time they missed. Towards the end, when the Canadians were approaching, the ferry boat was eventually sunk. Three weeks before the Canadians liberated us my hosts went on a big drinking session. Some German soldiers heard them bragging and they barely got away with their lives. Charles decided to have me moved after this incident. He put me in with a couple who had a small child. I stayed on the second floor of their three-storey house for three weeks. During that time there was incessant noise from artillery barrages and exchanges between the Germans and the advancing Allies. It got so bad on some occasions that we hid in some caves nearby which were used as air raid shelters.

'I was the first American many of the French townspeople had ever seen. My heart went out to the simple people who had truly saved my life at the risk of their own. Eventually, we were liberated by Canadian troops. They wanted me to hop on their tank and leave the area but I could not because I had to get my ID tags back from the underground. I sent word to the fellow who had them, and £16. He turned out to be the mayor and at first refused to hand the money and tags over to me. The Canadians suggested I tell him that if he did not hand them over they would drive a tank right through his darn house! That did the trick and I was given back my ID tags and money.

'Word went through about my plight and later a small unit came through to pick me up. They apparently picked up all shot down airmen. I was shipped back to Cherbourg, where we took a C-47 to London and SHEAF headquarters. I was interrogated and after several days I was returned to Thurleigh. There I met my co-pilot, Wilbur C. Pensinger, who had been picked up almost immediately by the Underground, but the other seven in my crew had been captured.'

Part 3
HOME BY CHRISTMAS

14 Sagan summer

Fortunately for the crew aboard *Squat N' Droppit* and for Bob Starzynski, once they were rescued by the French Underground, the outcome of their shooting down in June 1944 ended happily for all concerned. The events surrounding Lieutenant Loren E. Jackson, aircraft commander of *Crash Wagon III* in the 551st Bomb Squadron, 385th Bomb Group, after he was shot down on his tenth mission on 12 June 1944, are quite different.

This day the 385th, based at Great Ashfield, Suffolk, was part of the Third Air Division force which was engaged in bombing lines of communication around the Normandy bridgehead. The B-17s were tasked with bombing the marshalling yards at Montdidier. Although he did not know it at the time (his German interrogator would later confirm as much), *Crash Wagon III* was the highest Fortress in the 8th Air Force, flying in the high squadron, high group in the bomber stream. [*Crash Wagon III* had been named 'rather retroactively' because Jackson's first B-17 had crashlanded in Northern Ireland at the end of the flight from the USA when the landing gear refused to function and his second B-17 was lost on his crew's first mission two weeks later when they were forced to ditch in the English Channel.]

The short mission across the Channel to the beachhead became even shorter, when, approaching the target, flak disabled Jackson's number two engine. 'Ross M. Blake, my co-pilot from Great Neck, Long Island, and I, were unable to feather the propeller. It kept windmilling and making a rather unsettling racket. We continued on course but began to lag behind the main formation. Shortly thereafter, a flak hit in our number four engine disabled it but we were able to feather the propeller. By now we were considerably behind the formation.

'When fire broke out and enveloped the entire left wing I rang the emergency bell and instructed the crew to bale out. I was eager to get out too, but hit a snag. I was wearing a parachute harness and had stowed my parachute under my seat. I reached over to get the 'chute but it was hooked on something under the seat and I was unable to free it. I wrestled with it and finally got it loose. As I was attaching it to the harness, I looked out the left window and saw that the fire was out. (I suspect that as I leaned forward

Lieutenant Loren E. Jackson, pilot 551st Bomb Squadron, 385th Bomb Group (Jackson).

with my shoulders pressed against the control column, I put the airplane into a shallow dive. Apparently, the increased air speed blew out the fire.)

'I called the crew on interphone to see if anyone was still aboard but I received no answer. I flew along alone for about ten minutes, following the formation in the distance. When the fire erupted again and had the number two engine and the left wing obscured by flames, I left my position in the left seat and went out the nose hatch.

'The smoking, flaming B-17 circled me twice resembling a huge wounded bird. As I was descending, I plotted my escape route. I was falling into a clear field and could see a thick cluster of trees not far away. I planned to head for the trees and hide until nightfall. I landed in tall grass and lay on my back to disengage my parachute harness. I got up and started walking casually toward the forest. Then I heard a shout. "*Halt*!" I pretended not to hear it and continued towards the trees. Again the command to halt. I turned around and saw a German soldier on one knee with his rifle pointed at me. I threw up my hands. He came toward me, still holding his rifle on me and said the words I dreaded to hear, "For you the war is over".

'He could not believe that I was not armed. He took me to a small building which I suspect was the annex to a barn or similar structure. There was nothing in the room except two chairs. He put the chairs in diagonal corners of the room and told me to sit in one of them which he designated. He occupied the other chair with his rifle still trained on me. He had already searched me and relieved me of a Hershey bar, a pack of gum, some English coins, a pack of cigarettes, my lighter and my wrist watch. As we stared at each other across the room, he said. "If you move, I'll kill you." And I certainly believed him—I had no intention of moving but my bowels almost did. He calmly ate my Hershey bar, helped himself to a stick of gum and then lighted up one of my cigarettes. The urge to smoke was overwhelming so I asked him if I could have one. "No!" he thundered with great bitterness. "You are our prisoner, not our God-damn guest." He had me there.

'After about a half hour with this jolly host, two German soldiers came in an army sedan and drove me away. We were on a lonely country road which deteriorated into a one-way dirt track out in the wilds. They stopped the car by a crumbling wall which surrounded an ancient cemetery. I couldn't help but speculate on how awesome were the prospects for a good murder. They began to argue in German, which I could not understand. But somehow, it came to me that they were trying to agree on a place to shoot me and toss my lifeless body. And this cemetery was certainly an ideal location. They argued back and forth, getting louder and louder, for a good five minutes as the sweat trickled off my brow (I kept thinking that one of them wanted to go a little further and the other one wanted the execution to take place right there.) But my fears were for naught; they had simply taken the wrong fork in the road a few miles back. I 'died' a little in that five minutes.

'They turned around and we took the other fork. Shortly, we met up with another small German convoy. It contained a brand new prisoner of war, my bombardier, Joe Haught. We were glad to see each other; a friendly face does wonders in such a situation.

'We were promptly taken to a headquarters area in a German staff car where we sat and waited. In the front seat was an unarmed driver and beside him sat a guard with a rifle. Joe and I were in the back seat and between us was another German guard with a rifle. As we sat in the car, a German soldier ran up to the driver, said something to him in German, and we started to drive away. One of our guards said to us in English, "General von Schwerin has asked to see the American officers who were just shot down."

"Neither of us knew General von Schwerin by name nor by reputation but we did not relish the thought of facing a high-ranking enemy officer on his turf. We drove a few miles to a large, impressive chateau and were admitted by an aide to a large living room. From the opposite end of the room strode a tall, handsome man in civilian slacks, a white wool turtleneck sweater and bedroom slippers. As he neared us, two frightened and bewildered Second Lieutenants, he extended his hand and said, warmly, and in perfect English, "Good morning, I am General von Schwerin."'

The General was very courteous and offered them food and drink. The two Americans refused. (Although they had not eaten for eight hours Jackson feared he might be trying to poison them.) An offer of cigarettes was also politely refused. The General engaged them in small talk, informing them that he had toured 35 states in America and had attended Stanford University. At this point the General faltered, searching for the name of the town.

Jackson was asked if he knew its location. 'Yes I do,' he replied.

'Well?'

'I can't tell you,' replied Jackson very seriously. ('I was not about to lose the war by telling this scoundrel that Stanford was at Palo Alto!')

'The General paused a moment as though stunned, looked intently at me and at Joe, and then began to laugh. "Oh!" he said, "name, rank and serial number only. Is that it? Oh, very well. I can see that you have assumed that this is an interrogation but it really isn't. You are simply obeying your orders. I can assure you that you will be interrogated later on, but I only wanted to chat with you for a few minutes.'''

The General did not detain them further but congratulated Jackson and Haught for being 'good soldiers'. He shook hands and hoped that their stay in Germany would be 'as pleasant as possible under difficult circumstances'.

Puzzled, Jackson and Haught were returned to the waiting vehicle and driven away to Beauvais. Twenty years later Jackson sought out General von Schwerin and discovered him living in Bonn. 'The General met me at the front door with his hand extended. ''Palo Alto'' I said. At first my greeting puzzled him, but then, recalling the incident of two decades before, he laughed heartily as we shook hands.'

General von Schwerin relived his wartime experiences, saying that he had been relieved of command shortly after Jackson's and Haught's visit. He had been posted to Italy where he later commanded the 'Greyhound Division'. An anti-Nazi, the very day that SS troops were on their way to Hamburg to obtain evidence which would incriminate him in the assassination attempt on Adolf Hitler an American bombing raid on the city destroyed the only documents which could prove it conclusively. Since that time, General von Schwerin has always said that 'American bombers are not all bad!'

The General was captured in March 1945 just before the war ended and interrogated. He was released from confinement in Dachau at noon on Christmas Eve 1947; just over two and a half years later. Three years earlier, Loren Jackson and Joe Haught were just about to begin their confinement with a first, sad night in jail at Beauvais. Jackson explains: 'My navigator, Gerald Shaffer was killed on 12 June when his parachute failed to open. I saw the Germans bury his body near Beauvais. Some French women onlookers tossed flowers on his grave. The Germans showed me his dog tags and asked me if I knew him. I said, ''No.'' They said, ''You should; he was on your crew''.

'Fred Martini my assistant flight engineer/gunner, evaded capture for some time, masquerading as a Catholic priest in France. He was finally betrayed, however, and sold out to the Germans. He was incarcerated in the concentration camp at Buchenwald for some time until he was able to convince the authorities that he was an American military man. Sam Pennell, one of the wasit-gunners, also did a stint in Buchenwald with Martini. They evaded together, were captured together and spent time together in that infamous camp. Felipe E. Muzquiz, my Mexican ball-turret-gunner, Ted Dubenic, the tail-gunner, Ervin Pickerel, the radio operator, Blake and Armando Marsilii, my flight engineer, all survived the war.'

After accumulating a busload of PoWs Jackson and Haught were taken to Brussels where they spent a week in solitary confinement before a prison train took them to Dulag Luft. 'After a few days,' recalls Jackson, 'We boarded another prison train and went to Stalag Luft III at Sagan via Cologne and Frankfurt. I can remember seeing the grandeur of the great cathedral at Cologne and marvelling at how it had stood in the midst of the rubble of that city. In the railroad terminal at Frankfurt a group of civilians recognized us as ''terror bombers'' and, gathering strength and fermenting hatred, they closed in on us. We were in a corner and they were poised for attack. Our guards shouted to them and pointed their rifles at them but we all knew they would never shoot their own countrymen to protect us. As they got closer they saw one of our number who had been very badly burned. He was on a litter and his face and hands were burnt almost black. Apparently, the sight of this helpless, pitiful individual sparked some compassion in them and the mob melted away.

'During the same confrontation I noticed a young man of about twenty in the forefront of the mob wearing a leather A-2 jacket, the type worn by American flyers. He was so close I could have touched him. He caught my eye and winked at me. I have always wondered about him. Surely an American would not walk around in the heart of Germany wearing an A-2 jacket?

'Asked what were my most terrifying moments, I would reply that there were three terrifying moments in my life and they all happened on the same day, 12 June 1944. The first occurred as I was descending by parachute and the flaming, screaming airplane made two passes at me. It didn't miss me by much either time. The second was when I looked behind me and saw the German soldier in a kneeling position with his rifle trained on me. And the third happened on the outskirts of that ancient cemetery as my captors argued vehemently about whether to 'shoot me right there or go further down the road.

'I was imprisoned at Stalag Luft III from the summer of 1944 until the end of January 1945. My stay at Sagan was most uneventful; very boring and routine. I did a lot of reading, playing cards and walking around the compound. Another favourite pastime was computing one's back pay. (I was fortunate in that respect because all the computing I did was based on the premise that I was a Second Lieutenant, whereas in reality I had been promoted to First Lieutenant the day before I was shot down. I did not know this until after I returned to Allied control but the added pay was welcome).

'One of my most poignant memories is of Christmas Eve 1944. The Germans permitted us to be out until 9 o'clock that night (normally we were locked up in our blocks at 6.00 pm). We were visiting back and forth, greeting our friends and wishing each other a Merry Christmas. We expressed our strong conviction (and ardent hope) that the Germans just could not hold out much longer. One memory in camp during the Yuletide season is the 'Kriegie' parody on the song *I'll Be Home For Christmas.*

''*We won't be home for Christmas,*
Don't depend on us.
We'll have snow
But no mistletoe
Or presents on the tree.
Christmas Eve will find us
Standing at appell,
We won't be home for Christmas,
We know that very well.''

'After we were finally locked up at about ten o'clock, we heard music coming from the centre of the compound. It was an American brass quartet with a trumpet, Alto, baritone and a trombone. The group played *Silent Night.* I will never forget that moment and how the strains of that beautiful carol permeated the cold, black chill of that winter night in the heart of Germany.'

15 Barth—the final days

On 30 November 1944 Bernal 'Rusty' Lewis, co-pilot of a Fortress crew in the 527th Bomb Squadron in the 379th Bomb Group at Kimbolton, was also destined to become a 'guest of the Germans' when concentrated flak brought down his B-17, *Sad Shack*, on the mission to synthetic oil targets at Zeitz, south-west of Leipzig.

The mission began badly as 'Rusty' Lewis, who was flying his twenty-second mission, recalls: 'In order to maintain visual contact with the ground, our group leader dropped down through thick cloud, putting us in the low squadron at 23,000 ft. Major Theodore G. Ramsdell, the pilot, and I, attempted to relinquish the lead to the deputy lead, who was my ex-aircraft commander, on my right wing, but he ignored the green light. We were without radio communication so we pulled back and attempted to stall the aircraft so that we would slide ahead of us. Unfortunately, he stalled right with us. (I found out later that his co-pilot's control yoke was laying in his lap.)

'At last the deputy lead crew realized that we wanted them to take over the lead. We made a turn to the right, making sure we had not passed the target. Maybe we had gone a little bit beyond it when we made a swing to the right and passed near Leipzig where we encountered flak. During the 190 degree turn onto our secondary target at Merseberg, the deputy lead aircraft finally took over. We completed a 270 degree turn, taking us right back over the target area where we were again showered by flak. The secondary target was obscured by cloud so we headed for the third target at Fulda.

'On the bomb run Maurice M. Gropper, our "Micky" radar operator, screamed over the interphone that the target was to the left. Then I heard, "No, we're on the bomb run itself." They were checking checkpoints but when we arrived over the target area the target was not there! We heard some explosions off to our left and realized that the Germans had camouflaged the checkpoints to fool our visual men in the nose. Most crewmen at the time always believed their eyes and instruments and not the "Mickey" sets of which little was known except by the technicians who used them.'

In the resulting confusion the formation broke up and scattered in complete disarray. Bernal Lewis continues, 'We got a fire in the number four engine and we had to shut it down. Aircraft from our squadron were going down all around us and we only had three aircraft left in the formation. [*Take Me Home, Dimples* and Lewis' ship; which were all lost together with: *Landa, Lucy* and *Miss Lace,* which had already gone down.]

'Our intercom was dead. All electrical supply to the top turret was dead, we lost another engine and the propeller ran away. I looked out across the wing and saw that all the oil tanks appeared to have been riddled by rifle fire, although it was obviously flak. The oil ran low and the engines began overheating. Finally, a third engine went out and we had another runaway propeller. We were now flying around 4,000 ft with lost power. It was time to leave the ship.

'I held the aircraft level, looking down between my knees through the escape hatch below me until the hills came up underneath. John W. McDermott, the navigator, had been hit in the head and was unconscious. It was my intention to take him out with me in my arms with his "D" ring in my hands so that when we jumped out the airspeed would hit him and pull him away. Luckily, he regained consciousness just prior to our jump.

'We were over Heligolandstock, south of Hannover when I went to bale out and I could see right over the town. I noticed it had a high pointed steeple. I had always rehearsed parachute jumping in my mind and had day-dreamed about getting hung up on a steeple.

'I thought I might as well enjoy the parachute jump but all of a sudden, I realized I had left the aircraft at only 4,000 ft! I quickly pulled the ripcord. I was wearing a 28 ft back pack 'chute and its opening created a very big impact. The ring fell out of my hand and I thought, "Oh Hell, I won't be able to get into the "Caterpillar Club" without it. Then I noticed that those who had jumped before me were just opening their 'chutes! I thought how smart they were because they would not drift over the town like I was going to thanks to the prevailing wind. (It was only later that I found that three of the crew had to claw their 'chutes out of their chest packs with their fingernails after the rings had failed.)

'I landed right on the edge of Heligolandstock where people were waiting with pistols. I gave my parachute to a pretty girl in the group. There was rapid firing. Did I make it back this close to the front lines? I asked a young German soldier, who was about sixteen years old and had a broken arm, if we were in Holland or Germany. A little nine-year-old German kid laughed and said, "No, Germany". The rapid firing was only the ammunition exploding in our burning Fortress.

'An old man took me to his house and put on a hat with a feather in it. I guess he was "*Volkstrum*". I was led through the streets but people were becoming mean and angry and I got kicked in the crotch from behind. (This caused some bad urinary bleeding problems later). I was taken to a police station and joined by a German enlisted man called Eddie Stang. He used 1930s slang, saying things like, "These fellers want to bump you off. They think you dived your aircraft on the village and I want to help you". (We had decided to crash our airplane rather than let the Germans get our "Mickey" set.) I said I understood all this, although I didn't believe a word of it. I told him I could not give him any information other than my name, rank and serial number. He tried to con me that he had visited the USA before the war and had lived in Chicago. I stuck to the "name, rank and serial number" routine.

'Later, a 6 ft 5 in German with a shaved head visited me. It turned out he was the burgomeister. He asked me through an interpreter what target we had bombed but I said I could tell him nothing. He mouthed and slapped me with his bare hand. I figured if he really wanted to hurt me he would have used his fist. I looked him straight in the eyes and said to myself, "Don't look scared". In my mind I called him every dirty name I could think of. He gave up. Stang returned and said the crowd outside were calling for my blood because I had dived our 'plane into their village.

'About six hours later the Germans started bringing in the rest of my crew, including Major Theodore G. Ramsdell who had been flying with us. He was quite a soldier and the Germans recognized that they had a prize catch. The next day we were despatched to Frankfurt by train. We stood on the platform at the packed Bahnhof and I had the urge to escape until I saw a guard with his eyes locked on me waiting for me to attempt an escape. Had I tried to get away I would have been shot.

'By tram we were taken to Oberussel, about twenty miles from Frankfurt. However, about half way the tram broke down and we had to walk the rest of the way. At Oberussel we were herded into an overcrowded basement. Most were friends from my squadron, ten out of the twelve ships having been shot down. Next day we were put in solitary confinement. We had been shown a movie about Dulag Luft in England so we knew what to expect.

'It had said that there would be a Red Cross form and that we were to give only our name, rank and serial number. It also warned us that the Germans would try and peg us as extrovert or introvert. We were told, "Be as blasé as you can." Nevertheless, putting my ear to the wall I could hear men being sucked in by the Red Cross form, writing name, rank and serial number and then carrying on with information about where they had trained, their squadron and group details and so on. Because it had "Red Cross" at the top of the form, people were filling it in and getting out of Dulag Luft in about a day. They inadvertently told the Germans all they wanted to know.

'During my interrogation I refused to give the Germans any information. I said I understood the Germans to be good soldiers and I was one too. I had been ordered to stick to "name, rank and serial number". My interrogator, a German Captain, said, "We don't know if you are a spy. Your dog tags don't mean anything. We have to have more information about you and you will remain here until we get it."

'After four days in solitary confinement it became very tough going. Before the war I had been a psychiatric technician and having studied quite a bit about psychology I felt I could follow the dictates of my confinement and interrogations. I had been a "pumpster" all my life and I wanted to write a book about my religious beliefs. After about seven days' solitary confinement I think I would probably have become mentally ill had I not had the training in mental discipline. I could see where people had tried to scratch some messages on the wall with their finger nails and they had probably gone mad eventually. In the next cell to me was Count Daceagunsac. "Zac" was a Free French fighter and had been in solitary confinement for 56 days. Despite this he was still able to shout encouragement and taught me to sing *Allouette* and so on. Although I never met him face to face I have always considered him a friend.

'After solitary I was taken before a '*Hauptman*'; another shaven-headed type. As I entered his office I saw a complete mock of up a "Mickey" set. He asked me questions but I still stuck to the "name, rank and serial number" routine. On the wall was a board showing the squadrons in the 379th Bomb Group.

The *Hauptman* gave me a propaganda lecture and began by saying that my squadron CO was called the "Monster". (This was true; Major Crosby was a West Pointer and the men called him the "Monster" because of his size.) This was just to impress upon me that he knew all about us. He added, "You will win the war but not as soon as you think. (Unknown to me the "Battle of the Bulge" had just started.) It won't be long after this war that you'll be fighting the Russians and we'll be on your side."

'Later, I found out that Major Ramsdell had been given the opposite treatment. The Germans discovered that it had been his birthday and gave him a big champagne party. One of the Germans got up and toasted him, saying, "Five or ten years ago I was in the United States enjoying myself". The Major returned the toast, saying, "One, two or three years from now I'll be in the United States enjoying myself". This showed the different type of treatment we were getting.

'On my twenty-first day at Dulag Luft I was told that if I did not give more information, I would be left to rot. I said, "OK, I'll give you my birthday, but that's it." The *Hauptman* laughed and said, "OK". A Lieutenant-Colonel I later talked to told me that during his interrogation he was shown a clipping from his home town newspaper, printed a month before, giving his promotion. My home town newspaper had stated that I had flown 21 missions. My parents were able to pin down how many missions I flew because I had a little code system going with them. When we had gone overseas we had painted a nude on our B-17 and called her the *Sad Shack*. I said I was going to kiss her fanny everytime I got back from a mission. When I wrote that I had seen "fanny" that day they knew I had completed another mission. At one of the interim camps on the way to Stalag Luft I, I was allowed to write a message that would be sent over the "Red Cross" radio. All I wrote was, "All crew OK; am fine." A ham radio picked it up.

'After giving this information I joined a muster in a hall. My electric flying suit was returned to me and I found a piece of chewing gum in one of the pockets. Later, I tried to pass it through the door to "Zak" but a guard sneaked up from behind and got me by the scruff of my neck and the seat of my pants. He threw me across the room. Having been an accomplished boxer, my first reaction was to hit him but my crew shouted otherwise. I had taken a beating because the German thought I was a Jew.

'I was put on a long train journey across Germany. I was completely amazed at the German railway network. I saw there was no way we would ever knock out their railway system in the war. Every forest had camouflaged equipment, screw tracks and so on. At this time the Air Force effort was aimed at wiping them out and strafing trains was common. On Christmas Eve our train was strafed. Our guards jumped from the train and scrambled into ditches. They trained their guns on us while we stayed in the cars. They were especially angry that the Allies had strafed and bombed on Christmas Eve! Finally, we reached Stettin and East Prussia and went on to Stalag Luft I at Barth.'

'Rusty' Lewis arrived at Barth in Pomerania the day after Christmas 1944. The camp was sited near the town which lay in the Zingst Hoff, a large inlet sheltered from the Baltic by the sandy, forested arm of the Zingst Peninsula. In strict contravention of the Geneva Convention, Luft I was built near a German anti-aircraft regimental school for army recruits. Barth's huge, ugly, square-shaped church with its spire dominated the area. The camp itself held between nine and ten thousand Allied prisoners of war in four separate compounds. Lewis was put into North Compound 3.

Many of Luft I's population were RAF prisoners, some of whom had been held captive since the first months of the war. Flight Lieutenant (later Air-Vice-Marshal) Harry Burton, a 149 Squadron Wellington pilot shot down on 6 September 1940, became the first Allied prisoner to escape from a German PoW camp when he got clean away from Luft I in May 1941.

Despite this and other successful escapes the vast majority of RAF and American prisoners were destined to remain at Barth until the end of the war. Luft I seemed to bring together many colourful characters who would leave their indelible stamp on those around them. Lieutenant-Colonel Charles Ross Greening, or 'CRG' as he was known, had been at Barth since January 1944. Before the war he planned to become a professional artist and he continued in his spare time after joining the USAAF in 1936. On 18 April 1942 he took part in the raid on Japan mounted by B-25s from the US carrier, *Hornet*. All the Mitchells took off safely from the rolling deck of the carrier and none were lost over their targets but two crews crash-landed in China. Three men were executed by the Japanese and a third died in PoW camp. Greening and the crew of *Hari-Karier* were forced to bale out over China but he evaded capture for several weeks and finally reached safety with the help of Chinese guerilla forces.

In 1943 'CRG' was in North Africa, leading a group of B-26 Marauders. On a mission to Naples on 17 July Greening was again shot down when a German 88-mm shell hit his right engine. As if that was not enough 'CRG' parachuted out and landed on the slopes of Mount Vesuvius! Luckily, a kind wind blew him away from the volcanic crater and deposited him in the midst of some enemy soldiers who made

Col. Charles Greening Dies at 42; Pilot in Doolittle Raid on Tokyo

WASHINGTON, March 29 (AP) —Col. Charles Ross Greening, U. S. A. F., a survivor of the Doolittle raid on Tokyo during World War II, died today at the Bethesda (Md.) Naval Hospital. He was 42 years old.

Colonel Greening was a captain when he piloted a B-25 bomber off the storm-pitched deck of the aircraft carrier Hornet in April, 1942, on the raid led by then Col. James Doolittle. He parachuted to the China mainland after the raiders had dropped their bombs on Japan.

Later Colonel Greening served in North Africa and Italy. He was shot down in Italy and captured by the Germans. Escaping twice, he was recaptured each time and was a prisoner of war in Germany at the end of the conflict.

Colonel Greening's last assignment was as air attaché in Australia, where he developed heart trouble last year.

He is survived by his widow, Dorothy, who lives in Bethesda.

Col. Charles R. Greening, when a captain in 1942.

Talent for Design

Colonel Greening made a seemingly incongruous switch from the art courses in which he had majored at Washington State College when he joined the Army Air Forces in 1936.

But he put his talent for design to use. He devised a simple bombsight, which cost 20 cents to produce, so that the Doolittle raiders could leave the then secret Norden sight safely out of Japanese reach.

With many of his companions in the Tokyo raid, Colonel Greening, by then a major, was assigned to North Africa. On his twenty-seventh mission there, he was shot down near Mount Vesuvius, Italy, on July 27, 1943.

He managed to escape detection for two months, staying with the family of an Italian innkeeper in Pescantina, who was housing German officers under the same roof.

Attempting escape, he was caught in Yugoslavia and sent to Stalag Luft I, north of Berlin, on the Baltic. There his inventiveness again came into play, when he saw other fliers showing the effects of their long confinement. He organized an arts and crafts program, against his captors' wishes, and aided fellow-prisoners to produce artifacts with glass, tin cans, pins and bed slats.

By the time Russian troops reached the camp on May 1, 1945, enough violins, cameras, stoves, model homes and portraits had been produced to fill fifty-six packing cases. Colonel Greening managed to obtain three Flying Fortresses to take the articles to the United States, where he toured with them.

He also fulfilled a promise made to 9,000 fellow-prisoners to compile a book of pictures of scenes with which they were familiar. More than 6,000 copies of the book of water-colors were sold.

Among Colonel Greening's decorations were the Silver Star, the Distinguished Flying Cross, the Air Medal with Cluster and the Chinese Order of the Celestial Cloud.

him prisoner.

After spending two months in an Italian PoW camp Greening and four English friends saw their chance to escape when the PoWs were moved northwards to Germany and away from the Allied advance in Italy. They got clean away during a bombing raid and Greening remained free for nine months. His four friends were captured and shot for being in civilian clothes and Greening was finally cornered in a cave in Yugoslavia and sent to Stalag Luft I—where he passed much of the time painting and sketching

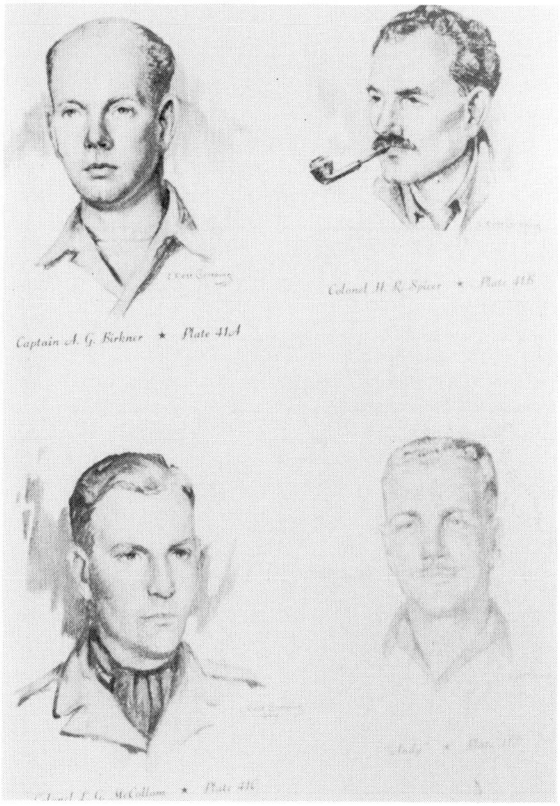

Above *Newspaper clipping detailing life of Colonel Charles Greening.*

Above right *Lieutenant Colonel Loren G. McCollom poses beside his P-47,* Butch, *during his time with the 56th Fighter Group* (Harry Holmes).

Right *Four portraits of well-known faces at Barth, painted by Colonel Charles Greening. Top left, Captain A. G. Erkner; top right, Colonel H. E. Spicer; bottom left, Colonel L. McCollom; bottom right, 'Andy'.*

Right *Duane Beeson points out the damage to his P-15B* 43-6819 *on 5 March 1944* (Harry Holmes).

Below *Four portraits of well-known faces at Barth painted by Colonel Charles Greening. Top left, John 'Red' Morgan; top right, 'Gabby' Gabreski; bottom left, Colonel Hubbard; bottom right, Major Gerald Johnson.*

other prisoners in the camp.

The large American contingent at Barth also boasted some very well-known fighter pilots who had been shot down towards the end of 1943 and throughout 1944. The first was Colonel Loren G. McCollom, commanding officer of the 353rd Fighter Group based at Metfield, Suffolk. On 25 November 1943 McCollom and fifteen other P-47 Thunderbolt dive-bombers each carrying a 500 lb bomb, headed for the airfield at St Omer-Ft Rouge in France. Heavy ground fire bracketed the formation as it approached the target and McCollom's P-47, *Cookie,* received a substantial hit underneath the fuselage, ripping away a large area and setting fire to a fuel tank. McCollom baled out and was taken prisoner. He was sent to Barth and for a time became the Senior American Officer in the camp.

On 5 March 1944 Colonel Henry R. Spicer, commanding officer of the 357th Fighter Group at Leiston, Suffolk, was also brought down and sent to Barth. During a sweep over the Cherbourg Peninsula his P-51 Mustang, *Tony Boy* (named after his young son) was hit in the coolant by light flak and crashed into the Channel. Spicer was washed ashore after two days and nights in the water unable to walk or avoid capture.

Later that month, on 18 March, the 20th Fighter Group at King's Cliffe, Northamptonshire, also lost its commanding officer. Lieutenant Colonel Mark E. Hubbard became a guest of the Germans and was despatched to Barth. For six months he was commanding officer of Group IV and was later attached to the Wing Staff after the camp was re-organized in November 1944. He was a capable, energetic and efficient officer and well liked by the men at Stalag Luft I.

As if these losses were not bad enough, on 27 March 1944 Major Gerald W. Johnson of the 56th Fighter Group, an ace with eighteen confirmed kills, was shot down during a strafing attack on a road convoy. Light flak hit his Thunderbolt and he followed the path of other fighter pilots into the bag at Barth, where he became the Security Officer for North Compound 3. He was joined shortly afterwards at Barth by Major Duane Beeson of the 4th Fighter Group, a leading ace, who was shot down by ground fire on 5 April, also during a strafing attack.

On 20 July 1944 the Germans caught one of their biggest fish yet. Colonel Francis S. 'Gabby' Gabreski of the 56th Fighter Group at Boxted, Essex, was the leading ace in the European Theatre of Operations with 28 victories, tying with his commanding officer, Colonel Hubert A. Zemke. During an attack on a

Left *'Rusty' Lewis, co-pilot of* Sad Shack.

Below left *Famous Four in the 56th Fighter Group at Boxted (L-R): Hub Zemke; Dave Schilling; Francis Gabreski and Christensen* (Harry Holmes).

Bottom left *'Red' Morgan, Medal of Honor recipient, ladles out hot water at Stalag Luft I* (Barth).

Right *Crew of* Bette La Belle, *100th Bomb Group. Standing (L-R): Unknown; Fortney; Pace; Numack; Nelson; Herbert. Kneeling (L-R): Blackman; Repole; Freshour; Sterrett* (Sterrett).

German airfield 'Gabby' pressed down the nose of his Thunderbolt to fire at a Bf 109 just taking off. The American ace was too low and his propeller touched the ground. Gabreski scrambled out unhurt and managed to evade capture for five days. Two Hitler Jugend overpowered him by an onslaught of reserves and he was sent to Stalag Luft I where he became commanding officer of North Compound 3.

Three months later, on 30 October 1944, his former Group Commander, 'Hub' Zemke, now in charge of the 479th Fighter Group at Wattisham, Suffolk, was also brought down. This brilliant fighter leader, with 17 ¾ confirmed kills in the air, was probably on his last mission before being transferred to a desk job at wing headquarters. North of Hannover his Mustang was thrown over on its back by violent winds and it entered a dive in which the wing parted from the fuselage. Zemke baled out before the Mustang disintegrated, was captured and sent to Barth where he became the Senior American Officer.

Of the bomber contingent at Barth, perhaps the best known was Lieutenant John C. 'Red' Morgan, who had won the Medal of Honor, America's highest decoration, in July 1943. On 6 March 1944 Morgan was shot down flying with the 385th Bomb Group which was leading the Third Bombardment Division over Berlin. Morgan was one of only four men who survived from the twelve-man crew after their B-17 was hit by flak. The B-17 exploded and Morgan was pitched out of the bomber still holding his parachute under his arm. He tried to get it on as he fell feet first but the pressure kept pushing it up too high. Then he fell head first and it pushed it past his chest. Morgan finally got it on when he was on his back and a few seconds later he landed in a tree. He fell 30 ft from its branches and was picked up by soldiers from a flak battery.

Throughout 1943 and 1944 the full-scale American daylight raids from England and Italy produced many PoWs and a large number found their way to Barth. Richard Olsen, a 19-year-old radio operator in the 451st Bomb Group of the 15th Air Force in Italy, arrived at Barth in January 1945. He had been shot down on 11 December 1944 on his tenth mission, to the marshalling yards at Vienna. Although it was only their tenth mission Olsen's crew was already a lead crew. It serves as an indication of

the heavy losses that the 15th Air Force was suffering at that time.

His Liberator, *Round Trip*, was hit by flak over Vienna and the pilot, Captain William A. Harris, nursed the bomber as far as Goya, Hungary where the thirteen-man crew baled out. The crew's silent descent was quickly shattered by ground fire which put fourteen holes through Olsen's 'chute and killed the rear-gunner, Melvin G. Schwulst. Once down on the ground Olsen was surrounded by Hungarian soldiers, one of whom was riding a horse. Olsen raised his arms and the horseman rode forward and relieved him of his GI 'hack' watch and ID bracelet. However, he missed Olsen's escape kit which included fifty dollars, hidden in his left trouser leg.

The surviving members of the crew were taken to Komron and interrogated. The Hungarians realized they had captured an important bunch of fliers because only a lead crew would have thirteen men aboard. Next day they were stripped and the Hungarians would all stop and stare at Olsen in his electric suit with its wires protruding everywhere.

After moving to Gyor and Parpau in four-wheel boxcars riddled with bullet holes from constant air atacks, Olsen and six others in the crew were sent to Germany on Christmas Day. On the way they went through Vienna, their target only three weeks before. Vienna from the ground looked different from the view obtained through a bombsight and Olsen noticed that 'chaff' dropped from their bombers was used as a substitute for tinsel on Christmas trees in the streets! While in Vienna, the bombing raids continued and the Viennese were very hostile towards them. They threw stones, hurled abuse and spat at them. One Austrian cursed Olsen for bombing his house three times!

At Oberussel Olsen's escape kit was discovered and it was confiscated along with his other apparel. During their short stay at Frankfurt the RAF made them feel at home with several bombing raids. However, the RAF always dropped a magnesium flare in the centre of the compound at Stalag IIIB, a PoW camp nearby, to prevent the accidental bombing of PoWs. Olsen and his compatriots were not sorry to leave the havoc and destruction of Frankfurt and on 11 January they arrived at Barth, their officers having been sent to an officers' camp in Germany.

The following day William M. Sterrett, a navigator on a Fortress in the 100th Bomb Group of the 8th Air Force based at Thorpe Abbotts in East Anglia, entered the forbidding barbed wire compound at Barth. Eleven days earlier, on 27 December, his Fortress was one of twelve shot down on a mission to Fulda. Sterrett recalls: 'I baled out and two men who got to me first had quite an argument over who should get the credit for capturing me. Finally, one of them told me to gather up my 'chute and put it on the back of their bicycle and push it down the road in front of him. A crowd built up and followed us. I thought they were going to lynch me but I was taken into the burgomeister's office and stayed there until 6.00 pm when a Major came in to find out my name, rank and serial number.

'An hour later the German guard returned and told me to pick up my 'chute and go with him. He and another guard put me in a buggy and sleigh combination pulled by a single horse and we started down the road. We rode about a half mile and then turned off into some woods. I thought for a moment they were going to dispose of me. However, I was taken to a German airfield and reunited with two of my crew. On 2 January we were put on a train for Frankfurt.

'The trip took two and a half days on about six different trains. We really had a scare at noon on the second day. We were approaching Fulda, our target on 31 December, when the train stopped. We heard the sound of sirens and aircraft engines but couldn't see any 'planes because of cloud. Everyone jumped from the train and lay in a ditch as bombs began to fall. It sounded like the earth was falling apart. When the raid was over the train could not move because the tracks had been destroyed directly in front of it. We had to walk all the way through town to get on another train. Bombs had dropped all over the place, killing lots of people and setting the whole place on fire. Some people wanted to lynch us but our guards would not allow that.

'At Frankfurt (Oberussel) we were put in solitary confinement, interrogated and accused of being spies unless we gave the information our interrogators needed. I said my dog tags were proof enough and refused to answer any questions. Finally, I was handed a piece of paper with answers to most of the questions and told to sign it. I refused and was taken back to my 8 × 13 ft cell. The truth was they knew more about what was going on than I did. After a couple of days I was put on a train for Wetzlar where we had our first contact with the Red Cross. We were given a "Joy Kit" containing cigarettes, clothes and toilet articles. I was at Oberussel only two days before going to Stalag Luft I. We finally arrived on 12 January 1945, the day the Russians started their drive out of Warsaw. We felt we would not be at Barth long but the Russians only came so far and then stopped.'

'Rusty' Lewis recalls: 'The old time prisoners thought the war would never end. We had a radio in the camp and every night someone would come round and give us the BBC news. I remember how joyful we were when the Allies arrived at the Rhine and then for months and months when there was no movement, we got very pessimistic. Six months does not sound a long time but we didn't know if we would ever make it back. When we heard troops had crossed Remagen Bridge we were happy again.

'We were so hungry that we could not keep our minds off food and recipes. We all became expert cooks in our minds and our conversations often centred on food. Everyone got out their little blue Red Cross books and wrote down marvellous menus. Our diet consisted of four thin slices of very black bread, only about an eighth of an inch thick, and a bowl of soup a day. As a consequence, I lost about 45 lb in weight.

'I saw a cat covered in sores and the thought passed my mind about catching and eating him. He disappeared so someone must have eaten him, sores and all. I also saw a black raven that someone later caught and ate. Even though I am half-Norwegian I gave away some stinking lumberger cheese about half an inch thick because I could not stand it. I got a chocolate bar from a Red Cross parcel and chewed it one little square a day. One guy said, "Can't you just eat the whole bar or let us have it; it's driving us nuts." I said I wouldn't sell it for less than twenty five dollars. He said "sold" and wrote me out a cheque on a piece of toilet paper. Later, I had an operation to remove an ulcer and had most of my stomach cut out because of my PoW diet.'

William Sterrett recalls: 'Two men were given one Red Cross parcel once a week plus some German food. On 28 February we were given six parcels for 24 men and were not given any more until 1 April. This was the roughest period of the whole episode. The Germans gave us 1/7th of a loaf of bread, a cup of Ersatz coffee and a cup and a half of stew a day. This is equivalent to about 1,000 or 1,200 calories a day; just enough to keep a person alive. Cigarettes were also scarce. Our morale was at rock bottom so someone would start a rumour just to build up morale.

'On Easter Sunday we were given some Red Cross parcels plus some potatoes and we really had a big feed. Some of the fellows ate too much and about 90 per cent of the camp went sick with dysentery.'

Tension increased when it became known in April 1945 that the Russians were nearing the camp. The presence of the British and American armies on the Elbe and the Russian encirclement of Berlin made everyone at Barth feel that liberation was not far off. When the Russians began a new, concerted drive, across the lower Oder towards the Baltic ports, tension reached fever pitch. In the *Vorlager* panic set in and the Germans were no longer interested in guarding the prisoners. On 29 April confidential reports were hurriedly put to the torch and the Germans even attempted to destroy the nearby airfield and flak school so that equipment would not fall into the hands of the Russians.

Finally, late in the afternoon, Group Captain Weir and Colonel Hubert Zemke, the Senior British and American officers respectively, were called to a conference with the camp Kommandant, Colonel Warnstedt. He told the two senior officers that he had received orders to move the entire camp westward. Colonel Zemke stated that he had no intention of moving and asked in that case what the Germans attitude would be. Warnstedt replied that he would not tolerate bloodshed in the camp and if the PoWs refused to move then he and his men would evacuate and leave the 'Kriegies' in sole possession.

At approximately 13.00 on 30 April 1945, Major Stienhauer informed Group Captain Weir and Colonel Zemke that the Germans had evacuated the camp. When they awoke that morning the prisoners discovered they were no longer under armed guard and comparatively free. However, the Russian forces were still not within sight so it was decided to send out scouting forces to make contact. An American Major, a British officer who could speak German and an American officer who could speak Russian, set out with a German in a German staff car with an American flag and a white flag to investigate the real situation in Barth. They were then to proceed to the main Stralsund-Rostock road about fifteen kilometres south of the camp and wait there for any Russian spearheads in the proximity of the front line. However, the patrol returned in the early evening with no sign of news of the Russian Army.

Meanwhile, the few Americans at a working party in Barth watched it become an open city and an open grave. The city had been in decay long before the Russian's imminent arrival. The streets were peopled only with children and old men. Most of the males were infirm; some lame, others blind. Shop windows were empty and in the baker's shop a sign said, 'Cake is not sold to Jews or Poles'. Now the shop would never again make '*brot*' for Stalag Luft I. However, there were good things to be found in the larders in Barth. Many were requisitioned items like Nestles milk from Denmark, wines looted from France and baking powder from Holland.

Once the first explosions reverberated through the streets of Barth, red flags and white sheets began to appear in the windows of the 'gingerbread' houses. The populace, or what remained, stood querulously in their doorways, wringing their hands and weeping, fearful of their fate. They could not take flight; there was nowhere to run to. All they could do was take down their pictures of Hitler and scatter the torn pieces to the wind.

At about 8.00 am on 1 May, Major Braithwaite and Sergeant Korson, two of the Stalag scouts, raced to a cross-roads about five miles south of Barth. They searched southward for the Russians despite a rumoured curfew which meant that anyone seen moving would be shot on sight. Meanwhile, another patrol led by Wing Commander Blackburn had reached Stralsund. His telephone crew rang numbers in the city hoping a Russian would answer the call. It was suggested that they telephone the Burgomeister of Stralsund but a girl, who was still manning the Barth exchange, told them he had long since fled.

Major Braithwaite and Sergeant Korson had better luck. They pushed on another three miles from the crossroads and met up with the first Russian they had ever seen. He was a chunky, small, man who loomed up brandishing a variety of lethal weapons. 'Engliski' shouted the scouts and without further ceremony they were taken to the nearest Russian officer, First Lieutenant Nick Karmyzoff, an infantryman from Tula. He had fought through to Barth from Stalingrad and three years of war across Russia, Poland and Germany.

Karmyzoff and the first vestiges of the Russian Army entered Stalag Luft I through the main gate. Zemke and Weir received him and Schnapps flowed freely. Toasts were exchanged and glasses were smashed against Hitler's picture. The 'Kriegies' had rigged up their radio to the camp loudspeaker system to hear the BBC *Lucky Strike* hit parade on Saturday night. The first song they heard was, appropriately, *Don't Fence Me In*.

Now began the transition from German occupation to one of Russian occupation. The PoWs had not known how the Russians would treat them so just prior to their arrival they had dug slit trenches inside the compound. The Russians asked why no black armbands were being worn as a mark of respect for the late President Roosevelt. Contrary to regulations the Russians gave orders that the 'Kriegies' were to wear them while they inspected the prisoners. Although the Russians and prisoners drank toasts to the 'destruction of Germany' and the 'solid and enduring friendship' between America, Russia and Britain, the opposite appeared to be true.

'Rusty' Lewis recalls: 'On 2 May the Russians began arriving in full force. The first one I saw was part of a bunch of Mongolian paratroops who were terrorizing the countryside. One shot a woman who was running away with her five-week-old baby. They fought, drunk, were completely undisciplined and lived off the land. The only equipment they had was American and British. They drafted 75 of our officers to work on a ship in a local port even though the war was not yet over and did not come under any reparations clause. It was rumoured that they would not let Allied aircraft fly us out. It was also rumoured that they were going to march us a thousand miles to Odessa on the Black Sea. We could not have walked fifty miles without keeling over.

'But when the high echelon troops came through they brought with them a dancing troupe and singers to entertain us. We rounded up cattle and potatoes and each man had a barbecue fixed up in the compound. The Russians brought in Red Cross parcels that they had been hoarding, saying that they had been delayed because of transportation problems. We ate and ate and almost gained our original weight.'

The Russians' apparent resolve to transport the PoWs to Odessa worried Colonel Zemke. Some PoWs succeeded in reaching the American lines to

Top *PoWs from Barth march to B-17 Flying Fortresses waiting to fly them on the first leg of their route home to the USA* (379th Bomb Group Association).

Above *Lancaster* 'S' for Sugar *sits patiently at Lubeck airfield waiting to transport Allied ex-PoWs back to England* (Imperial War Museum).

Left *Queues of ex-Allied PoWs form next to B-17 Flying Fortresses of the 452nd Bomb Group from Deopham Green at Camp 'Lucky Strike', France* (Holden).

the west and they were promised that the PoWs would be flown out. However, some men could not wait for aircraft to arrive so they left the camp, trading with local people and picking up souvenirs en-route. They finally got through to the Allied lines themselves. Rumours filtered through that some had been shot by the Russians. 'Rusty' Lewis recalls, 'It was said some Americans had their cigarette lighters stolen by the Russians and when they protested they were shot. I heard that 26 people who left the camp never made it back.'

On 12 May the Russians finally permitted some Flying Fortresses to fly in over a five-mile wide corridor to airlift the PoWs to France and home. William Sterrett was among them. 'This really made us happy. B-17s in formation came in over the field and peeled off. We were waiting on the ground in groups of thirty ready to hop on the plane as soon as the wheels stopped rolling.'

John A. Holden, a pilot in the 452nd Bomb Group, flew in from Deopham Green.

'We put plywood floors in the bomb bays so we could carry twenty passengers at a time. During take-off and landing fourteen of these had to ride in the bomb bay and six in the nose because of the centre of gravity. We flew in and out of hastily constructed metal strip landing grounds several times a day until the task was completed.'

Sterrett continues, 'We flew over Hamburg and the Ruhr at about 1,000 ft and really got a good view of all the damage done by bombs. The first night we stayed at Rheims. Next day we were put on C-47s which took us to Le Havre and then we were taken to Camp ''Lucky Strike'' at Fecamp. ''Lucky Strike'' was in a bit of a mess because 90,000 men were brought in without any notice.'

'Rusty' Lewis recalls, 'We were detained at ''Lucky Strike'' for almost thirty days. We were re-started on our PoW diet after eating properly for two weeks and we almost starved to death. General Eisenhower came through and walked up to one of the fellers and asked how they were treating him. He said, ''Goddamit Ike, they're starving us to death.'' Ike took him over to the mess tent and told the cooks to fill up his mess tin with chicken!'

Sterrett, Lewis and many thousands of other PoWs sailed on troopships for the long journey home to the USA. It gave them time to readjust and recall their past experiences at the hands of their German captors and more recently, their Russian 'allies'. 'Rusty' Lewis recalls: 'I felt that we would be at war with Russia within five years and as bad as I wanted to get home I felt that we should have gone right on through and cleaned them out. I came home from the war hating the Russians much more than the Germans.'

16 Journey from Krems

For prisoners like 'Rusty' Lewis and William Sterrett, liberation had come at last. However, for thousands like them, still languishing in Stalags further south, it was a different story. They too expected liberation but the Germans took steps to move them westwards, away from the Soviet advance.

One man, who more than most, wanted the war to end quickly was Lawrence Jenkins, a co-pilot in the 2nd Bomb Group, 15th Air Force. Jenkins had arrived at Stalag 17B in October 1944 after a long and harrowing existence in a German hospital following the loss of his Fortress during a mission to Vienna on 16 July. Already a veteran of fourteen missions, including one to the oilfields at Ploesti, two to Budapest and one to Vienna, Jenkins had had every reason to hope that a second trip to the Austrian capital would be without incident. 'It was a beautiful day. You could see for a hundred miles in any direction. We could see Vienna one hour away with a heavy black cloud hanging over it. All of us had seen this before and we knew what it was. Several times you could see bright flashes and flames shoot out from the black cloud and then your heart would sink just a little lower 'cause you knew ten more men had met their fate.

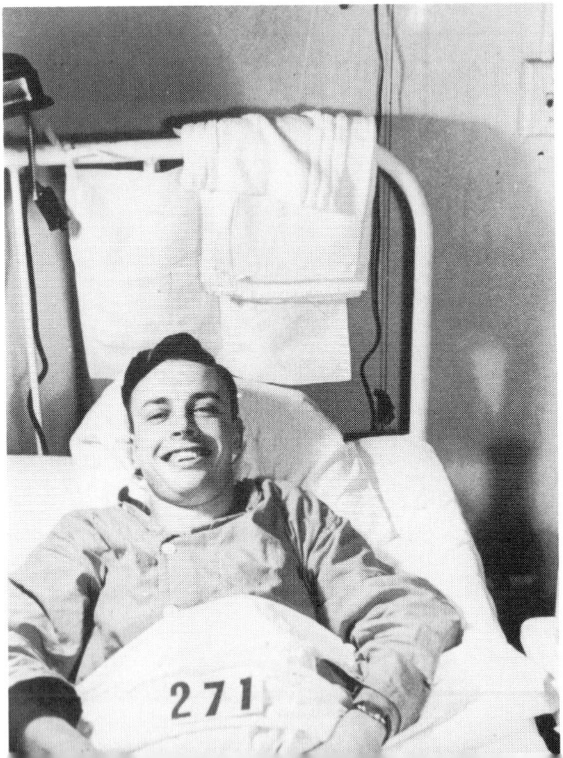

Lawrence Jenkins at Percy Jones Hospital, Battle Creek, Michigan 1946 (Jenkins).

'We turned on to the IP and adjusted our flak suits. By now the first bursts were coming up so I pulled my helmet a little lower to shade my eyes from most of the flak. They were tracking us and each burst seemed to come closer. I watched the bomb release light and counted to see if all twelve 500 lb GP bombs were released. The bomb bay doors were closing and we made our turn to the left. I was breathing better now as the flak was beginning to thin out. Then there came a loud crash and a ripping sound. Everything happened in the matter of seconds.

'I knew we had been hit hard but I could not see. The oxygen had burst and my eyes were flash burned. I could hear the engines whining at a terrific speed and the fire burning like a large blow torch. I ripped my flak suit off, reached under my seat for my 'chute and fastened it, tore my safety belt loose and jumped up. I fell back down in my seat when both legs collapsed. Hard luck, both my legs were broken. I tried walking and pulling myself until I reached the bomb bay. By this time my power was gone and I fell into the bomb bay only to find the doors closed. I was too weak from the loss of blood and oxygen by now so I lay there and said to myself, "It won't take long and everything will be over with."

'In my mind I had drawn a picture of the ship hitting the ground. Luck! I felt a hand reach my shoulder and tried to lift myself up but it was no use. I was too weak to help. I pointed in the direction of the bomb bay emergency release. Soon I started to roll and found myself falling into space. I pulled the rip cord and passed out. I owe my life to Sergeant Ray

Voss, one of the gunners, who stayed there and got me out, while the ship was burning and tearing itself for the earth.

'I woke up with my 'chute pulling my nose through a ploughed field. I heard voices and felt hands grab me. I knew they were Jerries and passed out again. I woke up hours later in a first aid station and by that time I could see. There were three Germans around me. One spoke a little English and said, "For you the war is over". He also asked me who would win the war. I looked at my legs which were wrapped in paper and drenched with blood. He told me both legs would have to come off but I didn't care for the pain was terrible.

'They came and picked me up in a truck, using a parachute to carry me in. There was great pain as the bones rubbed back and forth. In the main hospital they found one of my arms was also cut bad by flak. I was given a shot and sent to a room with ten other Americans. The windows were all barred and the door locked with a guard at it all the time. I became unconscious again and didn't wake up for three or four weeks. My legs were wrapped in paper with metal trays to support the bones. The swelling was so bad they could not put them in casts.'

Jenkins endured several Allied bombing raids while at the hospital, using a mirror to look out of a window as he lay on his back. German doctors carried out three operations on his legs and in September 1944 he was told he would spend the winter at Krems. However, bombing raids on Vienna put the city in turmoil and he was unable to be moved out. Finally, Jenkins was carried from bus to bus and station to station until a train could be found going west.

'We spent all day getting out and half the night going thirty miles. The train made so many stops for people and repairs, I thought we would never arrive at our destination. At Krems they laid me on a cart to transport me to the camp. It was dark and I was cold when it started to snow. Would I live through the night? At about 4 o'clock in the morning a truck, run by steam, picked me up. Every five miles it would stop and they would put more wood in the engine. Finally I arrived at my new home—Stalag 17B.'

'I was put in a room with a Rumanian who could not understand me nor I him. He was very ill and I found out later this was where they put men just before they died. They would also bring the dead men in and leave them until they could find some way of disposing of them. Some Frenchmen came in with water and food which wasn't much. They gave me an American flying suit so I could keep warm but it wasn't long before the Gestapo came after it. I quickly tore the zipper up and got into trouble with the Gestapo. Fortunately, I became so sick they couldn't move me and the Gestapo took their police

Above *Prisoners from Krems waiting to board B-17s for France* (Holden).

Below *Guard tower at Stalag 17B.*

Left *Tearing up the barracks to provide fuel to heat water.*

Below left *A typical barrack block with its outer wooden coating removed to provide fuel.*

dogs and left. I never did get warmed up until spring came.

'When I got well enough they moved me into a bigger room with five Americans, two Russians, four Rumanians, one South African, two Arabs and one blind Italian. The room kept changing as men became well or passed away. They put me next to McCabe, a Lieutenant from Montana. McCabe could walk a little with a full length cast. We pooled our black bread and Red Cross parcels as he became chief cook and bottle washer. We also had the help of a Russian General who would bring us water and assist in other chores.

'The overseer of the hospital was a Frenchman named Ligneres. He helped with dressings and medicine which was given out. We had nothing for pain and could only keep the wounds clean. I got to know and love each helpless individual like a brother no matter what his race was. Some of these people had legs off, others arms. Some couldn't see and others were slowly starving. One young Russian Lieutenant had the Russian Star Medal which kept him in good spirits. He lay in about one inch of pus which finally ate the skin off his back. He was as stiff as a board yet lived on. One American from the Bulge yelled so much at night we couldn't sleep but he soon passed on. Another froze all his toes off and they clipped the bones off with shears.

'It really hurt to see some of the people come in like a few who were caught in a train by American bombers. Not too many lived and this was a blessing. Our beds were made from straw which helped to keep us warm. The Germans gave us a few clothes to put over us and expected us to stay warm. It's a good thing we grew into the cold as we were able to stand freezing weather. In the Austrian Alps the snow comes early. Sometimes the water would freeze up and we lived on snow.

'When Christmas 1944 came we wanted to get some of the spirit so my cook traded some cigarettes for a couple of eggs. He tried to make a pudding which he invented with a bit of chocolate and the eggs. It was good because it was the most food we had had for sometime. Once he tried for some beans but it was hard to do as farm labour could not come into the hospital very often. We cut whatever wood we could from beds, floors, tables and buildings to make hot water for brews. We had to watch out for wood in the black bread because slivers didn't go down well. Our barley soup was so full of weeds that when you cleaned it out there wasn't much left. The potatoes were so

Right *A barracks' window with shutter.*

Below right *Palliasses out in the sun to kill bugs.*

watered and full of dirt we would leave them all day to dry out.

'The doctors wanted to get me out of bed but my bones would not mend. Under great torture they removed both casts. It took four men to hold me down while they pushed a needle in my back. They cut holes in both legs and drilled holes through the bone to let the marrow grow. One of the drills broke off and they had quite a job removing it. This didn't help as the food was so poor no calcium could form. They put new casts on which were so tight my feet became infected. I finally tore holes in the cast to show them what was taking place before they would help me. I had to wait for a warm spring day to take a bath in ice water. It was the only way to stop the bugs from eating you up.

'It had been several months since my operation when they decided to make walking casts to support the unmended bones. They were made from strips of plaster held tight by the knee bone. This was better than nothing but it made me nervous to feel the bones moving around. My knees were stiff and my feet so tender I yelled for help when they tried to stand me up. After several weeks of work they could stand me up for just a few minutes. I had licked the problem. After eight months in bed I could stand again. Now to break the knee joints by the help of weights and moving them back and forth eight hours a day for nearly a month. I could only walk with crutches just a short distance but this meant I was superior to a lot of other people.

'One day I reached our door and opened it. The fresh air just about knocked me down. I would never have believed the room was so stinking from all kinds of infections. SS boys of between twelve and sixteen would come around and show off by spitting in our faces or calling us names. They always carried sub-machine-guns and 'potato mashers' in their belts. They called their home one of the ancient castles built on the mountain tops near us.'

The arrogance on the part of young SS boys and the older camp guards would not last long. The sounds of war were beginning to creep ever nearer and at night prisoners at Krems could see the flashes of big guns firing into Vienna. The prisoners knew they would not have to spend another Christmas behind barbed wire.

Red Cross Christmas food parcels were slow getting through and prisoners did not receive them until 2 January 1945. Three days later the Germans repatriated some of the prisoners from Krems and they

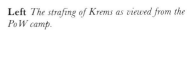

Left *The strafing of Krems as viewed from the PoW camp.*

Right *Kriegies brewing up in front of one of the hangars at Poking, Bavaria.*

were returned to England via Sweden. For those that remained behind the wire, living conditions deteriorated with ever worsening weather. Ten inches of snow fell on 15 January and by the end of the month there was no coal or wood left to burn in the stoves of the huts.

In February 1945 food supplies, which had always been scarce, were beginning to dry up altogether. There was no coal and the bread ration was cut to one loaf between seven men per day. By 16 February there were only enough food parcels left for three more weeks. To make matters worse on 5 March the bread ration was reduced to one loaf between eight men per day. On 9 March John Hurd wrote, 'Our barley ration to the kitchen has been cut 28 per cent and spuds 15 per cent. There are enough Red Cross parcels for a couple more issues and they are being given out one for two men per week. Most of the time we get spuds once a day. The other two meals we get hot water. Living conditions are poor. There is good news from the fighting fronts. Maybe we won't be here much longer.'

On 16 March P-38 fighters buzzed the camp and three days later contrails from hundreds of American bombers and fighters could be seen. John Hurd recorded it thus: '21 March. First day of spring. The sun is out with clouds in the sky. The planes made contrails in all directions, filling the sky everywhere. . .' Although it was a morale boosting sight, food was never far from his thoughts and he added, '. . .Will be glad to get a good meal under my belt again.'

On 30 March the prisoners' concealed radios confirmed that the Russians had crossed the Austrian border. Air raid sirens sounded the following day and on 2 April American bombers devastated a target several miles away and 'over a hundred' hit the town of Krems itself. Orlo Natvig recalls, 'When they made their turn I thought they were going to run in over the camp and bomb us. However, they were after the railway station at Krems. P-38s also strafed the area and the prisoners waved at them as they flew low over the camp. They were in the area to do strafing jobs on local railways and targets of that nature.'

The Germans realized that it was only a matter of time before they were overrun. They preferred surrender to the Allies in the west, rather than to the Russians. On 6 April it was announced that the prisoners would be marching 80 kilometres into Germany itself. Orlo Natvig recalls, 'A guard told us that an order had come through telling all camp Kommandants that all PoWs were to be shot. We didn't know how much truth there was in it.'

Ralph Ernst heard the news on his illegal radio set. 'Towards the end Hitler was getting desperate and his speeches on Vienna Radio stated that all PoWs would be executed and all guards would be sent to front line duty. We kept this news quiet to prevent an uprising among the "Kriegies" but plans were laid for action in the event Hitler kept his word.'

Orlo Natvig explains: 'A series of meetings were held and it was decided that all prisoners would hit a certain section of the fence en-masse in the hope that most would get away. Faced with total annihilation one had to take every advantage and opportunity that presented itself even though the chances were slim.'

But the order to kill the prisoners did not materialize. Instead, on Sunday 8 April, the prisoners were told they were to be moved out and thus 'be saved from the Russians'. Gunfire could be heard in Vienna, thirty miles to the south-east. In the camp bonfires were started and everything was done to prevent the move taking place until the Germans took action, as Marshall Hamer recalls. 'Guards burst into our barracks and ordered us to evacuate the camp immediately. We knew that it was against International law to move prisoners under such circumstances. We at first refused to as it seemed inhumane for us to have to endure a difficult journey after a year and a half of starvation rations. However, we reasoned it would be better to go with the guards than deal with Russians, so we braced ourselves for a forced march.

'Fires were burning in Vienna as civilians and troops moved out of the city heading west past our camp. We reasoned that it was in the best interest of the Germans to protect us so that when we met the American forces, we would say that they had acted responsibly.'

For eleven hours about 4,000 American prisoners in groups of 500, covered about seventeen kilometres, resting for the night in the hills near Ostra. The cold was intense and frost covered their blankets as men huddled together for warmth.

The prisoners continued their forced march on the ninth, resting all day on the tenth and then resuming again on the eleventh. On 13 April the column reached Grein, an Austrian town on the Danube. Bill Morris recalls, 'All along our route villagers let it be known that if the Russians advanced too far east they were going to throw themselves in the Danube. I have no doubt that several hundreds did.'

John Hurd saw a sign which said that Grein was 78 kilometres from Krems but they had travelled along the back roads so the distance was probably longer. 'While walking near an airfield one day some P-38s flew low over us. We would wave white handkerchiefs so friendly aircraft wouldn't attack us. On 25 April we arrived at Braunau; Hitler's birthplace and ended our march in a wooded area west of the town. We set up camp on the south bank of the Inn River. American Army units were advancing toward this area.

'On 2 May an American jeep with a Captain came into the camp. The Captain talked to our leaders and the Germans and then left. We were no longer PoWs. On 6 May we walked to an abandoned aluminium factory near Braunau and spent the night there. I ate a couple of eggs and got a little sick. I guess they weren't too fresh. Next morning army trucks brought us some chow. On 7 May we were trucked through Braunau and across the Inn River to an airfield in Bavaria.' C-47s flew the PoWs to Camp 'Lucky Strike' where they boarded a hospital ship for the USA.

Twelve men were left behind at Krems when the main contingent of prisoners pulled out. One of them was Lawrence Jenkins. 'No one knew what was to happen. I sat outside one morning when two American ambulances drove up. We all began to yell and then started to cry, even those who couldn't speak English. One of the drivers gave us several loaves of

Standing by the door of a C-47, a planeload of Kriegies await the order to board.

bread and we tore into it like wild animals until not a crumb was left.

'We had to hurry back to the American lines forty miles away as the Russians were confused about their coming. About ten miles from camp we came across two American ambulances which were coming in for us several weeks before but were shelled by the Russians and destroyed. We found dead horses and people along the way but no one to bury them. We were searched whenever we met the Russians. Small groups of Russians would make us drink a toast to them. Finally, at Linz we had to try three different bridges before we could bribe the guards to let us across. Once across, I felt for the first time like a free man.'

17 Death march

The prisoners at Krems estimated that they had marched at least 400 kilometres from Stalag 17B. Meanwhile, the Red Army had penetrated deep into Poland and were approaching Breslau, about ninety kilometres due east of Stalg Luft III at Sagan. Some 'Kriegies' feared that the Germans might shoot them. Bob O'Hearn recalls, 'We had a contingency plan for mass escape; storming the fence while a crew under Major Jerry Sage, would disable the guards. The plan was hairy but it seemed better than getting exterminated. At least some should survive.'

However, the ''Kriegies'' fears proved groundless. Colonel Braune, the German Kommandant, suggested to Brigadier-General Arthur W. Vanaman (now SAO at Sagan), that all prisoners should start taking as much exercise as possible in preparation for a forced march due west. A directive was issued by the Allied camp staff stating that all PoWs were expected to talk ten laps around the inner camp perimeter each day. Soon the camp perimeter became very crowded with some prisoners even carrying prepared packs to simulate actual marching conditions. On 26 January the Red Army attempted a crossing of the Oder at Steinau, just thirty kilometres from Luft III. German Panzers halted the advance by blowing the Russian tanks off the bridge but they had come too close for German comfort.

On Saturday, 27 January the German Kommandant summoned General Vanaman and issued a thirty-minute evacuation order. At 9.30 pm Colonel Charles G. Goodrich, SAO of the South Compound, received the order to be ready to march. O'Hearn remembers that Goodrich, who was shot down in North Africa in 1942, 'though aloof, was much concerned for our welfare. As the buffer between us and the German Kommandant, he earned the admiration and respect of the PoWs.'

Goodrich immediately rushed over to the South Compound theatre, right in the middle of a performance, of appropriately, '*You Can't Take It With You*', boarded the stage and gave the order for all the prisoners to prepare to leave at once. In the West Compound, the SAO, Colonel Darr H. Alkire, issued the same order to his men.

The men of the South Compound were the first to leave Stalag Luft III. Jim O'Brien wrote in his diary; 'Pulled out of camp with escort at 1.00 am. Don't know where we are going. Uncertainty.' After considerable delay the 10,000 American and RAF prisoners left in a single file column, each man carrying a Red Cross food parcel tossed to him from the parcel warehouse as he walked past.

Colonel Braune headed the evacuation column as it marched south-westwards. Following behind him were his executive officer, Major Simolite, a professor in civilian life who had been at Luft III since the beginning in April 1942, Lieutenant Wigginhouse, the *Lager* officer of the South Compound, Captain Golotovics, the *Lager* officer of South Compound C and Feldwebel Hohendal.

Normally, Sunday mornings would have been peaceful but on this occasion the calm was shattered by the sound of artillery fire coming from the north-east. Snow, which had been falling as they left, increased and the temperature dropped to ten degrees below zero. The prisoners marched until noon and then stopped for a five-hour rest. They stopped in the streets of a little German town without shelter from the freezing conditions and howling wind. Guards surrounded the column as men ate cold meat they had brought with them and snatched what rest they could lying in the snow.

With the transition from 'sack artists' to 'foot soldiers' many cherished belongings were discarded en-route. Frank Cotner recalls, 'There were quite a few PoWs that had previous military experience before they became air crew. I had been in the infantry for three years prior to going in the Air Force. I had a pretty good idea of how to take care of myself in situations like this. Before leaving Sagan I had made a hat from a pair of long johns. It covered my head and face and I cut two eye holes. I was in slightly better condition than some of the others who were inexperienced.

'Later that afternoon we stopped marching and rested near a forest. During the stop there was a horse-drawn wagon which was filled with German records. These were contained in trunks with metal supports on each corner. One of the horses froze to death in its traces. When the traces were pulled clear it alarmed the other horse which bolted. The metal edges on the boxes started making a noise like machine-gun fire. The guards thought the Russians were upon them and they started firing their machine-guns indiscriminately. We jumped off to the side of the road and lay in ditches for twenty minutes. During that time our body heat melted the snow so that when we continued the march our clothing on our fronts was wet.

'When we stopped for our five to ten-minute rest each hour, many of the inexperienced PoWs would kneel in the centre of the road and start rocking back and forth on their hands and knees, not knowing they were freezing to death. I and some others did everything we could to get them back on their feet. We dragged them, kicked them in the ''fanny'', swore at them—anything that would cause a spark to get them moving.'

Bob O'Hearn adds, 'The Germans said they would shoot stragglers. Very tired, I kept numbly plodding like the others, concentrating on each step.'

The column walked 17 kilometres to Halbau and eleven more to Freiwaldau; eleven hours from Sagan. About six miles from Freiwaldau there was some confusion and shooting to the rear of the column and several men were shot in the legs as they dived for cover after an air raid strafing alarm was given. None was seriously injured. At Freiwaldau the PoWs were billeted in concentration camp buildings. There was not enough room inside so men took it in turns warming themselves while others waited in blizzards outside. The march began again at 6.00 pm on 28 January in the relentless driving snow and extreme cold. Artillery fire could still be heard to the north.

Exhausted groups began leaving the line for shelter in barns during the early hours of Monday, 29 January as the temperature fell to below zero. About six inches of snow fell and continued falling. The column made several stops but by mid-afternoon the leading groups reached Muskau at 8.00 am. Ron Kramer recalls, 'Everyone was barely able to move and many were hysterical'. They had marched about forty miles in 27 out of the past 32 hours.'

Bob O'Hearn recalls. 'Colonel Goodrich made the famous demand to the Germans that they would have to shoot us because we weren't moving. We all seemed to agree. We were let into a foundry with open-hearth type furnaces. The heat felt good until I noticed that the place looked like Dante's *Inferno* with lots of smoke and lit only by the flames of the furnaces. Very tired, I struggled to climb up on a furnace platform to dry out. An unknown ''Kriegie'' gave me a hand. I forgot to let go of his hand until he said, ''OK, that's enough guy!''

'The heat was too much to stand for long. I overheard a guard saying there was room for fifty people in another factory that had lights and other niceties. Room-mate Jack Moyer and I moved to where we would be in line when the announcement was made. The factory was an improvement: clean tile floors, electric lights and wash basins. Jack traded my cigarettes for two bottles of good beer. For the moment we were relatively content.

'Four young ladies, possibly Poles or Czech, appeared at a window and indicated that they would like to come in. Someone talked with them but we were all too exhausted to consider the delights of female company.'

Frank Cotner, meanwhile, was billeted in a pottery. 'It was an opportunity to remove my pack and two others I was carrying for other marchers.' His arms and legs had been frostbitten and he began to double with pain. That night some prisoners, exhausted by the day's exertions, froze to death where they lay.

The marchers remained in Muskau for two days and on Wednesday 31 March, at 1.00 pm, the trek began again. Although a thaw was in the air snow was still falling and men tried to keep their feet on sheet ice in darkness. The prisoners passed many wagon-loads of Polish refugees fleeing from the east. Many small wagons piled high with their possessions had broken down and old people sat motionless by the sides of the roads staring blankly ahead while young children huddled together for warmth.

The column walked eighteen kilometres, arriving in Graustein at about 6.00 pm. Prisoners tried to swap cigarettes and soap for knives, apples or eggs from the German townspeople. Next morning, Thursday 1 February, the prisoners were given some bread and one and a half potatoes each before the march began again, to an infantry camp at Spremburg. The eight-kilometre march began in spring-like weather. Unfortunately, this preevented the use of sleds which had been tugged by bearded men with canes tied to the rear of their belt straps as they hobbled along slippery roads.

The column began reaching the outskirts of Spremberg at around noon. One group of about 2,000 men were herded into a field near a large, square building that the Germans used for training radio men and were forced to stand there for two hours. Many thought that any minute machine-guns would open up but the Germans were simply taking a head count. Ron Kramer spent the night in a large gymnasium. 'A German officer said that the Russians had broken through the German lines and were nearing Berlin. He said they could not stop them and

Crowded barrack conditions at Moosburg.

that the Americans would also be unable to stop them at the west wall. He added ominously that all Europe would be overrun by Bolshevism.'

The forced march had lasted six days, during which time the prisoners had walked an agonizing 62 miles. Colonel Delmar Spivey recalls, 'The march was a nightmare. Our German guards were as miserable as we were and many wanted to escape with PoWs but we had orders to remain together as a group.' (When roll call was taken at Stalag Luft VIIA, Moosburg, 31 South Compound men were missing, having escaped using 'X' committee maps, compasses and equipment distributed before the march began.)

At Spremberg the prisoners were issued with hot barley and meat soup; the first attempt the Germans had made to issue hot food since leaving Stalag Luft III. Each man received only a cupful but at least it was a change from the huge chunks of frozen bread and margarine that had tasted like cake and ice-cream. Colonel Braune informed the senior American officers that the prisoners would stay at Spremberg until they were overrun by the Russians. But later and without warning, the RAF prisoners were ordered to march on to Stalag III-A, Luckenwalde and on Friday, 2 February, the American contingent was ordered to walk the two kilometres through Spremberg to the railway station where prisoners were allowed to fill their containers with cold water before being locked in boxcars. The train pulled out at 7.00 pm that night.

The two-day trip was almost as wretched as the gruelling march. With fifty prisoners to a wagon, there was barely room for anyone to sit down. Men who had survived the rigours of the forced march broke down completely under the terrible conditions in the wagons. Many fought, argued and passed out, turning blue with cold. Others cried like children. Sleep was almost impossible. An attempt to string blankets across the top of the wagons as hammocks failed when the occupants were jolted and thrown on top of other weary prisoners lying on the hard wooden floors.

On Sunday 4 February the train steamed into Nuremburg but not all the prisoners were allowed to disembark. There was not the capacity at Stalag XIII-D for all the prisoners so some were sent further south to Stalag VII-A, Moosburg, about 40 km north of Munich.

Ron Kramer was among those who were sent to Nuremburg. 'The camp had only just been vacated by Italian PoWs and it was crawling with bed bugs, lice and general filth. Buildings were in a state of extreme disrepair. There was no coal and then we had to tear down boards from the wash-houses for burning. The Germans threatened disciplinary action but look outs were posted to observe the comings and goings of the guards.'

German food rations were practically non-existent and in the general unhygenic and unhealthy conditions, men soon became very ill. Dehydrated vegetables were consistently wormy and only two types of 'soup' were available: the 'green death' and the 'grey death'. Both were made from an insipid tasting flour. German-made black bread and a few potatoes only served to increase the dysentery and diarrhoea epi-

Left *Second Lieutenant Frederic 'Dusty' Worthen.*

Below left *Rosacker crew of the 328th Bomb Squadron, 93rd Bomb Group, Hardwick, which was shot down on 28 January 1945 on the mission to Dortmund. Back row (L-R): Bennie Hayes (gunner); 'Dusty' Worthen (bombaimer); Joe Rosacker (pilot); Glenn Tessmer (co-pilot). Kneeling (L-R): C. J. Philage (gunner); Chas Conley (gunner); 'Cobb' Gibbs (gunner); John Pace (navigator); Otis Hair (engineer); Sid Metro (gunner)* (Worthen).

demic. Ron Kramer was one of many who spent four days in Nuremburg with dysentery and continual vomiting.

To add to the general discomfort, Stalag XIII-D was strategically located only three quarters of a mile from the huge marshalling yards at Nuremburg and the PoWs had to endure several raids by both the RAF and 8th Air Force. On 20 February the 8th flew a large scale raid against Nuremburg. Although the bombs fell very near the camp it was a great thrill for the prisoners to see it all from the other end of the bombsight as 'Dusty' Worthen, a bombardier in the 93rd Bomb Group, who had been shot down on a mission to Dortmund on 28 January 1945, recalls: 'Bombs hit close to our camp but caused no problems for us. After turning from the target the bombers flew right over us. Of course we kept waiting for a stray bomb to go off that was kicked out of some fool plane. A few planes went down over the target. One B-17 went straight down into the flames in Nuremburg. Some 'chutes could be seen. However, one did not come down with the rest; it just floated away over the horizon. You knew the airman didn't fasten the harness through his legs and the 'chute pulled right away from him.' The 8th Air Force returned the following day and bombed through overcast skies.

Nuremburg was pretty well destroyed and all electricity to the camp was cut off. Frank Cotner recalls: 'Sometimes our barracks would be moved off the foundations by four or five inches and the next day be moved back again. The windows were shattered. The Germans said we could not seek shelter during the raids and kept us in the huts at gunpoint. We replied, "Up Your Bucket," dug little trenches outside our huts with "Klim" cans and jumped out the broken windows during air raids straight into the trenches. We even removed the wooden covers from the windows and used them to shield ourselves in the trenches from flying debris. We could see all the devastation being wreaked on Nuremburg and more than once we said, "Isn't it wonderful that when we get home we'll have the United States and the German PoWs will have all this to come back to.'

On 22 February two P-51 Mustangs banked nonchantly over the camp at 3,000 ft, contemptuous of the frenzied German anti-aircraft barrage which exploded behind them. On 26 February sixteen P-51s returned and strafed lines of communication to the

A Red Cross train in Germany transporting food for PoWs (believed to be the summer of 1944).

north of the camp. That night RAF Mosquitoes flew over singly and at high speed and dropped a string of yellow flares which formed a corridor the length of the city. These were followed by red and green flares marking the centre of the target. They came in so fast they were overhead before the camp lights could be extinguished. Many prisoners were caught unawares: buildings rocked and windows were broken as wave after wave of Lancasters dropped their bombs on the flares and turned the city into a blazing inferno. Prisoners watched from their trenches transfixed. An amplifier blared out the position of the bombers from zone to zone and searchlights frantically probed the sky for a trace of the bombers. The earth shook with each explosion and the city was left to burn that night and all next day.

On the night of 27 February the RAF returned to stoke up the fires caused by the previous night's bombing. Broken glass and bits of plaster crashed onto the floors of the prisoners' huts while the PoWs sought refuge under their beds. One Mosquito was seen to crash near the camp.

On 28 February Colonel Darr H. Alkire, the SAO at Nuremburg, issued a set of complaints to the Kommandant after conditions continued to deteriorate. He claimed that Germany had violated the Geneva Convention of 27 July 1929 by siting Stalag XIII-D so close to a marshalling yard. He went on to complain about the food situation, which was now so bad black marketeers were selling two slices of cake and two slices of pie for $135 a slice. Fuel was low and illness was reaching epidemic proportions. The situation never did improve.

Without Red Cross parcels and medicine several hundreds of PoWs would have starved to death or died of disease. Colonel Spivey recalls: 'Hitler had placed Obergruppenführer Gatlob Berger in charge of all PoWs and displaced persons; nine million according to him. Berger was a Waffen SS officer and a good one; a friend of Hitler's and Eva Braun. Berger arranged to get Red Cross food to PoWs during the last months of the war and tried to get Vanaman and myself to act as couriers to deliver messages to General Eisenhower proposing that the west front Germans surrender to the western Allies so the Ger-

Major John Egan (left) and Major Gale 'Bucky' Cleven of the 100th Bomb Group pictured at Thorpe Abbotts (Thorpe Abbotts Tower Association).

mans would be free to take on the USSR. Berger got Red Cross parcels and medicine through the front to the PoWs.'

On 14 March 1945 three trucks brought Red Cross parcels into the camp after running the gauntlet in the havoc in and around Nuremburg. Other shipments filtered through by rail and road and a large quantity of American insecticide got through by rail from Switzerland to alleviate the lice problem. After the war, at the Nuremburg War Crimes trial, General Vanaman and Spivey testified on Berger's behalf. Spivey continues, 'The British and American judges voted to acquit him. France and the USSR voted to hang him. He eventually got fifteen years but was pardoned after serving part of his sentence.'

During March 1945 the weather grew worse. On eight consecutive days, from the second to the ninth, it snowed continuously and turned the camp into a quagmire. Fuel was not forthcoming and barracks went unheated. Among all this deprivation and degradation there was always the glimmer of hope that the war would soon be over. Although the 'Kriegies' were kept informed of the war situation, albeit from the German's point of view via OKW (Official Kommunique Wehrmacht) broadcasts over the camp tannoy, a secret radio set tuned to the BBC gave them the news they wanted to hear. On 10 March even the Germans were forced to admit that the Allies had crossed the Rhine at Wesel and Bonn.

Two days after Easter Sunday, on 3 April 1945, it was reported that the American 7th Army was only sixty miles from Nuremburg. But on 4 April with liberation so close, the PoWs were shattered to learn that they were to be marched in the opposite direction once again. Their destination would be Moosburg, 145 km distant and about 40 km north-west of Munich.

The evacuation at Sagan had largely been unprepared but the 'Kriegies' were able to take some precautions for the march to Moosburg. Colonel William Aring and Major Gale 'Buck' Cleven were assigned duties by Colonel Alkire which would come into effect at the first sign of trouble. Major John Egan was Provost Marshal. Cleven and Egan were old friends, having served together in the States with the 100th Bomb Group, which had also been commanded by Alkire for a time. At Thorpe Abbotts, England, both Cleven and Egan had been squadron commanders and had been shot down within two days of each other in October 1943. Both had agreed that Egan following Cleven down into Germany was going a little too far, although Cleven's first words to Egan upon meeting in prison camp had been, 'You're late. What detained you?'

The German Kommandant insisted on night marches but after an argument with their captors, Alkire and his staff reached an agreement that the prisoners would not travel more than 20 km by day or night. Frank Cotner recalls, 'Our officers also created a "commando group". I was selected along with some others, to march directly behind the senior American officers and the German Major in charge. Our job was to save the lives of as many PoWs as we could if their lives were in danger. We also had some bed sheets to spread out in a field in the letters "PoW" or wave white flags if American fighter planes discovered the column.'

On the morning of 4 April, at 11.30 am, the prisoners began leaving the camp in barracks formations, three abreast. There was no snow but the column had to contend with teeming rain for several days. Early that first afternoon the head of the seven and a half mile column reached Feucht. The PoWs were allowed no respite and continued walking towards Ochenbruk. At 3.30 pm that afternoon, while some of the leading elements stopped to rest, some of the prisoners at the rear of the column were still in Feucht when Thunderbolts bombed and strafed the town.

At around 9.15 pm that night the column began arriving in Polling, a small town almost sixteen miles from Moosburg. Barns were opened up and the lucky ones managed to get some sleep inside. The following morning the prisoners set off again. They stopped at Neumarkt while seventeen miles away, massive formations of bombers struck at Nuremburg again. Vapour trails criss-crossed the sky above and shock waves rippled from the target area. Flares cascaded

Prisoners drag their sledges in appalling conditions during the forced march from Sagan to Stalag VII-A, Moosburg.

onto the city like ribbons and when the wind blew them away, others were dropped to replace them. Many fighters roared overhead and the occupants of Neumarkt fled in terror to the open fields. The Germans issued cups of soup, a ninth of a loaf of bread and a minute portion of synthetic honey to each prisoner before re-commencing the journey.

The column passed through Berching, Beilingries and Paulushofen, stopping for ten-minute rest periods every hour. The German guards were very lax and the 'Kriegies' did almost as they pleased. Many traded cigarettes with local villagers for eggs, milk, coffee and bread. On the night of Friday 6 April the column stopped at Barnsdorf and stayed there until Sunday morning. When the time came to leave warm sunshine broke through the clouds and cheered the ragged, weary column.

At 5.00 pm that evening the leading elements of the column reached the town of Marching on the River Danube. Before crossing it the prisoners were allowed to rest overnight. The bridge was mined and guns were being set up on its banks. Major John Egan noted that Aring and Cleven had altered their appearance and was not surprised to learn that Colonel Alkire had given them permission to escape. That night, as Egan was busy pumping water on a rusty old pump to cover their escape, Cleven and Aring slipped away in the darkness. Nine nights later both men made contact with the US 45th Division and they were flown to England.

Meanwhile, the column of prisoners had entered Neustadt. People lined the streets and directed their hostility towards the airmen they felt were responsible for all that they had suffered from Allied bombing raids. Just beyond the city the 'Kriegies' stopped for food. Shortly thereafter American fighters launched an attack on Neustadt. The 'commando group' quickly set up white sheets in the form of letters 30 ft high displaying the word, 'PoW'. After circling a few times, the fighters flew away. Soon afterwards the column dragged itself to its feet and headed for Mulhausen and Schweinbach. The countryside now was more picturesque and a welcome change from the wartorn towns and cities of southern Bavaria.

'Dusty' Worthen enjoyed the change of scenery. 'Being on the road was great by comparison to a prison camp. We were marching (really a leisurely walk) on dirt roads through farming country. Most nights we would stay in barns on the farms. The first thing we would do is raid the potato cellars. We would put potatoes in an open fire to cook and eat them right out of the skin—this was gourmet eating. The farmers were really nice about all this, but also, what could they do? Many times this seemed so strange: a short time ago we were bombing these people and now we were walking among the SOBs.'

From the night of Tuesday 10 April until Thursday 12 April the prisoners rested in barns at Gammelsdorf. Just before noon on Friday 13 April the leading elements of the column reached Stalag VIIA, Moosburg. The march had involved ten gruelling days and had carried them approximately 91 miles.

Moosburg was in an even greater state of decay than Nuremburg but practically vermin free. The barracks were dingy, poorly lit and furnished with very few three-tier bunks so many were forced to sleep on the floors. Layers of wood shavings on the floor served as matresses. There were advantages as 'Dusty' Worthen recalls, 'When we got to Moosburg the first thing was into the showers; the only one in two and a half months. It went through our minds though, was this one of those gas chambers?'

Another plus was that Moosburg was a supply centre for Red Cross food parcels in southern Germany and an issue of one parcel per week per prisoner was put into effect. Stalag VII-A was a very large camp with thousands of prisoners of all nationalities from camps throughout the Reich. Jim O'Brien and hundreds of others had been in the camp since early February when they had continued the journey south from Nuremburg. He told some of the inquisitive newcomers that despite the privations the food at Moosburg had been very good and on 19 March full Red Cross deliveries had started. However, rumours were circulating that soon the prisoners might have to make ends meet with 'Reich

Rations' and even 'K' rations.

So many prisoners were coming into the camp that it was bursting at the seams. For seven days beginning on 8 April, the men were suddenly rousted out of their huts and moved into tents in other compounds. Conditions were filthy and overcrowded. On 24 April the camp was alerted to move out within 48 hours but the following day the alert was cancelled after agreement between the Swiss, German and Allied authorities not to move the PoWs. Jim O'Brien wrote, 'This is a ringside seat for diplomatic and military affairs. Lots of bombing and artillery fire. Most pleasing thing is the gamble our hut took in building a little stove instead of a cart as we now enjoy wonderful stews, fish chowders, bread puddings and grilled limberger cheese sandwiches 'till the GI field kitchen arrives.'

On 25 April Me 109s and Fw 190s were seen daily at tree-top level as they tried to escape detection by the ever increasing American presence over Germany. Heavy raids were made on Munich to the south and B-26 Marauders made attacks on towns on all sides of the camp. Artillery fire rocked the countryside and at night flashes could be seen. Some PoWs estimated their distance from the camp by checking the time it took for the sound to reach them after each flash. On 26 April LC-5 light aircraft scoured the area and sometimes buzzed the camp. Then a P-51 Mustang appeared and performed a slow roll overhead. The prisoners rushed from their barracks and poured into the compound, jumping, cheering and hugging each other with emotion.

At 3.00 pm on 27 April the prisoners took over the camp interior. Good food was plentiful; pork chops and prime chocolate pie. O'Brien wrote, 'This is the only way for this whole business to end.' The end indeed was not far off. On Sunday 29 April John Egan wrote, 'We have more or less taken over the camp. Germans are about but things are going our way. Last night Colonel Good and the CO of the SS met and planned to make this camp neutral ground. Colonel Good took a Red Cross truck and went through the lines to Allied headquarters, where he met a West Point classmate. The American Command said "HELL NO, we'll fight for it!" The "Kriegies" are in the middle again. Right now a fair-sized war is going on all around us. Light arms, tanks, heavy guns, mortars, etc. . .'

As Mass finished in the centre of the recreation field bullets began to whistle through the camp amid the clatter of rifle and machine-gun fire. Frank Cotner recalls: 'I was sitting peeling potatoes when a bullet entered the tent and missed my head by a few inches. There was some commotion outside so we tumbled out to see what the problem was. There was a light aircraft flying over the camp. I believe they wanted everyone out of the tents into slit trenches.

'As I looked out to the east there was a column of American tanks on a hill, moving to the south. We hit the trenches and the war began again. The tanks started their bombardment and the Germans fired in reply. It lasted into the night and next day we were told that some SS troopers had gone into a barracks and told the Wehrmacht that they should resist to the end. They were a bunch of middle-aged farmers who did not care one way or the other about the outcome of the war. They made it clear to the SS that they were not going to fight it out to the end. The SS fired a few rounds from a bazooka into the barracks, killing quite a few of the Wehrmacht troops, then took off when the sound of American artillery could be heard close by.'

The American prisoners were ordered inside but the Russians in the camp stayed on the roofs cheering. Outside the camp they could see American tanks exchanging fire with the Germans and for fifteen minutes shells whistled over the camp. Then suddenly, all was quiet. The American PoWs raced outside to the barbed wire fence. White flags, sheets and anything else the civilians could lay their hands on, fluttered from every window in Moosburg. Early in the afternoon all resistance ceased and the dreaded flag with the hated Swastika was lowered from the mast at Moosburg town hall.

John Egan wrote: '14.05. General Smith of the Third Army just entered the camp in a jeep followed by an armoured vehicle. Further identification was impossible because it was covered with "Kriegies". 19.00. We are free! The infantry has not arrived but

Liberation: 29 April 1945.

the tank boys assure us ''Allus is gut''. Heavy guns continue to shake the buildings. Highlight of the day was a Corporal Mahoney, a tank man, whose son, a Lieutenant, was a prisoner in the camp. . .'

A Sherman tank crashed through the camp gates followed by another and another. GIs riding on the sides threw cigarettes and candy bars to the shrieking, delirious mob many of whom had waited years for this moment to arrive. General Patton entered the camp at the lead of the 14th Armoured Division and was greeted by a thunderous and emotional ovation from the PoWs. It was the most beautiful sight the 'Kriegies' would ever wish to see. Bob O'Hearn recorded that it was, 'a most wonderful day; the 609th day of imprisonment. The war was still going on but for us, as the German lady wistfully said on the day I was captured, ''For you der war is over''.'

Jim O'Brien wrote later, 'No-one could fathom the amount of cheering and shouting that went on when the tanks, jeeps, GI trucks and GI uniforms came rolling in the front gate. Many an iron heart broke down into tears when the ''Stars and Stripes'', the ''Union Jack'', the ''Tricolour'', the Russian flag and other odd national banners were hoisted over the camp. The ''Kriegies'' cheered, wept and then laughed as the ''Stars and Stripes'' was hoisted up-side down and they wept and cheered again as it was raised the right way up.' 'Dusty' Worthen had a lump in his throat 'the size of an orange'.

John Egan wrote his entry for 30 April: 'Soldiers all over the place. Goons putting up resistance about 1 ½ miles from here. Alkire's regiment, of which I am Exec, goes into action. We take over a warehouse to billet our troops, who are commando work parties. We are going to France by air in seven to ten days. Heard that Colonel Aring is back home in the States. . .no word of Cleven. If he's home I'll be late for the wedding. We picked up three barrels and small amount of ''spirits'', also fresh eggs.'

A few days after liberation the prisoners saw their first American girls. American nurses visited the camp and stayed on to work in the hospital. Red Cross girls also visited the camp and passed out doughnuts and chewing gum. Oddly enough, the prisoners just stood and stared as though they had never seen a woman before.

The GIs gave away their 'K' ration packs to the prisoners who treated them like rare gifts. Although ordered to stay inside the barbed wire, some 'Kriegies' ventured to Ingolstadt, Munich and Landshut, wandering through forests and into the hills, supplementing their rations with a little foraging and liberating of their own. Bob O'Hearn came upon a US Ordinance Detachment in a nearby town and acquired a sword with ruby-eyed lion's head and swastikas on a gold coloured handle; it had

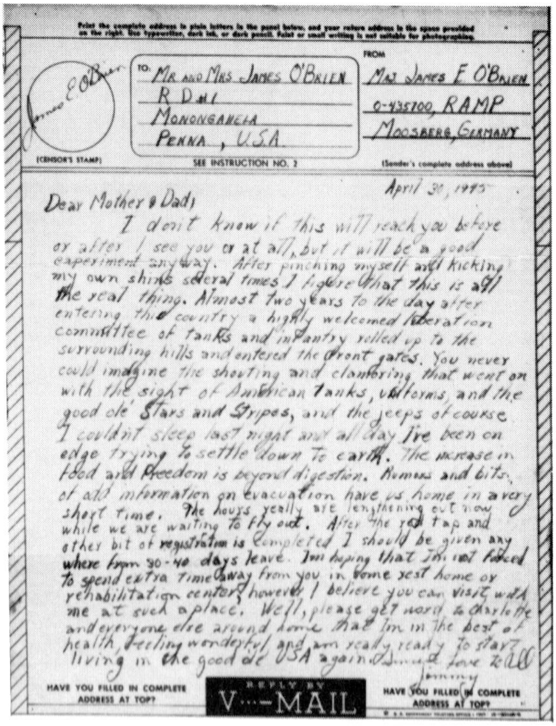
TO: MR AND MRS JAMES O'BRIEN
R D #1
MONONGAHELA
PENNA, U.S.A.

FROM: MAJ JAMES E O'BRIEN
0-435700, RAMP
MOOSBERG, GERMANY

April 30, 1945

Dear Mother & Dad,

I don't know if this will reach you before or after I see you or at all, but it will be a good experiment anyway. After pinching myself and kicking my own shins several times I figure that this is all the real thing. Almost two years to the day after entering this country a highly welcomed liberation committee of tanks and infantry rolled up to the surrounding hills and entered the front gates. You never could imagine the shouting and clamoring that went on with the sight of American tanks, uniforms, and the good ole' Stars and Stripes, and the jeeps of course. I couldn't sleep last night and all day I've been on edge trying to settle down to earth. The increase in food and freedom is beyond digestion. Rumors and bits of all information on evacuation have us home in a very short time. The hours really are lengthening out now while we are waiting to fly out. After the red tape and other bit of registration is completed I should be given anywhere from 30-40 days leave. I'm hoping that I'm not forced to spend extra time away from you in some rest home or rehabilitation center, however I believe you can visit with me at such a place. Well, please get word to Charlotte and everyone else around home that I'm in the best of health, feeling wonderful and am really ready to start living in the good ole USA again. Love to all

Jimmy

Above *V-Mail message sent from Moosburg by Jim O'Brien to his parents on 30 April 1945* (O'Brien).

Below *Major Dave Lyster (L) and Major Robert Rosenthal (R) welcome Major Cleven home to Thorpe Abbotts after his escape from captivity in April 1945. Cleven was shot down on 8 October 1943* (Thorpe Abbotts Tower Association).

The boot on the other foot. Aerial view of PoW camp at Ludwigshafen shows German prisoners held at the end of the war.

been 'liberated' from the walls of the Munich beer hall, scene of Hitler's ill-fated 'Beer Hall Putch' in 1923. Chickens, pigs, rabbits, horse-drawn wagons and even a shiny silver BMW racing car, appeared in the compound.

Lots were drawn among the 45,000 prisoners and they were deloused with DDT and transported by road to Landshut, about ten miles to the north-east, where they were flown out in C-47 transports to France. On 3 May 1,500 prisoners were evacuated and on 6 May 19,500 were flown out from four airfields to Camp 'Lucky Strike' and on to Le Havre. On 22 May Colonel Agee, his senior staff and some members of the 'commando group', John Egan and Frank Cotner among them, were put aboard the USS *Monticello*, one of two Italian liners that had been confiscated by the Allies.

Cotner recalls: 'The minute I hit the gang plank I began to feel sea sick. For twelve days I was in a miserable condition. I couldn't eat, I couldn't sit down or stand up. I couldn't lie down. The only relief I got was at night when the barber's shop closed. I had made a deal with the barber so that I could sleep in his swivel chair. I would tilt it in a certain way and I could get some rest.'

On 2 June the convoy of 100 or so freighters, liberty ships and tankers arrived on the US East Coast. Jim O'Brien, aboard the Navy transport, *La Jeune*, saw the Statue of Liberty loom up out of the haze of a June thunderstorm and realized he was really home.

Frank Cotner landed in Boston. 'We were taken to Camp Miles Standish, Massachusetts, where we were fed steak, mashed potatoes, pie, milk; anything we wanted, by German PoWs. Personally, I couldn't eat anything except potatoes without gravy. The German PoWs ate with us, heaping up their plates and sitting in their own section of the dining hall. They would gobble down everything we had and I sat there watching them while I ate nothing!

The returned American PoWs spent some time re-adjusting to their new surroundings before new careers lay ahead. Their thoughts would never be entirely free of their experiences 'behind the wire'. To quote from a poem written by J.B. Boyle while in PoW camp, 'So here's to happy days ahead. When you and I are free. To look back on this interlude And call it history.'

Appendix

RESTRICTED

INSTRUCTIONS FOR OFFICERS AND MEN OF THE EIGHTH AIR FORCE IN THE EVENT OF CAPTURE

AG 8 AF NO. 1.
21 *July*, 1942.

THIS DOCUMENT MUST NOT BE TAKEN INTO A PLANE.

1. The information contained in this document is not to be communicated, directly or indirectly, to anyone not in the armed forces of the United States.

2. C.O.'s are to see that a copy of this publication is issued to every member of the 8th Air Force whose duties might take him over enemy territory.

By Command of Major General SPAATZ.

B. L. DAVIS,
Colonel, A.G.D.,
Adjutant General.

RESTRICTED

Inevitably some members of the Eighth Air Force will be captured by the enemy. This document contains instructions and information for their guidance. It should be preserved and read from time to time so that its contents will not be forgotten.

I.—GENERAL INSTRUCTIONS

Any officer or enlisted man who becomes a prisoner of war remains in the military service of the United States. He is to escape when practicable, to perform other military duties when ordered and to obey his American military superior in the prison camp. No parole is to be given to the enemy except with permission of the senior American officer or non-commissioned officer and then only for periods of several hours duration and for special purposes. No broadcasts are to be made from prison camps for any purpose.

Prisoners of war have many rights. These are fully stated in the Geneva Convention of 1929, which the United States and all the great powers except Japan have signed and ratified. According to its terms a copy of the treaty should be available in every prison camp. Insist on this being done. Study it and insist on your rights. There is a neutral Protecting Power to whom all serious complaints can be addressed by the senior American officer or non-commissioned officer through the Camp Commandant.

II.—WHAT INFORMATION SHOULD BE GIVEN TO THE ENEMY

A prisoner must give his **Name, Rank** and serial **Number**. This is required by the Geneva Convention of 1929. No further information of any kind should be given.

III.—WHAT THE ENEMY WILL TRY TO FIND OUT FROM YOU

The American Air Force is a new factor in the war,

so the enemy will try desperately to ascertain its strength and capabilities. They will want to know:-

1. The number, strength and location of your squadron or unit.
2. The location of other squadrons and of airdromes.
3. The length of time you have been in England and the way you travelled from America.
4. The training you have received.
5. The size of the American Air Force.
6. The types of aircraft used with their performances and armament.
7. The signals and radio equipment used.
8. The tactics used by the American Air Force.
9. Anything and everything about A.A. defences and Air Defence organization.
10. Anything and everything about the Ground Forces of the American Army.
11. Any facts about the R.A.F. or its co-operation with the American Air Force.
12. Anything about conditions in Great Britain and in America—food supply, politics, moral among civilians and the armed forces, production of war supplies, etc.

IV.—HOW THE ENEMY WILL TRY TO LEARN THESE THINGS FROM YOU

There are only three sources through which the enemy can obtain information from you. They are:-

1. Your aircraft and its equipment.
2. Your papers—either official such as maps and documents, or personal such as letters and diaries.
3. Your talk.

The enemy cannot add to the information provided by your plane or papers, **but he can do a lot to make you talk**. The first Americans captured must expect the most rigorous interrogation, and must be prepared for all the tricks that the Germans have used. Among the methods which the enemy has employed to get people to talk, and which have been reported by prisoners of war who actually experienced them, are the following:-

(*a*) Direct interrogation, sometimes for long periods in the hope of wearing you down and sometimes renewed long after capture.

(*b*) Indirect interrogation through casual conversations about flying and the war in general—shop talk—in the hope of having you reveal something.

(*c*) He will try to impress you with his great knowledge about yourself, your plane and the American Air Force in the hope you will think he knows everything already, and therefore there is no "harm" in talking freely. He may suggest that others have already told everything so your silence is no longer necessary.

(*d*) He will appeal to your vanity by letting you show how much you know.

(*e*) He will try to arouse you to angry protest by ridiculing the war efforts of the United States.

(*f*) He will flatter you with special attentions, inviting you to parties with German airmen of great prominence. A spirit of good sportsmanship will prevail and liquor will flow.

(*g*) He will reveal all sorts of German facts and secrets to you in the hope that you will feel like a heel if you do not tell him something.

(*h*) He may try to intimidate you with threats.

(*i*) On first arriving at a prison camp a "Red Cross" official, really an enemy officer dressed up, may give you a blank to fill out which will ask you to supply you squadron number and location. He may say your capture will not be reported or your mail transmitted if you refuse to fill out the blanks.

(*j*) Enemy officials may dress in Allied or American uniforms and engage genuine prisoners in conversation.

(*k*) Hospital nurses or attendants may try to gather information after being very sympathetic.

(*l*) Microphones will certainly be used as they are a favourite German device and may be expected in every room at every stage of your imprisonment.

(*m*) In addition to the above much-used methods the enemy will resort to many other tricks to extract information from you.

V.—HOW YOU CAN DEFEAT THE ENEMY

1. Destroy, if possible, your aircraft, maps, etc., by fire if brought down. You have instructions. Do not forget to follow them.
2. Do not carry and do not allow anyone else to carry any unauthorized papers, official or private, on a flight. An envelope, a bill or the stub of a movie ticket may give away the location of your squadron. In writing letters

after becoming a prisoner do not address them in such a way as to reveal the location of your squadron or any other unit. Use the official A.P.O. or write c/o War Department.

3. (*a*) **Tell only your Name, Rank and Serial Number**. If you answer any other questions you are helping the enemy. Say "I cannot answer," or "I do not know," or following the advice the enemy gives his own airmen, say "Would you answer that question if you were me?" By sticking to these you win.

(*b*) Do not talk shop with the enemy. He is not really anxious to talk with a fellow flyer. He wants to gain knowledge which will help him in the war. Do not try to deceive him with lies. Remember he is an expert interrogator and among your lies he will find some truths. **You can outwit him only by saying nothing**.

(*c*) Don't be impressed with his knowledge, which may have come from papers or markings in your plane. It may partly be a guess or he may want you to confirm something. **No facts are harmless**. They may be used to persuade the next prisoner that all is known and he may as well talk.

(*d*) Don't try to prove to the enemy how big you are by telling him what you know. He will only think you are small, and you will be much better satisfied with yourself afterwards if you have told only your name, rank and number.

(*e*) It is good to be patriotic, but you can best prove your patriotism by keeping silent and not by telling how much the United States is doing.

(*f*) The enemy will not treat you nicely and offer you drinks because he likes you. Remember he treats any likely prospect that way. He is after information to use against us. Among the "good sports" will be one or several interogation officers waiting to seize on any chance remark you may let slip. It is not good sportsmanship but a stupid mistake to go on parties with the enemy.

(*g*) Never believe anything you are told from enemy sources. Even if he should give you correct information, it is reasonably safe for him to do so, while **any fact you reveal may cost your friends their lives**.

(*h*) Threats are bluff. The enemy will not dare to carry out threats, he knows that reprisals would follow.

(*i*) In order to have your capture promptly reported and your mail delivered you need only tell your **Name, Rank and Number**.

(*j*) Remember the person to whom you are talking may be an enemy. The only friend you can be sure of is the man you knew before capture.

(*k*) Tell no enemy person, however sympathetic, anything except your **Name, Rank and Number**.

(*l*) Because you cannot find a microphone do not think there isn't one. We know that there is and that the enemy, who has had years of experience in eavesdropping, is listening. If you have plans to discuss with friends, do your talking outdoors and even there be careful.

(*m*) You can defeat every effort of the enemy by **keeping silent**.

VI.—WHAT ELSE YOU CAN DO TO DEFEAT THE ENEMY

1. You can plan to escape. Opportunities will be offered. Even attempts which fail are worth while as they have an appreciable nuisance value and the information collected will make later attempts successful. If you succeed in escaping and arriving in friendly territory do not discuss your experiences with anyone, in military service or out, until you are interviewed by the proper military authorities. And never, **under any circumstances, mention the name of any person who may have helped you to escape**.
2. You can damage enemy morale by spreading proper ideas and correcting misinformation among the prison guards and such civilians as you may be able to reach.
3. You can, if you are an enlisted man and go out of the camp on working parties, do as little work as possible and you may be able to do real damage.
4. You can keep your eyes and ears open at all times. We want information. Help us to get it.

(S.O.214) P.573 10M 8/42 H & S, Ltd. Gp 393

Index